AEPS

Assessment, Evaluation, and Programming System for Infants and Children

Edited by **Diane Bricker, Ph.D.**

VOLUME 3

AEPS Measurement for Three to Six Years

AEPS

Assessment, Evaluation, and Programming System for Infants and Children

VOLUME 3

AEPS Measurement for Three to Six Years

Edited by

Diane Bricker, Ph.D.

and

Kristie Pretti-Frontczak, Ph.D.

College of Education
University of Oregon

Content developed by

Ruth Kaminski, Ph.D., Kristine Slentz, Ph.D.,
Melinda Buhl, M.S., Lizann Hupp, M.S.P.A., Betsy Seth, M.S.
Susan Janko, Ph.D., and Susan Ryan, Ph.D.

·P A U L·H·
BROOKES
PUBLISHING Cº

Baltimore • London • Toronto • Sydney

Paul H. Brookes Publishing Co.
Post Office Box 10624
Baltimore, Maryland 21285-0624

Copyright © 1996 by Paul H. Brookes Publishing Co., Inc.

Typeset by Signature Typesetting & Design, Baltimore, Maryland.
Manufactured in the United States of America by
BookCrafters, Chelsea, Michigan.

The following AEPS forms, found in Appendix D, can be purchased separately; these separate
packages are printed in different colors.
  AEPS Data Recording Forms, Three to Six Years (printed in black; sold in packages of
  10)
  AEPS Family Report, Three to Six Years (printed in brown; sold in packages of 10)
  AEPS Family Interest Survey (printed in blue; sold in packages of 30)
  AEPS Child Progress Record, Three to Six Years (printed in green; sold in packages of
  30)
To order, contact Paul H. Brookes Publishing Co., Post Office Box 10624, Baltimore, Maryland
21285-0624 (1-800-638-3775).
Please see page ii for information about other volumes in the AEPS series, all available from
Paul H. Brookes Publishing Co.

Portions of some chapters in this book appeared originally in Bricker, D. (Ed.). (1993). *Assessment, Evaluation, and Programming System for Infants and Children: Vol. 1. AEPS Measurement for
Birth to Three Years.* Baltimore: Paul H. Brookes Publishing Co.

The Assessment, Evaluation, and Programming System for Infants and Children was developed in part with support from Grants #G008400661 and #H024C80001 from the U.S. Office
of Education and Grant #09DD0019 from the Department of Health and Human Services to
the Center on Human Development, University of Oregon. The content, however, does not
necessarily reflect the position or policy of DOE or the University of Oregon, and no official
endorsement of these materials should be inferred.

Library of Congress Cataloging-in-Publication Data
Assessment, evaluation, and programming system for infants and
    children / Diane Bricker, editor.
        p.   cm.
    Includes bibliographical references and index.
    Contents: v. 1. AEPS measurement for birth to three years.
    ISBN 1-55766-095-6 (v. 1)
    1. Assessment, Evaluation, and Programming System   2. Child development—Testing.
3. Child development deviations—Diagnosis.   I. Bricker, Diane D.
RJ51.D48A87   1992
155.4'028'7—dc20
                                                                    92-6690
                                                                    CIP

ISBN 1-55766-187-1   Vol. 3
British Library Cataloguing-in-Publication data are available from the British Library.

CONTENTS

CONTRIBUTORS

THE EDITORS

Diane Bricker, Ph.D., Early Intervention Area, 5253 University of Oregon, Eugene, Oregon 97403-5253. Dr. Bricker is Professor of Special Education and a highly respected, well-known authority in the field of early intervention. She has directed a number of national demonstration projects and research efforts focused on examining the efficacy of early intervention; the development of a linked assessment, intervention, and evaluation system; and the study of a comprehensive, parent-focused screening tool. She presently directs the Early Intervention Area, and is Associate Dean for Academic Programs, College of Education, University of Oregon.

Kristie Pretti-Frontczak, Ph.D., Assistant Professor, Early Intervention Area, 5253 University of Oregon, Eugene, Oregon 97403-5253. Dr. Pretti-Frontczak recently received her doctoral degree from the College of Education, University of Oregon, with a specialty in early intervention special education. She has coordinated a major research project that examined the treatment validity of the AEPS, has conducted a large number of training workshops on the AEPS, and has been involved in the preparation of graduate-level early interventionists. She is Assistant Professor at the College of Education, University of Oregon.

CONTENT DEVELOPED BY

Ruth Kaminski, Ph.D., Assistant Professor, School Psychology Program, University of Oregon, Eugene, Oregon 97403

Kristine Slentz, Ph.D., Associate Professor, Early Childhood and Special Education Department, Western Washington University, 318B Mail Stop 9090, Bellingham, Washington 98225

Melinda Buhl, M.S., Special Educator, Developmental Disabilities Center, St. Luke's Roosevelt Hospital, 428 West 59th Street, New York, New York 10019

Lizann Hupp, M.S.P.A, Speech/Language Pathologist, Patina Design, 10256 Hyla Avenue NE, Bainbridge Island, Washington 98110

Betsy Seth, M.S., Learning Specialist, Mt. Angel School District, Mt. Angel, Oregon 97338

Susan Janko, Ph.D., Assistant Professor, College of Education, University of Washington, Miller Hall, Box 353600, Seattle, Washington 98195

Susan Ryan, Ph.D., Assistant Professor, Special Education Department, University of Alaska at Anchorage, 3211 Providence Drive, Anchorage, Alaska 99508

ACKNOWLEDGMENTS

As noted in Volume 1, the Assessment, Evaluation, and Programming System (AEPS) for Infants and Children has taken years to develop, test, and refine. The AEPS Test for Three to Six Years, as it appears in this volume, is the culmination of years of effort by many people. This combined effort has been both a strength and a weakness. Contributions by multiple people have helped to make the test broad, comprehensive, and useful while at the same time the participation of many individuals has necessitated compromise and negotiation to accommodate the variety of perspectives and suggested changes. From time to time we have found ourselves going full circle.

In addition to the many contributors to the AEPS Test for Three to Six Years, there are three individuals who deserve special mention. Summer Hsia conducted a comprehensive study of the items to help establish selected psychometric parameters of the test. Her conscientious efforts have helped determine the test's reliability and validity. The contributions of Karen Lawrence and Casie Givens should also be recognized. They have been responsible for typing the many versions of the AEPS Test as well as completing many other tasks, large and small, that have made it possible to publish this volume.

Without consistent support in the form of grants from the federal government, the development of the *AEPS Measurement for Three to Six Years* would not have been possible. Nor would the completion of this project have been possible without the support of hundreds of early childhood special education and early intervention personnel who have used the test and provided helpful feedback to project personnel.

PREFACE

At the October 1974 organizational meeting of the American Association for the Education of the Severely and Profoundly Handicapped, which is now called The Association for Persons with Severe Handicaps, a group of frustrated people convened. My recollection is that the meeting was not planned but occurred spontaneously in a dining room over breakfast. The topic of conversation was the need for a functional and accurate measurement tool for young children with severe disabilities. The conversation was a magnet that drew people from adjoining tables as well as those who happened to be passing by. It seemed everyone within earshot who worked with young children was feeling a strong and urgent need for some alternative to the use of standardized norm-referenced tests or homemade tests with questionable validity and reliability. The interest was as intense then as it has been for me and many others during the long life of this project.

From 1974 to 1976, conversations continued periodically among a group of people who were highly motivated to address this pressing measurement need. In the spring of 1976, professionals from six universities met in New Orleans to discuss the possibility of developing a tool that was specifically designed for children who ranged developmentally from birth to 2 years of age and that would yield educationally relevant outcomes. In addition, we discussed the possibility of developing this tool through a consortium effort. Personnel from five of the six universities agreed to work toward a collaborative effort to fill this measurement gap. The initial participants included Diane Bricker from the University of Miami; Dale Gentry, Owen White, and Robin Beck from the University of Washington; Lizbeth Vincent from the University of Wisconsin; Verna Hart from the University of Pittsburgh; and Evelyn Brown-Lynch from the University of Indiana.

A second meeting was held in Madison, Wisconsin, in June 1976, when the group, whose constellation had changed slightly, formalized responsibilities and adopted the name Consortium on Adaptive Performance Evaluation, or CAPE. Two other meetings were held in 1976, one in Kansas City in October and one in Pittsburgh in November. During these meetings, plans were formulated to write an application to be submitted to the Research Branch of the Division of Innovation and Development, Bureau of Education for the Handicapped (now the Office of Special Education Programs). The grant application, written primarily by Dale Gentry and Owen White, was submitted in December with the American Association for the Education of the Severely and Profoundly Handicapped as the sponsoring agency.

The application was approved and funded, permitting formal continuation of the work begun by the consortium members. During the 3-year period of the grant, a number of individuals from the five participating universities shared in the development of the instrument. The major players during this period were Dale Gentry, Diane Bricker, Owen White, Lizbeth Vincent, Evelyn Brown-Lynch, and Verna Hart, although many other individuals made important contributions, in particular Gene Edgar, Margaret Bendersky, and Jeff Seibert.

During this period, conceptual as well as empirical work was undertaken. The principles underlying the tool were refined and the first data collection on the preliminary instrument conducted. It was perhaps at this time that members of the consortium began to realize the magnitude of the task they had set for themselves. I recall that Owen White argued that we should develop one domain, test it, and make the necessary modifications before tackling other test areas. Although he was outvoted, hindsight suggests he was probably correct, and development might have proceeded more rapidly had we followed his suggestion. The size of the task was particularly intimidating because none of the major players could allot sufficient time to the project because of other commitments. In addition, although the consortium players could agree on the need for the tool, we often disagreed on the form and content for such a tool. Attempting to negotiate compromise between developmentalists and behavior analysts was time consuming and exhausting and often led to contentious meetings. Again, hindsight suggests that much of the strength of the ensuing instrument was the result of divergent views represented by consortium members.

In 1980, under the leadership of Dale Gentry with the able assistance of Katie McCarton, a supplemental award to the Handicapped Children's Early Education Project grant to the University of Idaho provided continued support for the project. (By this time Gentry had moved to Idaho and Bricker to Oregon.) During this period, the first complete and usable assessment/evaluation tool became available for comprehensive field testing. The tool was called the Adaptive Performance Instrument (API). The data and informal feedback on the API were extremely interesting but troublesome. The tool had more than 600 items for the developmental range of birth to 2 years. This depth of coverage provided detailed and useful descriptions of children's behavioral repertoires but also took 8–10 hours to administer. Thus, the tool's strength—generation of detailed behavioral profiles—was also its weakness—excessive administration time.

At the termination of the federal supplemental grant, consortium members considered seeking a commercial publisher to disseminate the API. However, several consortium members believed that adequate psychometric data had not been collected on the test and thus continued study was in order. Also, there was the nagging problem of administration time. A complete copy of the API was sent to the U.S. Bureau for the Education of the Handicapped as part of the final project report. In addition, copies of the API that had been made during the granting period were distributed to interested parties as long as the supply lasted.

With the termination of the grant funds, support was no longer available for the consortium to meet or for the continuation of a coordinated and organized research effort. After almost 10 years and the lack of a solidly defensible instrument, several of the original members lost their enthusiasm for the project. Who could blame them?

The Idaho and Oregon group retained their interest and found creative ways to maintain support for the project. During 1983 and 1984, the API was modified considerably. The number of test items was reduced from more than 600 to less than 300, and the developmental range was extended to 36 months. Most items were rewritten and the presentation format changed. The modifications were so extensive that the measure was renamed the Comprehensive Early Evaluation and Programming System (CEEPS). A dissertation conducted by E.J. Bailey (Ayres) at the University of Oregon examined the psychometric properties of the CEEPS and was completed in August 1983.

Using the Bailey-Ayres dissertation data as a base, a research grant was written and submitted to the field-initiated research program of the Division of Innovation and

Development, Office of Special Education Programs. In October 1984, a 3-year grant was awarded to the University of Oregon. During the ensuing 3 years, another extensive revision was conducted on the instrument and the name was changed to the Evaluation and Programming System: For Infants and Young Children, or EPS. In addition, an associated curriculum was developed and field tested.

From 1984 to 1989, extensive data were collected on the EPS Birth to Three Years and have been published elsewhere (Bailey & Bricker, 1986; Bricker, Bailey, & Slentz, 1990; Cripe, 1990; Notari & Bricker, 1990). In 1993, the EPS Test for Birth to Three Years and its associated curriculum were published by Paul H. Brookes Publishing Company. At that time the name was changed to the Assessment, Evaluation, and Programming System (AEPS) for Infants and Children to reflect accurately its purpose and use. The AEPS for Birth to Three Years is composed of a test (*AEPS Measurement for Birth to Three Years*) and an associated curriculum (*AEPS Curriculum for Birth to Three Years*). The success of the AEPS Test and Curriculum for the developmental range from birth to 3 years served as the major impetus for expanding the AEPS to cover the developmental range from 3 to 6 years.

From the time of the first field testing of the EPS Birth to Three Years, there was pressure to expand the system to cover the entire preschool age range. In 1985, work was begun on the development of a test and associated curriculum to address the developmental range from 3 to 6 years. The first version was field tested by Slentz (1986). The results from this study served as a basis for extensive revisions of the test. The revised test was called the Evaluation and Programming System for Young Children—Assessment Level II: Developmentally 3 Years to 6 Years (Bricker, Janko, Cripe, Bailey, & Kaminski, 1989). Selected psychometric properties of the revised test were examined by Hsia (1993). The findings from this study were encouraging and suggested only minor modifications in test items were needed in the third revision, entitled the *Assessment, Evaluation, and Programming System Test for Three to Six Years* (Bricker, Ayres, Slentz, & Kaminski, 1992). A review of the psychometric data on the AEPS Test for Three to Six Years is contained in Appendix A of this volume.

As with the AEPS Test for Birth to Three Years, the AEPS Test for Three to Six Years will likely benefit from further study; however, the considerable pressure from the field for easy access to the test and curriculum has resulted in their release to Paul H. Brookes Publishing Company for commercial publication. We anticipate and encourage continued study of the AEPS. Currently the University of Oregon's Center on Human Development has a field-initiated research grant from the National Institute on Disability and Rehabilitation Research to examine the reliability and treatment validity of the AEPS Test for Three to Six Years.

Although my colleagues and I will continue to study and improve the AEPS Tests and Curricula, we are extremely grateful to have the major product development phases behind us. This brief historical recounting of the AEPS only highlights the enormous effort expended by a dedicated group of people over the years. Lately I have heard that teachers and therapists are asking for an extension of the AEPS to cover the developmental range from 6 to 9 years. That work, if undertaken, will have to be directed by someone else.

Although acknowledging that it has problems and weaknesses, I am, for the most part, pleased with the efforts of our work on the AEPS. Now it is time to move on to other concerns and projects. For me this is the closing of an era—one that has been satisfying and rewarding. I hope that our work will serve as a solid and useful basis for others to expand the system or to develop more effective, useful, and efficient measurement and curricular tools for infants and young children who are at risk for or have disabilities.

Diane Bricker
August 1996

REFERENCES

Bailey, E., & Bricker, D. (1986). A psychometric study of a criterion-referenced assessment instrument designed for infants and young children. *Journal of the Division of Early Childhood, 10*(2), 124–134.

Bricker, D., Ayres, E.J., Slentz, K., & Kaminski, R. (1992). *Assessment, Evaluation, and Programming System Test for Three to Six Years.* Eugene: University of Oregon, Center on Human Development.

Bricker, D., Bailey, E., & Slentz, K. (1990). Reliability, validity, and utility of the Evaluation and Programming System: For Infants and Young Children (EPS-I). *Journal of Early Intervention, 14*(2), 147–160.

Bricker, D., Janko, S., Cripe, J., Bailey, E.J., & Kaminski, R. (1989). *Evaluation and programming system: For infants and young children.* Eugene: University of Oregon, Center on Human Development.

Cripe, J. (1990). *Evaluating the effectiveness of training procedures in a linked system approach to individual family service plan development.* Unpublished doctoral dissertation, University of Oregon, Eugene.

Hsia, T. (1993). *Evaluating the psychometric properties of the Assessment, Evaluation, and Programming System for Three to Six Years: AEPS Test.* Unpublished doctoral dissertation, University of Oregon, Eugene.

Notari, A., & Bricker, D. (1990). The utility of a curriculum-based assessment instrument in the development of individualized education plans for infants and young children. *Journal of Early Intervention, 14*(2), 117–132.

Slentz, K. (1986). *Evaluating the instructional needs of young children with handicaps: Psychometric adequacy of the Evaluation and Programming System—Assessment Level II (EPS-II).* Unpublished doctoral dissertation, University of Oregon, Eugene.

AEPS

Assessment, Evaluation, and
Programming System for
Infants and Children

Edited by **Diane Bricker, Ph.D.**

VOLUME 3

AEPS Measurement
for Three to Six Years

Introduction

The importance of early experience for young children has long been recognized and has been the foundation for early intervention programs designed for young children who have or are at risk for disabilities. Beginning with unclear expectations and a narrow focus, early intervention programs have evolved into comprehensive approaches that produce positive change in the lives of participating children and their families. In large measure, the increasingly positive outcomes engendered by early intervention programs have occurred because of the growing sophistication of personnel, curricular materials, and assessment/evaluation tools. The assessment, intervention, and evaluation system described in this volume and other volumes is an example of this growing sophistication, which will, in turn, enhance future intervention efforts with young children in need of services.

Accompanying this enhancement in quality has been the growth in the number of early intervention programs. This growth has been systematically spurred on by the passage of important federal legislation, beginning with the Education for All Handicapped Children Act (PL 94-142), which was signed into law in 1975. This landmark legislation required public schools to accept all school-age children no matter how severe their disability, and it introduced the concept of the individualized education program (IEP). In 1990, PL 101-476 reauthorized the Education for All Handicapped Children Act and changed the name to the Individuals with Disabilities Education Act (IDEA). Eleven years after the original enactment of PL 94-142, the Education of the Handicapped Act Amendments of 1986 (PL 99-457) extended the mandate for public school programs to 3-, 4-, and 5-year-old children with disabilities and offered states incentives to serve infants and toddlers. PL 99-457 strongly urges the inclusion of families as partners in the development of intervention plans, known as individualized family service plans (IFSPs), and in the delivery of services to their children. The most recent amendments, the Individuals with Disabilities Education Act Amendments of 1991 (PL 102-119), further encourage family participation, permit states to discontinue the use of categorical labels for preschoolers, and strongly urge the inclusion of children at risk for disabilities in early intervention programs. Accompanying this series of important federal enactments have been an increasing number of state mandates to provide services to infants and young children who have disabilities and to their families.

As noted, accompanying the growth of early intervention programs has been an increasing sophistication in the delivery of services. Personnel are better prepared, curricular content is improved, intervention techniques are more effective, and assessment and evaluation approaches are more appropriate and useful. Importantly, there has been a move to develop approaches that are cohesive, coordinated, and comprehensive. Approaches that treat program components as isolated and unrelated units are being replaced by approaches that systematically link the major components of assessment, intervention, and evaluation. The Assessment, Evaluation, and Programming

System (AEPS), presented in this volume, is one such linked approach. The components of this system are displayed in Figure 1.

WHAT IS THE ASSESSMENT, EVALUATION, AND PROGRAMMING SYSTEM?

The AEPS is an assessment and evaluation system that has an associated curriculum. The AEPS is more than an assessment measure; it is a comprehensive and linked system that includes assessment/evaluation, curricular, and family participation components. As shown in Figure 1, the AEPS is divided into two developmental ranges: birth to 3 years (Volumes 1 and 2) and 3–6 years (Volumes 3 and 4). Each developmental range is covered by two volumes, one that contains measurement information and a second that contains associated curricular information. The test and associated measurement materials are contained in Volumes 1 and 3, whereas the curriculum materials are contained in Volumes 2 and 4.

Volume 1, *AEPS Measurement for Birth to Three Years,* is divided into three sections. Section I provides a comprehensive description of the Assessment, Evaluation, and Programming System. Section II presents the AEPS Test items, which are divided into six domains that cover the developmental period from 1 month to 3 years. Section III describes how to involve families in the assessment and evaluation process as well as how to provide specific strategies and guidelines for doing so.

Volume 1 also provides useful appendices to assist in the implementation of the AEPS. Appendix A contains summarized psychometric information on the AEPS Test that has been collected since the early 1980s. Readers requiring more detail are referred to specific published articles. Appendix B contains a series of IEP/IFSP goals and objec-

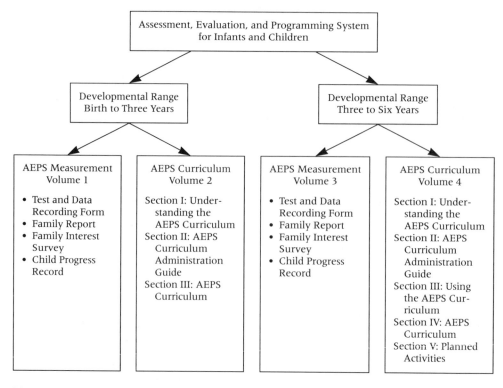

Figure 1.   Components of the Assessment, Evaluation, and Programming System for Infants and Children.

tives specifically related to each item on the AEPS Test. Appendix C contains a set of Assessment Activity Plans. Appendix D contains examples of the AEPS Data Recording Forms, the Family Report, the Family Interest Survey, and the Child Progress Record.

Volume 2, *AEPS Curriculum for Birth to Three Years*, is also composed of three sections. Section I describes the relationship between the AEPS Test described in Volume 1 and the Curriculum. The numbering system for the AEPS Test and Curriculum permits efficient movement between the two. Procedures for general use of the AEPS Curriculum are also described in Section I. Section II explains in detail how to use the AEPS Curriculum separately or in conjunction with the AEPS Test. Section III presents the AEPS curricular activities, covering the fine motor, gross motor, adaptive, cognitive, social-communication, and social domains. For each item on the AEPS Test, an associated set of curricular activities is described, including cross-references to the AEPS Test, the item's importance to a child's development, procedures for using an activity-based intervention approach as well as more structured approaches, cautions, and teaching suggestions.

Volume 3 is described below. Volume 4, *AEPS Curriculum for Three to Six Years*, is composed of five sections. Section I describes the relationship between the AEPS Test described in this volume and the Curriculum. The numbering system for the AEPS Test and Curriculum permits efficient movement between the two. Section II explains how to use the AEPS Curriculum separately or in conjunction with the AEPS Test. Section III describes the use of the AEPS Curriculum in the context of an activity-based intervention approach. Section IV presents the AEPS curricular activities, covering the fine motor, gross motor, adaptive, cognitive, social-communication, and social domains. For each item on the AEPS Test, an associated set of curricular activities is described, including cross-references to the AEPS Test, the item's importance to a child's development, and procedures for using an activity-based intervention approach as well as more structured approaches, cautions, and teaching suggestions. Finally, Section V presents a series of planned activities that most children enjoy and that can be used to embed individual children's goals and objectives.

INTRODUCTION TO VOLUME 3

Volume 3, *AEPS Measurement for Three to Six Years*, is divided into three sections. Section I provides a comprehensive description of the AEPS. Section II presents the AEPS Test items, which are divided into six domains that cover the developmental period from 3 to 6 years. Section III describes how to involve families in the assessment and evaluation process as well as provides specific strategies and guidelines for doing so.

Volume 3 also provides useful appendices to assist in the implementation of the AEPS. Appendix A contains summarized psychometric information on the AEPS Test that has been collected since 1985. Appendix B contains a series of IEP/IFSP goals and objectives specifically related to each item on the AEPS Test. Appendix C contains a set of Assessment Activity Plans. Appendix D contains examples of the AEPS Data Recording Forms, the Family Report, the Family Interest Survey, and the Child Progress Record.

The content in Volume 3 is focused on assisting interventionists and caregivers in assessment and evaluation. It describes a program-relevant assessment and evaluation system designed for interventionists to use on a regular basis. Use of this system will help ensure the appropriate assessment and evaluation of infants and children who are at risk for or who have disabilities and their families.

The developers of the AEPS strongly encourage users to become familiar with its underlying principles. Understanding the purposes of the measurement system and how it operates is fundamental to its appropriate use. Reading and understanding Section I of this volume is mandatory if the material contained in Sections II and III is to be maximally useful to interventionists, caregivers, and, ultimately, children.

REFERENCES

Education for All Handicapped Children Act of 1975, PL 94-142. (August 23, 1977). 20 U.S.C. §1401 *et seq.*
Education of the Handicapped Act Amendments of 1986, PL 99-457. (October 8, 1986). 20 U.S.C. §1400 *et seq.*
Individuals with Disabilities Education Act (IDEA) of 1990, PL 101-476. (October 30, 1990). 20 U.S.C. §1400 *et seq.*
Individuals with Disabilities Education Act Amendments of 1991, PL 102-119. (October 7, 1991). 20 U.S.C. §1400 *et seq.*

Understanding the Assessment, Evaluation, and Programming System for Infants and Children

SECTION

I

Portions of the material contained in Section I are a revision of Bricker, D., Janko, S., Cripe, J., Bailey, E.J., and Kaminski, R. (1989). *Evaluation and programming system: For infants and young children.* Eugene: University of Oregon, Center on Human Development.

Purpose and Value of Assessment and Evaluation

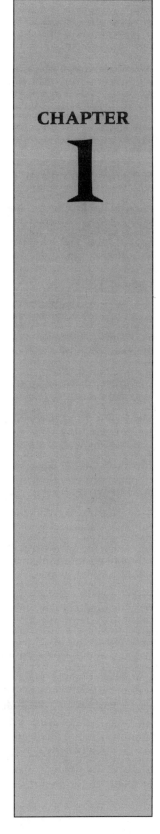

CHAPTER

1

The purpose and value of assessment and evaluation are fundamental to effective intervention. Without the systematic conduct of assessment and evaluation activities, early interventionists do a significant disservice to children and their families, who can ill afford to waste precious time and effort.

PURPOSE OF ASSESSMENT AND EVALUATION

To understand the Assessment, Evaluation, and Programming System (AEPS) for Infants and Children, the purposes for conducting assessment and evaluation activities should be discussed. Although many people use the terms interchangeably, we draw a distinction between assessment and evaluation.

> Assessment refers to the process of establishing a baseline or entry level measurement of the child's skills and desired family outcomes...Evaluation refers to the process of comparing the child's performance on selected intervention objectives before and after intervention, and to compare the progress toward established family outcomes. (Bricker, 1989, p. 236)

Evaluation makes a comparison over time; however, assessment determines the current performance status.

Given these definitions, the purpose of program-related assessment is to determine children's current developmental repertoires across a range of important domains of behavior. Specifically, such assessment is used to determine the skills and information children have and under what conditions they are used. In addition, assessment procedures should determine the next level of skills and information that children should be acquiring; these data are crucial in determining intervention targets. The information necessary to develop an appropriate IEP/IFSP document should come from the assessment activities.

The purpose of evaluation is to compare children's behavioral repertoires at different points over time following intervention or to monitor progress toward family outcomes. For example, following 3 months of intervention, the interventionist's measurement of change in child performance on selected goals and comparison of the performance to a previous measure would constitute an evaluation of child progress. Appropriate practice requires that children's repertoires in target areas be measured and compared at least quarterly to ensure adequate progress toward goals.

VALUE OF ASSESSMENT AND EVALUATION

Discussing the value of assessment and evaluation is important because many early intervention personnel do not systematically use objective measures to assess children's entry behaviors and to evaluate progress over time. Excuses for not conducting objective assessment and evaluation activities include not being a program priority as well as lack of time, lack of appropriate measurement tools, inadequately trained personnel, lack of necessary staff, and lack of financial resources. We would like to argue that none of these reasons provide adequate justification to preclude program-relevant assessment and evaluation.

An example may help explain our reasoning. Suppose you have just discovered that you have a winning lottery ticket; however, to receive your million-dollar prize you must present the winning ticket to an office located in Denver, Colorado, within 2 weeks. You then realize that you are standing in a wooded area without any signs to indicate your location. You do not know the state or county in which you stand. Because you do not know your present location, your two choices are to remain where you are, hoping to be discovered, or to begin walking in some direction. Let us say that you begin walking north. If you are located in Arizona, you might run into Denver; however, if you are located in Minnesota, you will miss Denver completely. If you begin walking east, you might hit Denver if you are located in Oregon, but if you are in Missouri, you will again miss your target completely. Even once you are headed in the right general direction, you may make many detours because you lack precise information on where you are and a reasonable set of directions to lead you to Denver. You may eventually get to Denver, but long after the lottery office is closed and your winnings are being spent by someone who knew where he or she was and had a system to measure his or her progress toward Denver (e.g., a map).

Failing to establish children's entering repertoires, select goals, and map how to reach those goals places children and families in wooded areas with little chance of successful escape. How can early interventionists select appropriate goals and objectives for children and families if they do not know what children can and cannot do and what families see as problems that need remedies? Furthermore, how can interventionists determine whether children and families are making systematic progress toward selected goals and objectives if their progress is not evaluated over time? These are, of course, rhetorical questions posed to emphasize the purposes of assessment and evaluation in early intervention programs.

We can see no adequate justification for not determining children's entering repertoires. Without such information, personnel simply cannot know children's developmental levels or determine the focus of intervention efforts. Beginning without adequate assessment likely leads to moving in the wrong direction and making many unnecessary detours. This, of course, results in wasted resources and time for children, families, and interventionists; therefore, excuses of inadequate time, personnel, and resources are simply not acceptable. Children must be assessed.

Equally important is the systematic evaluation of child and family progress over time. Without monitoring progress toward goals and objectives, interventionists and caregivers have no way of determining whether intervention is effective and change is in order. Again, to not evaluate change over time will likely result in wasted efforts and the poor use of limited resources.

REFERENCE

Bricker, D. (1989). *Early intervention for at-risk and handicapped infants, toddlers, and preschool children.* Palo Alto, CA: VORT Corp.

Linked Assessment, Intervention, and Evaluation Systems Approach to Early Intervention

The use of AEPS measurement components or other similar curriculum-based assessment/evaluation tools is fundamental to the adoption of intervention models that link assessment, intervention, and evaluation processes. These linked intervention models are the most appropriate and effective approaches currently available to early intervention personnel. In this chapter, a linked assessment, intervention, and evaluation approach to early intervention is described. Two outcomes for the reader are anticipated: 1) an understanding of a linked approach, and 2) an understanding of the importance of using a curriculum-based assessment/evaluation tool to employ a linked model.

An explanation of linked assessment-intervention-evaluation systems in early intervention programs is important for at least three reasons. First, many personnel who operate programs have not received adequate preparation on topics of assessment and evaluation or on methods for linking assessment, intervention, and evaluation. Second, descriptions of linked systems seldom appear in the literature. With few exceptions (e.g., Bagnato & Neisworth, 1991; Bagnato, Neisworth, & Munson, 1997; Bricker, 1989; Bricker & Cripe, 1992), descriptions focus on one element (e.g., assessment) and fail to extend the linkage to other program elements at the theoretical level and further fail to provide practical strategies to implement the linkage of assessment, intervention, and evaluation. Third, many available norm- and criterion-referenced instruments yield

Material in this chapter was taken from Bricker, D., Janko, S., Cripe, J., Bailey, E., and Kaminski, R. (1989). *Evaluation and programming system: For infants and young children.* Eugene: University of Oregon, Center on Human Development.

results that are not helpful for program planning for young children who are at risk for or who have disabilities. The common disparity among assessment, intervention, and evaluation efforts is partly due to the use of instruments that contain items with little relationship to program goals and objectives.

The assessment and evaluation of individual change and programmatic impact require that intervention methods and systems be supported with procedures appropriate to evaluating their efficacy. Assessment and evaluation should determine the format and success of intervention for individual children and determine the impact programs have on groups of children. These objectives require that assessment and evaluation procedures serve three distinct but complementary functions: 1) guiding the development of individual program plans, 2) monitoring the success of individual programming, and 3) determining the value of an intervention program for groups or subgroups of children (e.g., at risk; having mild, moderate, and severe disability). Underlying these three functions is the important concept that these separate assessment/evaluation objectives are linked into a unified systems approach.

The linked approach is composed of three processes: assessment, intervention, and evaluation. *Assessment* refers to the process of establishing a baseline or entry-level measurement of the child's skills and desired family outcomes. The assessment process should produce the necessary information to select appropriate and relevant intervention goals and objectives. *Intervention* refers to the process of arranging the physical and social environment to produce the desired growth and development specified in the formulated intervention plan for the child and family. *Evaluation* refers to the process of comparing the child's performance on selected intervention goals and objectives before and after intervention and comparing the family's progress toward established family outcomes.

Figure 2.1 provides an illustration of the linked assessment, intervention, and evaluation approach. The major processes are represented by boxes linked by arrows to indicate the sequence in which the processes should occur. In addition, the vertical arrows indicate the desired participation of professionals and families in each of these three processes.

The assessment, intervention, and evaluation systems approach can be divided into six phases:

Phase One: Initial assessment
Phase Two: Formulation of IEPs/IFSPs
Phase Three: Intervention
Phase Four: Ongoing monitoring for immediate feedback on individualized intervention procedures
Phase Five: Quarterly evaluation of children and families
Phase Six: Annual or semiannual evaluation of individual child and family progress and program effectiveness for total group and subgroups of children, such as those at risk for or those having mild, moderate, or severe disability

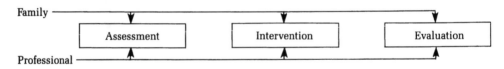

Figure 2.1.   Schematic of a linked assessment-intervention-evaluation approach to early intervention with joint professional and family participation.

As indicated in Figure 2.1, family input and participation should be encouraged throughout all three phases. The more families become involved in the assessment, intervention, and evaluation process, the greater the likelihood of improved outcomes for their children.

Phase One: Initial Assessment

The link among assessment, intervention, and evaluation begins with the entry of children into a program. The major objective of the initial assessment is to formulate a realistic and appropriate IEP/IFSP that has an accompanying individualized evaluation plan. Unfortunately, confusion exists about the purposes for initial assessment. In the present approach, the initial assessment procedures are predicated on previously established child diagnosis and program eligibility, as shown in Figure 2.2.

During screening (a quick assessment of the child), the objective is to determine if the child requires further, more comprehensive diagnostic evaluation, which is generally performed by a professional team. During diagnostic evaluation, standardized norm-referenced tests are often used to determine whether the child performs in a manner similar to his or her age-mates. In addition, specialty tests that attempt to document specific deficiencies may be given. The objectives of diagnostic evaluation are to determine if a child is eligible to receive early intervention services and, when options exist, to refer the child to the most appropriate intervention program. Once a child has been determined to be eligible for services, the final step in the initial assessment process is to administer program-relevant (e.g., curriculum-based) assessments to the child to determine the content of the IEP/IFSP. The content of the IEP/IFSP provides the road map for moving children from their beginning skills repertoires to the acquisition of skills specified as annual goals on their IEPs/IFSPs (Benner, 1992). For the family, this initial assessment should help determine priority interests that can develop into family outcomes.

The formulation of the IEP/IFSP is crucially dependent on an accurate assessment of the child's beginning skill level so that an intervention plan can be developed toward improving areas in which the child is deficient. In addition, the assessment strategies employed should yield information that precisely describes the child's behavior in the following ways. First, the assessment should include information about the child's performance of skills that are appropriate intervention targets. Norm-referenced tests do not typically include items that are appropriate or useful for designing intervention programs. Second, the assessment should include a scoring system that is sensitive to how the child performed the skill and that indicates if the skill was performed independently, with different people, or in different settings. A standard binary scoring system only provides information on whether the child's response was "correct" or "incorrect"; therefore, important information for developing educational programs may be lost (Cole, Swisher, Thompson, & Fewell, 1985). Third, the assessment measure should be designed to be administered by intervention personnel in the child's usual environ-

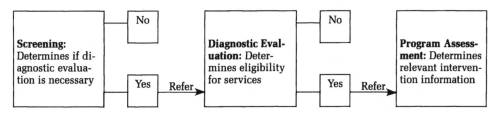

Figure 2.2.   Three-step screening, diagnostic evaluation, and program assessment process.

ment. Individuals working with the child should be able to use the test in the home or other environments in an unobtrusive manner. Fourth, the assessment should have some procedure for the formal inclusion of input from parents or caregivers. Finally, and most important, the information generated by the test should be directly usable in the development of an IEP/IFSP.

An assessment that measures functional skills and is sensitive to the conditions in which a child is most likely to perform the skills will facilitate the development of appropriate and realistic IEPs/IFSPs. This, in turn, will lead to child growth and development and will yield a sensitive measure of child progress throughout the intervention process.

Formulation of an IFSP requires specification of family outcomes as well as children's goals. Family assessment should yield program-relevant information that will aid in developing functional outcome statements, but it should not be seen as intrusive by family members. We recommend the use of a parent interest checklist followed by a structured interview to assist families in developing outcomes they see as relevant and important for the child and family.

Phase Two: Formulation of IEPs/IFSPs

The initial IEP/IFSP should be based primarily on information accumulated during the initial assessment period, although this assessment should be validated at the first quarterly evaluation or sooner. Relevant information should be obtained from parents' knowledge of their children as well as professional observation and testing. The initial information should be used to develop a plan of action for the interventionists and family to identify the specific content areas that the IEP/IFSP will address. The child's portion of the IEP/IFSP should contain goals, objectives, strategies for reaching objectives, and a time frame for meeting selected goals. The IEP/IFSP should be straightforward so that it can be used as a working guide for interventionists and caregivers. The IEP/IFSP can also be used as a criterion for evaluating the success of the intervention.

The family portion of the IFSP should contain a statement of family strengths and needs related to enhancing the child's development. This statement is based on information obtained from the family's assessment of their interests and needs. Priorities can be collaboratively established during a structured interview—meaning that the interventionist has developed a set of open-ended questions to which caregivers can respond (e.g., "How can program staff be most useful to you and your child?"). A set of outcome statements will evolve from these priorities, and activities and resources necessary for reaching outcomes, as well as a timeline, should be indicated (Zeitlin & Williamson, 1994).

Phase Three: Intervention

Once the IEP/IFSP has been formulated by family members and interventionists, the actual intervention activities can be initiated. The child's performance on the program assessment indicates where teaching should begin. Items that the child is unable to perform become the goals and objectives, which often require prioritization. If the assessment tool links directly to the curriculum, interventionists can easily locate the intervention activities that were developed to facilitate acquisition of specific goals and objectives. There is a direct correspondence between the assessment items (skills) identified as goals or objectives and the intervention content and strategies specified in the associated curriculum.

Phase Four: Ongoing Monitoring

A useful IEP/IFSP specifies both the tasks to be conducted and the manner in which the success of the intervention will be evaluated. A variety of strategies may be used for daily or weekly monitoring of child progress (e.g., trial-by-trial data, brief probes during or after intervention activities). The strategies selected should be determined by the specific goals or objectives, the program resources, and the need for daily or weekly monitoring as a source of feedback to keep intervention efforts on track. Weekly monitoring may enhance the prospects of demonstrating individual improvement and program efficacy at quarterly and annual evaluations by providing ongoing feedback that will allow interventionists to detect and remedy ineffective program targets and strategies that impede child progress. Ongoing monitoring also allows timely identification of child progress (e.g., reaching the specified criteria) so that children can proceed with subsequent objectives in the most efficient manner.

The IFSP requires specifications of activities and an associated evaluation procedure to be conducted for the family as well as the child. Parents and staff must arrive at a mutually agreed-upon procedure for monitoring progress toward selected family outcomes; ongoing monitoring is important for these outcomes. Family interests are dynamic and must be reviewed and updated to ensure their appropriateness.

Phase Five: Quarterly Evaluation

Quarterly evaluation should focus on determining the effect of intervention efforts on children's objectives as specified in the IEP/IFSP. This can be done by using the initial assessment measures in conjunction with the weekly data. Quarterly evaluations should be used to compare the child's progress with some standard or expectation for progress. Without assigning an expected date of completion to objectives, it may not be possible to determine if the progress made by the child is acceptable or unacceptable. For example, quarterly IEP/IFSP objectives should have accompanying timelines (e.g., the child is expected to reach criterion on objectives within 3 months).

By frequently plotting the child's progress toward the established objectives, interventionists can establish more realistic objectives. In addition, comparisons between expected and attained outcomes will generate information that may eventually allow the establishment of relevant and useful norms for subgroups of children who are at risk for or who have disabilities.

Quarterly evaluations provide information for revising the IEP/IFSP program. If all children fail to reach their established objectives in the gross motor domain, program staff or caregivers may not be providing enough intervention time in this area or the teaching may be ineffective. In either case, the quarterly evaluation may suggest that a modification of the program is in order. Information from quarterly evaluations provides feedback about the child's progress and clarifies where modifications or revisions in the IEP/IFSP may be necessary.

Similar procedures can be employed for monitoring family progress. Goal Attainment Scaling (GAS) is an effective strategy for helping families and professionals monitor progress toward established outcomes. GAS helps determine if progress is better than expected, as expected, or not up to expectations. Procedures for using GAS are found in Bailey et al. (1986). Dunst, Trivette, and Deal (1988) advocate the use of a 6-point rating scale to evaluate progress or determine if changes are necessary in family outcomes. The type of system employed should be useful for monitoring change but also should be nonjudgmental of the family's participation or progress.

Phase Six: Annual or Semiannual Evaluation

Although encouraged at the federal level through legislative policy and guidelines, implementation of appropriate evaluation efforts at the local or program level has fallen short. The generation of methods to produce objective evidence supporting program effectiveness has been a continuing problem for professionals who work with populations of infants and young children who are at risk for or who have disabilities (Dunst & Rheingrover, 1981; Guralnick & Bennett, 1987; Hauser-Cram, 1990; Odom & Fewell, 1983; Sheehan & Keogh, 1982; Strain, 1984). Many conceptual and methodological problems exist, such as incongruence between program philosophy and intervention procedures, population variability, inadequate instrumentation, inappropriate statistical analyses, and the use of assessment and evaluation systems that do not reflect program emphases (Bricker, Bailey, & Bruder, 1984).

To appropriately determine the impact of intervention content and procedures, a method of comparison should be used that takes into account child behavior prior to the intervention. For meaningful comparison, it is essential that the content of intervention programs is reflected in their evaluation procedures, and this requires a strong and continuing link among assessment, IEP/IFSP development, curricular emphasis, and evaluation (Bagnato et al., 1997).

Annual or semiannual evaluations can be used to evaluate the progress of individual children and families and the generic impact of the program (i.e., subgroup analysis). Without subgroup comparisons, it is difficult to know how to improve intervention strategies for subpopulations of children and families. Methodological design and measurement problems facing the field of early intervention make subgroup evaluations difficult; however, analyses of subgroups may yield important findings on the generalization of impact for certain groups of children and families.

SUMMARY

The six phases of the linked systems approach to early intervention exemplify the need to directly relate the processes of assessment, intervention, and evaluation. Employing such systems allows for efficiency of effort and use of resources, accountability in terms of program impact over time, and individualization through the design of programs specific to the needs of children and their families. Fundamental to the operation of such a system is an assessment/evaluation tool that yields the information necessary to devise appropriate intervention plans. This tool, the AEPS Test, is described in Chapter 3.

REFERENCES

Bagnato, S., & Neisworth, J. (1991). *Assessment for early intervention: Best practices for professionals.* New York: Guilford Press.

Bagnato, S.J., Neisworth, J.T., & Munson, S.M. (1997). *LINKing assessment and early intervention: An authentic curriculum-based approach.* Baltimore: Paul H. Brookes Publishing Co.

Bailey, D., Simeonsson, R., Winton, P., Huntington, G., Comfort, M., Isbell, P., O'Donnell, K., & Helm, J. (1986). Family-focused intervention: A functional model for planning, implementing, and evaluating individualized family services in early intervention. *Journal of the Division for Early Childhood, 10*(2), 156–171.

Benner, S. (1992). *Assessing young children with special needs: An ecological perspective.* White Plains, NY: Longman.

Bricker, D. (1989). *Early intervention for at-risk and handicapped infants, toddlers, and preschool children.* Palo Alto, CA: VORT Corp.

Bricker, D., Bailey, E., & Bruder, M. (1984). The efficacy of early intervention and the handicapped infant: A wise or wasted resource. In *Advances in developmental and behavioral pediatrics* (Vol. V, pp. 373–423). Greenwich, CT: JAI Press.

Bricker, D., & Cripe, J. (1992). *An activity-based approach to early intervention.* Baltimore: Paul H. Brookes Publishing Co.

Bricker, D., Janko, S., Cripe, J., Bailey, E., & Kaminski, R. (1989). *Evaluation and programming system: For infants and young children.* Eugene: University of Oregon, Center on Human Development.

Cole, K., Swisher, M., Thompson, M., & Fewell, R. (1985). Enhancing sensitivity of assessment instruments for children: Graded multidimensional scoring. *Journal of The Association for Persons with Severe Handicaps, 10*(4), 209–213.

Dunst, C., & Rheingrover, R. (1981). An analysis of the efficacy of infant intervention programs with organically handicapped children. *Evaluation and Program Planning, 4,* 287–323.

Dunst, C., Trivette, C., & Deal, A. (1988). *Enabling and empowering families: Principles and guidelines for practice.* Cambridge, MA: Brookline Books.

Guralnick, M., & Bennett, F. (1987). *The effectiveness of early intervention for at-risk and handicapped children.* New York: Academic Press.

Hauser-Cram, P. (1990). Designing meaningful evaluations of early intervention services. In S.J. Meisels & J.P. Shonkoff (Eds.), *Handbook of early childhood intervention* (pp. 583–602). New York: Cambridge University Press.

Odom, S., & Fewell, R. (1983). Program evaluation in early childhood special education: A meta-evaluation. *Educational Evaluation and Policy Analysis, 5,* 445–460.

Sheehan, R., & Keogh, B. (1982). Strategies for documenting progress of handicapped children in early education programs. *Educational Evaluation and Policy Analysis, 3(6),* 59–67.

Strain, P. (1984). Efficacy research with young handicapped children: A critique of the status quo. *Journal of the Division for Early Childhood, 9(1),* 4–10.

Zeitlin, S., & Williamson, G.G. (1994). *Coping in young children: Early intervention practices to enhance adaptive behavior and resilience.* Baltimore: Paul H. Brookes Publishing Co.

Using the AEPS Test

A linked assessment-intervention-evaluation approach is predicated on having a measurement instrument that permits the collection of program-related performance data on children that can be used to formulate IEPs/IFSPs and guide intervention efforts. It is also important that the instrument be able to monitor subsequent child progress.

An assessment/evaluation instrument should meet certain criteria in order to be appropriate for preschool children who are at risk for or who have disabilities and to provide useful programming and evaluation information (Bricker, 1989; McLean & McCormick, 1993). Instruments designed to assess children, monitor child progress, and assist in program evaluation should

1. Be used by those people who deal with the child on a regular basis (e.g., interventionists, aides, parents) in familiar settings (e.g., home, classroom)
2. Reflect curricular content of the intervention program
3. Provide a logical developmental sequence of items or objectives that can be used as training guidelines
4. Accommodate a range of disabilities
5. Specify performance criteria that indicate if a child has a particular skill and if the skill is a functional part of the child's daily repertoire
6. Be a reliable and valid measure

The AEPS Test[1] is a criterion-referenced tool developed for use by direct service personnel (e.g., classroom interventionists, home visitors) and specialists (e.g., communication specialists, occupational therapists, physical therapists, psychologists) to assess and evaluate the skills and abilities of young children who are at risk for or who have disabilities. The AEPS Test was designed to yield appropriate information for the development of IEPs/IFSPs, intervention programs, and program evaluation. The instrument was also developed to be used in conjunction with the AEPS Curriculum or other similar curricula

---

[1]The AEPS Test was developed, in part, from the *Adaptive Performance Instrument (API)* (CAPE, 1978).

(e.g., *The Carolina Curriculum for Preschoolers with Special Needs* [Johnson-Martin, Atter-meier, & Hacker, 1990]).

Items on the AEPS Test cover the developmental period from 3 to 6 years. Items are focused on determining a child's skill level across early critical processes. The AEPS Test is generally appropriate for children whose chronological age is from 3 to 9 years. However, significant modification may be necessary in the wording of the items, crite-ria, and suggested testing procedures to make them appropriate for a child who is chronologically older than 6 years of age.

In addition to the assessment/evaluation function, a set of accompanying materi-als is designed to enhance the AEPS Test. These materials include 1) a set of IEP/IFSP goals and objectives (see Appendix B), 2) AEPS Data Recording Forms (see Appendix D), 3) a curriculum composed of a comprehensive set of programming steps and suggested intervention activities (*AEPS Curriculum for Three to Six Years* [Bricker & Waddell, 1996]), 4) an assessment form designed to be completed by families (AEPS Family Report; see Appendix D), 5) an assessment of family interests (AEPS Family Interest Survey; see Appendix D), and 6) a child progress form (AEPS Child Progress Record; see Appendix D).

ADVANTAGES OF THE AEPS TEST

Personnel who work with young children who are at risk for or who have disabilities are often frustrated by attempting to use traditional instruments to assess and measure child progress. Frequently, outcomes from direct tests or standardized measures are not reflective of a child's actual abilities or progress and are not helpful in selecting appro-priate intervention goals and objectives. Furthermore, the progress made by children with disabilities may be slow and gradual, and the increments between items on tradi-tional assessment instruments often do not reflect small changes in behavior. Addition-ally, traditional standardized assessments often penalize children with communication, sensory, or motor disabilities by allowing only a single correct response. To counter these and other problems faced by personnel interested in assessing children who are at risk for or who have disabilities, the AEPS Test diverges from other available instru-ments in a number of ways.

1. The AEPS Test measures functional skills and abilities thought to be essential for young children to function independently and to cope with environmental demands. The focus on functional skills and abilities ensures that each test item is potentially an appropriate intervention target.

2. The AEPS Test is comprehensive in nature. The content of the AEPS Test cov-ers the major domains of fine motor, gross motor, adaptive, cognitive, social-communi-cation, and social development. The comprehensive nature of this instrument makes it valuable both as an initial assessment tool and in monitoring children's subsequent progress.

3. The primary and preferred method of obtaining assessment/evaluation infor-mation is through observation of the child in familiar and usual environments. This feature of the AEPS Test provides the assessor with critical information about what responses the child uses in a functional manner and when and how they are used.

4. To avoid interfering with the child's performance, the AEPS Test allows the user to adapt or modify either the presentation format of items or the stated criteria for children with disabilities. In particular, users are encouraged to find and use adapta-tions for children with sensory or motor impairments. For example, the user is free to

use sign language with children with hearing impairments and may allow children with motor impairments to use prosthetics to complete items such as "eats with fork or spoon." Freedom and flexibility in modifying the presentation or in the child's response are acceptable because the test results are not for comparative purposes but, instead, are used to generate appropriate intervention targets for individual children.

5. The items on the AEPS Test are written to reflect conceptual or response classes rather than singular, specific responses. For example, an item asks about hand–eye coordination rather than the child's ability to insert pegs in a pegboard.

6. The AEPS Test has an associated curriculum (*AEPS Curriculum for Three to Six Years* [Bricker & Waddell, 1996]). Results from the assessment can be used to locate and select intervention content for children. There is a direct relationship between the items on the AEPS Test and the curriculum materials.

7. A parallel family assessment/evaluation form (AEPS Family Report) is available for caregivers to assess their child to help promote involvement in the IEP/IFSP process. In addition, completion of a parallel family form (IEP/IFSP Planning Guide) assists the family in preparing to contribute to the IEP/IFSP meeting. Asking caregivers to complete an assessment form on their child clearly conveys that the professional staff consider their knowledge of their child to be an important contribution to the assessment and IEP/IFSP process. In addition, there is a parallel form to assist families in monitoring their child's progress over time (AEPS Child Progress Record).

8. An associated set of written IEP/IFSP goals and objectives is available that is keyed to individual assessment/evaluation items on the AEPS Test. These IEP/IFSP goals and objectives can be used to guide the development of IEPs/IFSPs and intervention plans.

9. An associated assessment form to determine family interests (AEPS Family Interest Survey) has also been developed. Using an unobtrusive format, parents or caregivers can indicate topics or areas of interest relevant to the child, the family, and the community and assign a priority to each selection.

These advantages make the AEPS Test an appealing choice for interventionists and specialists who are interested in obtaining comprehensive information on children's behavioral repertoires. Perhaps most appealing is the immediate and functional use of this information to develop intervention programs and monitor progress.

CAVEATS FOR ASSESSMENT

An examination of the AEPS Test reveals several characteristics that may initially appear to be limitations. These characteristics are addressed in anticipation of questions that may arise about administration and interpretation of the AEPS Test outcomes.

1. The AEPS Test does not provide norms for the test outcomes. Although this may seem to be a disadvantage, norms have not been developed so that the focus of intervention is on assisting children to acquire functional skills and information in logical order rather than on targeting items because they reflect the child's chronological age. For children with disabilities, the value of comparisons with developmental norms is, at best, questionable. Rather, it is more essential to determine the child's current level of functioning and work on the skills that will move the child toward selected developmental objectives.

2. Assessment with the AEPS Test requires an initial time investment. Users of the AEPS Test have found the administration time to vary as a function of 1) familiarity with the test (e.g., the more familiar the assessor is with the AEPS Test, the more quick-

ly assessments can be completed); 2) familiarity with the child (e.g., the more familiar the assessor is with the child's behavioral repertoire, the more quickly assessment can be completed); and 3) the child's level of functioning (e.g., a child with a limited repertoire can be assessed more quickly than a child with a more extensive repertoire). Such variations make it difficult to state precisely how rapidly the AEPS Test can be administered; however, interventionists familiar with the test and their children report that initial assessments require 1–2 hours, whereas subsequent assessments take one quarter of that time. Users unfamiliar with the test can expect the assessment to take longer; however, as familiarity increases, administration time decreases.

Some interventionists indicate that an expenditure of 1–2 hours or more on assessment or evaluation per child is unrealistic, given their programs' resources. We would argue that assessment/evaluation should not be viewed as a discrete activity that can be completed in a predetermined period of time. Rather, assessment/evaluation should be viewed as a continuous process that occurs across time and situations and allows for the development of a comprehensive developmental profile of a child. Hastily completed assessments or evaluations that do not include information about a child's performance across tasks, materials, people, and settings will yield results that are incomplete and often inaccurate. Comprehensive, detailed assessments are fundamental to the development of appropriate IEPs/IFSPs and to the quality of subsequent intervention. If IEPs/IFSPs are not based on comprehensive, accurate assessment data, they will be of questionable value and relevance to children.

3.   Unlike some assessment/evaluation instruments, understanding general developmental patterns is fundamental to the appropriate use of the AEPS Test. For example, items that assess the child's understanding of means–end relationships probably will not be properly scored and interpreted if the assessor does not have an adequate grasp of the means–end concept and its importance to a child's overall development. Individuals who do not have an adequate background in early child development should not administer the AEPS Test without careful supervision. Individuals who do have knowledge of early child development will find that the AEPS Test has a structure that permits them to capitalize on their expertise and apply it to the creation of sound intervention programs.

4.   In addition to being familiar with early child development, users of the AEPS Test should be familiar with the organization and content of the instrument. The AEPS Test is not a simple checklist that can be examined briefly prior to its use. The assessor should have read each item and studied its associated criteria and notes. In addition, the user should be familiar with the Data Recording Forms, including the scoring procedures and the qualifying notes. Use of the AEPS Test without accurate preparation may yield inaccurate and misleading results.

5.   The AEPS Test can be used by individual interventionists; however, the accuracy and quality of the outcomes will be enhanced if specialists (e.g., communication specialists, occupational therapists, physical therapists) participate in the assessment and subsequent evaluation. It is particularly important to involve a motor specialist if the child has a motor disability, a sensory specialist if the child has a sensory disability (e.g., hearing or visual impairment), and a communication specialist if the child has a communication delay or disorder.

Formulation of appropriate IEPs/IFSPs and subsequent intervention plans is fundamental to effective intervention. To accomplish this, the assessment process should generate accurate and reliable information on a child's behavioral repertoire in contexts that are typical for the child. Acquisition of such information requires an investment of time and effort, but it will yield accurate assessment data for developing appropriate IEPs/IFSPs.

TARGET POPULATION

The AEPS Test was designed to be used with children who are at risk for or who have disabilities. The developmental range of the test items is from 3 to 6 years. The AEPS Test has been successfully used with children who have Down syndrome, cerebral palsy, central nervous system disorders, seizure disorders, sensory impairments, and general developmental delays. In addition, the AEPS Test has been successfully used with children who are environmentally at risk (e.g., those with adolescent parents, those with substance-abusing parents).

Interventionists and specialists have also used the AEPS Test with children who have severe impairments. Successful use of the test with this population requires some general modifications. For children whose chronological age exceeds 6 years, items should be carefully evaluated to ensure their appropriateness for elementary-age children. The use of the *AEPS Test for Three to Six Years* is not recommended for children whose developmental levels are less than 3 years; rather, the use of the *AEPS Test for Birth to Three Years* should be explored.

The acquisition of new skills and information by children with severe disabilities is, by definition, slow; therefore, interventionists may wish to use the AEPS Test objectives as goals and develop new, simpler objectives to meet the adjusted goals. This shift will help adjust for the slower development seen in children with severe disabilities.

CONTENT AND ORGANIZATION OF THE AEPS TEST

Conducting assessment and evaluation with the AEPS Test allows interventionists to generate a comprehensive profile of the child's behavior in familiar environments, as opposed to a narrow description of one aspect of the child's behavior. The developmental range covered is 3–6 years. To collect comprehensive information on the child's developmental status, six broad curricular areas called *domains* are included: Fine Motor, Gross Motor, Adaptive, Cognitive, Social-Communication, and Social. Each domain encompasses a particular set of skills, behaviors, or information that is traditionally seen as related developmental phenomena. Each domain is divided into *strands*. Strands consist of related groups of behaviors organized under a common category. For example, behaviors relating to movement in standing and walking are grouped in the "balance and mobility in standing and walking" strand in the Gross Motor Domain. An overview of the six domains with their associated strands is provided in Table 3.1.

Items on the AEPS Test are sequenced to facilitate the assessment of a child's ability to perform a particular behavior within a developmental sequence of skills. Each strand contains a series of test items called *goals* and *objectives*. The goals were developed to be used as annual goals on a child's IEP/IFSP. The objectives represent more discrete skills and enable the user to accurately pinpoint a child's level within a specific skill sequence. Objectives can serve as short-term or quarterly objectives on the child's IEP/IFSP.

The number of strands varies by domain, as shown in Table 3.1. Strands and goals are arranged from easier or developmentally earlier skills to more difficult or developmentally more advanced skills whenever possible. The objectives listed under each goal

Table 3.1.   Overview of the domains and strands for the *AEPS Test for Three to Six Years*

Domains	Strands	
Fine Motor	A:	Manipulation of objects
	B:	Prewriting
Gross Motor	A:	Balance and mobility in standing and walking
	B:	Play skills
Adaptive	A:	Dining
	B:	Personal hygiene
	C:	Dressing and undressing
Cognitive	A:	Participation
	B:	Demonstrates understanding of concepts
	C:	Categorizing
	D:	Sequencing
	E:	Recalling events
	F:	Problem solving
	G:	Play
	H:	Premath
	I:	Prereading
Social-Communication	A:	Social-communicative interactions
	B:	Production of words, phrases, and sentences
Social	A:	Interaction with others
	B:	Interaction with environment
	C:	Knowledge of self and others

are arranged in a reverse sequence—the most difficult items occur first and the less difficult items follow sequentially. This was done to facilitate test administration. If a child performs a more advanced objective within a sequence of objectives (e.g., jumps in place within the developmental sequence of play skills), the assessment of earlier objectives within the sequence (e.g., balances on one foot, maintains balance in walking) is generally unnecessary. This procedure makes assessment more efficient and generally holds true unless the child's behavioral repertoire appears to be uneven (i.e., the child is inconsistent and performs a variety of splinter skills). In this case, assessment of a broader range of items is in order. The hierarchical arrangement of easy to more difficult strands, goals, and objectives is shown in Figure 3.1.

The content of the *AEPS Test for Three to Six Years* is less hierarchical than that of the *AEPS Test for Birth to Three Years,* reflecting an increase in the influence of individual experience and environmental factors on the preschool child's development. As children approach school age, they show increasing individuality and variability as they learn new skills.

The identification system associated with the strands (e.g., A, B, C), goals (e.g., G1, G2, G3), and objectives (e.g., 1.1, 1.2, 1.3) reflects this sequential arrangement and has been included to assist the test user in locating and referring to items. The organizational structure of the strands, goals, and objectives is presented in Figure 3.2.

INTERDISCIPLINARY TEAM ASSESSMENTS

Early intervention and early childhood special education programs have a variety of staffing patterns. Many programs have more than one interdisciplinary team specialist who is regularly available to children and families. Participation by these specialists in

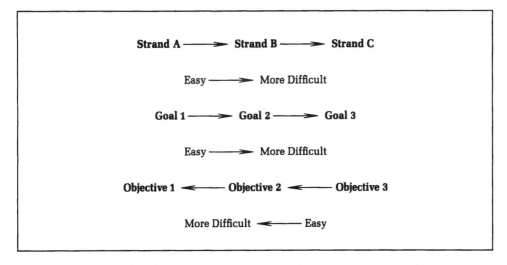

Figure 3.1. Hierarchical arrangement of strands, goals, and objectives on the AEPS Test.

the administration of programmatic assessments, such as the AEPS Test, is encouraged. Inclusion of specialists helps ensure the efficient and comprehensive completion of the programmatic assessment for children. The team members may choose to participate in group, center-based assessment by observing and interacting with the children at a particular station. For example, the communication specialist might record a language sample on the Social-Communication Recording Form, whereas the physical or occupational therapist completes the fine motor and gross motor portions of the AEPS Test. Another alternative is for the specialists to observe and score the domains pertinent to their areas of expertise while the interventionist moves children through a series of assessment activities. To increase the awareness of the strengths and needs of the child across developmental domains, results should be compiled and shared among the team members. Such sharing also helps eliminate the redundancy and inconsistency that occur when professionals complete separate assessments. Incorporating the observa-

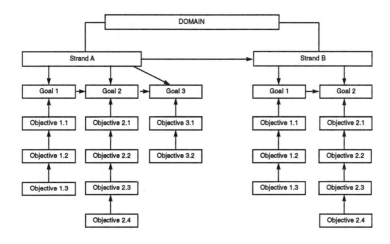

Figure 3.2. Organizational structure of assessment items on the AEPS Test.

tions of the specialists and interventionists into one assessment protocol leads to more efficient and functional program planning.

SUMMARY

The information in this chapter assists the user in understanding the general features of the AEPS Test that distinguish it from other available instruments. The overall organization and content of the AEPS Test are described to assist the user in appreciating its structure and coverage. Specific administration guidelines are contained in Chapter 6, preceding the AEPS Test items.

REFERENCES

Bricker, D. (1989). *Psychometric and utility study of a comprehensive early assessment instrument for handicapped infants and children.* Final Report submitted to the U.S. Office of Education, Office of Special Education Programs, Washington, DC.

Bricker, D., & Waddell, M. (Eds.). (1996). *Assessment, evaluation, and programming system for infants and children: Vol. 4. AEPS curriculum for three to six years.* Baltimore: Paul H. Brookes Publishing Co.

CAPE. (1978). *Adaptive performance instrument (API).* Seattle, WA: The Consortium on Adaptive Performance Evaluation.

Johnson-Martin, N.M., Attermeier, S.M., & Hacker, B.J. (1990). *The Carolina curriculum for preschoolers with special needs.* Baltimore: Paul H. Brookes Publishing Co.

McLean, M., & McCormick, K. (1993). Assessment and evaluation in early intervention. In W. Brown, S.K. Thurman, & L.F. Pearl (Eds.), *Family-centered early intervention with infants and toddlers: Innovative cross-disciplinary approaches* (pp. 43–79). Baltimore: Paul H. Brookes Publishing Co.

Family Participation in Assessment and Evaluation

Family input and participation should be encouraged in assessment, intervention, and evaluation. The greater the involvement, the greater likelihood of improved outcomes for children and for families in general. To enhance and help ensure family participation, the AEPS includes a set of materials that were developed to assist parents and caregivers in the assessment/evaluation of their child and to identify family interests. These family-guided materials can be used in conjunction with other AEPS materials. They include

AEPS Family Report
IEP/IFSP Planning Guide
AEPS Child Progress Record
AEPS Family Interest Survey

This chapter presents a general overview of the purposes and designs of these materials. Samples of the AEPS Family Report, AEPS Family Interest Survey, and AEPS Child Progress Record are contained in Appendix D of this volume.

AEPS FAMILY REPORT

The AEPS Family Report is a set of assessment/evaluation items developed to obtain information from parents and caregivers about their children's skills and abilities across major areas of development. It was designed to be used in conjunction with the AEPS Test—each item on the AEPS Family Report corresponds directly to a goal or objective on the AEPS Test, as illustrated in Table 4.1.

Structured procedures to obtain assessment/evaluation information from parents and other caregivers are

Material in this chapter was taken in part from Bricker, D., Bailey, E., Gumerlock, S., Buhl, M., and Slentz, K. (1986). *Administration guide: Experimental edition—I. Parent form level I: For infants and young children.* Eugene: University of Oregon, Center on Human Development.

Table 4.1. An example of corresponding items from the AEPS Test and the
AEPS Family Report

	AEPS Test	AEPS Family Report
Domain	Social	Social
Strand	A: Interaction with Others	
Item	G1: Has play partners	1. Does your child choose to play with other children?

important for several reasons. First, caregivers often have more opportunities to observe their children's behavior than do professionals. This rich source of information should never be overlooked. Second, accurate assessment and evaluation is dependent on gathering information from a variety of sources. The family's perspective about a child should always be included when gathering assessment and evaluation information. Third, caregiver and professional observations can be compared to determine points of agreement and disagreement. The points of agreement can serve as priorities for the development of IEP/IFSP outcomes. The points of disagreement indicate that additional information is needed. Fourth, asking caregivers to participate in the assessment/ evaluation process conveys an important message—program personnel believe caregivers can contribute to their children's intervention programs. Finally, the use of formal procedures to involve parents and caregivers may assist in their increased participation in the IEP/IFSP process and subsequent monitoring of child progress.

The AEPS Family Report has several important features. First, the AEPS Family Report corresponds directly to the AEPS Test, which is used by professionals. The AEPS Family Report items are simple paraphrases of the goals and, in some cases, objectives on the AEPS Test. This feature permits a direct comparison between the caregivers' and professionals' assessments of the child.

Second, the AEPS Family Report measures skills that are functional for young children; that is, only skills that may enhance the child's ability to cope with and adapt to the demands of his or her social and physical environments are included. This focus on functional skills ensures that all of the items have the potential of being appropriate intervention targets. This feature of the AEPS Family Report makes the assessment outcome of direct relevance and use to the development of the child's IEP/IFSP. The assessment information can be used to assist in developing the child's IEP/IFSP and to formulate subsequent programming to be delivered by an intervention team.

A third feature of the AEPS Family Report that makes it valuable both as an initial assessment tool and in monitoring the child's subsequent progress is the comprehensive nature of the instrument. The major developmental areas of fine motor, gross motor, adaptive, cognitive, social-communication, and social behavior are included in the instrument.

Fourth, although caregivers may complete the AEPS Family Report from their knowledge of and experience with the child, they are encouraged to verify their knowledge through observation of the child in familiar environments. This feature of the AEPS Family Report provides information about which responses the child uses in a functional manner and when and how they are used.

Caregivers are asked to score each item on the AEPS Family Report by selecting one of three responses that most accurately describes their child's current level of functioning: "Yes," "Sometimes," and "Not Yet." Interventionists can translate caregivers' scores to 2, 1, and 0, respectively. Parents or caregivers are informed that their child is not expected to perform all the skills listed on the form. Before scoring each item, caregivers are encouraged to observe children in situations that are likely to elicit the skill rather than score items from memory.

More information on the AEPS Family Report can be found in Chapter 10, and a complete copy of the AEPS Family Report is contained in Appendix D.

IEP/IFSP PLANNING GUIDE

The IEP/IFSP Planning Guide is a simple one-page form developed to assist families in preparing for their IEP/IFSP meeting. Parents or caregivers may or may not find completing this form to be useful. Whether to complete the IEP/IFSP Planning Guide should be the family's choice.

The IEP/IFSP Planning Guide is divided into three sections for recording information: IEP/IFSP logistics, strengths of the child and the family, and family priorities. The logistics section is used to enter the child's name and birth date, the family's name, the date of the IEP/IFSP meeting, the location, and the names of the people attending. The strengths section includes one column for listing the child's strengths and a second column for indicating the family's strengths. The final section, family priorities, provides space for writing the child's goals—those items that the parents noted as priorities on the AEPS Family Report. In addition, there is space to indicate the family interests that were noted on the AEPS Family Interest Survey (described later in this chapter). A copy of the IEP/IFSP Planning Guide is shown in Figure 4.1.

Parents or caregivers can complete the IEP/IFSP Planning Guide independently or in conjunction with a professional. Some families may find completing the IEP/IFSP Planning Guide to be a helpful step in preparing for the IEP/IFSP meeting.

AEPS CHILD PROGRESS RECORD

In addition to involving parents in the initial assessment of their child, it is useful to have parents and caregivers participate in the ongoing monitoring of their child's progress. The AEPS Child Progress Record was developed for this purpose.

As with the AEPS Family Report, the AEPS Child Progress Record parallels the AEPS Test. Each of the goals and objectives from the AEPS Test are listed hierarchically on the AEPS Child Progress Record by domain and by strand. As children meet the stated criteria for a goal or objective, that progress can be indicated by striking or shading through the particular goal or objective. This form provides parents and caregivers with a visual record of each child's accomplishments, current targets, and future goals and objectives. Figure 4.2 contains a partially completed strand from the Fine Motor Domain of the AEPS Child Progress Record.

The AEPS Child Progress Record should be updated quarterly in conjunction with quarterly administrations of the AEPS Test. For children with severe disabilities, interventionists may wish to add items to the AEPS Child Progress Record by scaling back the objectives to smaller, more discrete targets. Parents of children with severe disabilities may become discouraged if their child appears to be making no progress over time. A complete copy of the AEPS Child Progress Record is contained in Appendix D.

AEPS FAMILY INTEREST SURVEY

The AEPS Family Interest Survey is a self-assessment for families to identify their interests. This measure has been developed to assist in the IEP/IFSP process. The AEPS Fam-

---

IEP/IFSP Planning Guide

Child's Name: _____ Birthdate: _____ Family Name: _____
Date of IEP/IFSP: _____ Time: _____ Location: _____
Family Members/Professionals/Agency Representatives your family wishes to attend meeting:

_____

_____

_____

Strengths

Child Strengths
(Include recent progress or changes, favorite activities, special qualities)

Family Strengths
(Include available resources, special qualities, abilities, supports)

_____   _____

_____   _____

_____   _____

_____   _____

_____   _____

Family Priorities

Child Goals
(Taken from AEPS Family Report)

Family Interests
(Taken from AEPS Family Interest Survey)

1. _____   1. _____

2. _____   2. _____

3. _____   3. _____

4. _____   4. _____

5. _____   5. _____

Figure 4.1. Sample IEP/IFSP Planning Guide form.

ily Interest Survey is based on the philosophy that families should identify the outcomes they desire from their own and their child's participation in the program.

The AEPS Family Interest Survey is divided into three major categories: child, family, and community interests. These categories were derived from selected literature on family systems and ecologically based approaches to intervention (e.g., Bailey & Simeonsson, 1988; Bricker, 1989; Bronfenbrenner, 1979; Dunst, Trivette, & Deal, 1988;

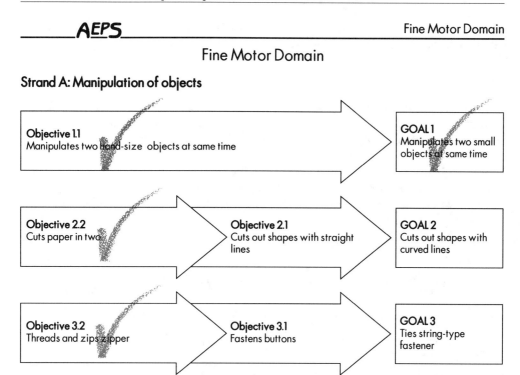

Fine Motor Domain

Strand A: Manipulation of objects

Figure 4.2.   Sample section from the AEPS Child Progress Record.

Krauss & Jacobs, 1990; Turnbull & Turnbull, 1991). These approaches promote recognition of the child as a member of the family unit and the understanding that what affects the child also affects other family members, as well as what affects the family also affects the child. In addition, these perspectives emphasize the interconnectedness among families, communities, and the larger society. Adoption of these approaches requires assessment and evaluation of the environmental factors that families perceive to be important. To accomplish this, the AEPS Family Interest Survey asks families to indicate their priority interests for the child and the family. This approach purposely avoids a problem, weakness, or need orientation that carries connotations of family pathology inappropriate to the majority of families participating in early intervention programs.

There are 30 items on the AEPS Family Interest Survey that are divided into the three survey categories. Each item is a statement designed to assist families in identifying interests pertinent to their child. The statements help families define interests in gathering information, support, and resources or in participating in activities offered by the intervention program, related agencies, and the community. An open-ended question at the end of the survey allows families to list additional interests. Each item is written as a positive, action-oriented statement that can be translated into a functional and measurable outcome.

Each item is followed by two sets of three boxes that parents or caregivers can use to indicate if the item is a priority interest, an interest but not a current priority, or not an interest at this time. The first set of boxes is to be used for the initial IEP/IFSP development and the second set is used for quarterly or semiannual reviews.

A copy of the AEPS Family Interest Survey is contained in Appendix D. More detail on its use is provided in Chapter 9.

SUMMARY

This chapter has described a set of family-guided materials that were developed to be used in conjunction with other AEPS materials. These materials were developed to be supportive rather than invasive (Bailey & Henderson, 1993). The assessment approach to families is designed to assist families in determining their needs and the priority of those needs and then to find acceptable strategies for meeting those priorities (Slentz & Bricker, 1992). The materials were also developed to enhance family participation, a value repeatedly stressed by early intervention professionals, policy developers, and parents themselves.

REFERENCES

Bailey, D., & Henderson, L. (1993). Traditions in family assessment: Toward an inquiry-oriented, reflective model. In D. Bryant & M. Graham (Eds.), *Implementing early intervention* (pp. 127–147). New York: Guilford Press.

Bailey, D., & Simeonsson, R. (Eds.). (1988). *Family assessment in early intervention.* Columbus, OH: Charles E. Merrill.

Bricker, D. (1989). *Early intervention for at-risk and handicapped infants, toddlers, and preschool children.* Palo Alto, CA: VORT Corp.

Bricker, D., Bailey, E., Gumerlock, S., Buhl, M., & Slentz, K. (1986). *Administration guide: Experimental edition—I. Parent form level I: For infants and young children.* Eugene: University of Oregon, Center on Human Development.

Bronfenbrenner, U. (1979). *The ecology of human development: Experiments by nature and design.* Cambridge, MA: Harvard University Press.

Dunst, C., Trivette, C., & Deal, A. (1988). *Enabling and empowering families: Principles and guidelines for practice.* Cambridge, MA: Brookline Books.

Krauss, W.M., & Jacobs, F. (1990). Family assessment: Purposes and techniques. In S.J. Meisels & J.P. Shonkoff (Eds.), *Handbook of early childhood intervention* (pp. 303–325). New York: Cambridge University Press.

Slentz, K., & Bricker, D. (1992). Family-guided assessment for IFSP development: Jumping off the family assessment bandwagon. *Journal of Early Intervention, 16*(1), 11–19.

Turnbull, A.P., & Turnbull, H.R. III. (1991). *Families, professionals, and exceptionality: A special partnership* (2nd ed.). Columbus, OH: Charles E. Merrill.

Linking Assessment, Intervention, and Evaluation

Developing the IEP/IFSP, Intervention Plans, and Evaluation Procedures

Since the passage of PL 94-142 (now PL 101-476) and PL 99-457 (reauthorized as PL 102-119), the IEP and IFSP have become an integral part of intervention services. The federal regulations governing the development and content of IEPs/IFSPs mandate many of the practices characteristic of quality intervention services, including individualized selection of objectives and procedures based on a child's current functioning level, family involvement in the planning process, use of objective evaluation procedures to monitor child progress, and educational placement based on child needs rather than on a disability label or administrative convenience.

The purpose of this chapter is to describe the process to be followed once the child and family assessment is complete. How can interventionists and caregivers translate assessment data into functional and usable IEP/IFSP documents and subsequent intervention plans? Although child and family assessment/evaluation are likely to be conducted simultaneously, this chapter deals with these topics separately. The first section covers 1) the recommended process to be followed for developing an IEP/IFSP for a child, 2) translation of goals and objectives into intervention plans, 3) an intervention approach that is activity based, and 4) evaluation of child progress over time. The second section of this chapter addresses family participation in assessment/evaluation, including 1) the translation of family assessment information into IFSPs, and 2) the subsequent evaluation of family progress over time. A general schematic for these processes is contained in Figure 5.1.

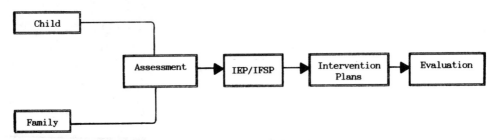

Figure 5.1.   Processes for linking assessment information to developing IEP/IFSP, intervention plans, and evaluation.

CHILD ASSESSMENT/EVALUATION

IEP/IFSP Development for the Child

As shown in Figure 5.1, the relationship between the program assessment instrument and the development of the IEP/IFSP provides an important link between assessment and intervention. Three features of the AEPS Test make this link between assessment and intervention direct and relevant. First, the AEPS Test is comprehensive and covers all developmental areas for programming (i.e., fine motor, gross motor, adaptive, cognitive, social-communication, and social). Second, each domain is composed of items that are, for the most part, hierarchically arranged from simple to increasingly complex, which is helpful in determining the sequence of skills to be taught. Third, each item on the AEPS Test measures a functional skill and is thus a potentially relevant intervention target.

The importance of family participation in a child's intervention program cannot be overemphasized; therefore, it is important to use an IEP/IFSP process that generates meaningful parent participation. Some ways of encouraging active parent and caregiver involvement are to provide parents and caregivers with an understanding of the IEP/IFSP process before the IEP/IFSP meeting is conducted and to develop strategies to assist caregivers in selecting and prioritizing appropriate goals for their child. As described in Chapter 4, the AEPS Family Report can be used in conjunction with the AEPS Test for this purpose.

The first step in developing an IEP/IFSP from the AEPS Test and AEPS Family Report assessments is *summarization of the results.* Items taken from the AEPS Test and AEPS Family Report are used by the team (e.g., interventionist, family members, specialists) as a basis for developing IEP/IFSP goals and objectives. The team reviews the results from each developmental domain. The caregivers present what was recorded on the AEPS Family Report and the IEP/IFSP Planning Guide, and other team members (e.g., interventionist) present the results of the AEPS Test assessment. The focus is on learned and unlearned skills rather than scores, and attention is given to selecting goals that can be organized into a comprehensive but manageable intervention program for the child and team. Intervention targets are selected from the goals and objectives on the AEPS Test and AEPS Family Report that the child does not demonstrate or demonstrates inconsistently. Family priorities are given first consideration, with additional input from other team members.

By using this procedure, goals and objectives selected for inclusion on the child's IEP/IFSP are taken directly from the child's programmatic assessment. This procedure provides a direct tie to assessment and a common basis for the selection of functional IEP/IFSP goals and objectives by caregivers and interventionists.

The second step in developing an IEP/IFSP from the AEPS Test and the AEPS Family Report is for the team to *prioritize the goals and their associated objectives*. It is often the case that children with disabilities may show impairments in several or all of the major developmental areas. Attempting to select several goals and objectives from each problem area may be unwise and unproductive. Caregivers and interventionists may become overwhelmed if they are responsible for intervening across many objectives and tracking child progress on 10–15 targets. An alternative and recommended approach is for caregivers and interventionists to prioritize goals and objectives and to select only the highest priorities as intervention targets.

Interventionists may be able to work on four to five objectives simultaneously; however, caregivers may find it more manageable to target only one or two objectives. Targeting additional objectives may be possible if, as indicated previously, they can be coordinated into a manageable intervention program (e.g., different objectives are targeted by different team members).

After the team prioritizes those goals and objectives that will be targeted first, the next step in developing an IEP/IFSP is to *write quality goals and objectives*. Quality goals and objectives should meet five criteria (Notari & Bricker, 1990; Notari & Drinkwater, 1991; Notari-Syverson & Shuster, 1995):

1. *Functional*—When determining the functionality of a goal or objective, it is important to determine if attainment of the targeted skill will allow children to be more independent within their daily environment. Functional goals/objectives allow the child to perform functions that would otherwise have to be completed by others (e.g., caregivers, teachers).
2. *Generalizable*—Generalizability of a goal or objective refers to whether the skill is from a broad response class that can be used by the child in a variety of settings with a variety of materials and people.
3. *Instructional*—It is important to consider the instructional context in which the goal/objective is expected to be targeted. Team members should consider their resources when writing goals and objectives. Interventionists can ask themselves the following questions: "Which settings (e.g., home, preschool, child care) will allow the child to practice this goal/objective?" and "What is manageable given existing resources (e.g., teachers, caregivers, time, materials)?" Goals/objectives that are targeted should fit into the child's and family's daily routine.
4. *Observable/Measurable*—Goals and objectives should be observable (i.e., the behavior can be seen or heard) as well as measurable (i.e., the behavior can be counted in terms of frequency, latency, or duration). It is important that the goals/objectives be written in such a way that members of the team can reliably agree that a behavior did or did not meet a stated criterion.
5. *Hierarchical*—Goals and objectives should be related. The objectives should ideally be the components that lead to the child's attainment of the goal. Objectives are the building blocks or the essential steps a child must progress through to reach a goal.

Interventionists should evaluate selected IEP/IFSP goals and objectives to ensure that they meet these five criteria.

The final step is to develop intervention plans for priority goals and objectives. Intervention plans should specify the intervention setting, type of intervention activities, child progress procedures, and decision rules (Bricker & Cripe, 1992).

Development of a Child Intervention Plan

Using the AEPS Test, Joey, a 4-year-old child with cerebral palsy, was observed, and his performance was scored across settings, people, and events. The results for the Social-Communication Domain are shown in Figure 5.2. Joey meets criteria for all of the objectives (items) within Strand A, Goal 1, and has met criteria for the simplest objectives within Strand A, Goal 2. Joey is beginning to meet criteria on the more difficult goals and objectives within Strand B, Goals 1–5. His parents reported similar findings using the AEPS Family Report; therefore, the team selected and will target Strand A, Goal 2: "Uses conversational rules" and its associated objective (2.4) "Responds to contingent questions." Table 5.1 shows the relationship between the selected AEPS item and its wording as an IEP/IFSP goal or objective taken from the list of associated IEP/IFSP goal and objective statements contained in Appendix B.

Once the goal has been selected, the next step is to develop an intervention plan for the selected goal and its associated objective(s). An intervention plan can follow a number of formats, but it should contain the following information:

1.   Identification information: child's name and interventionist's name
2.   Dates for initiation and expected completion
3.   Intervention area
4.   Type of setting where intervention occurs
5.   Goal and objective(s) specified
6.   Curricular program steps, if needed
7.   Child progress procedures
8.   Decision rules

An intervention plan should be developed for each selected goal and its associated objective(s) to provide a framework and guidance for choosing intervention activities. An example of a completed program plan is contained in Figure 5.3.

An associated set of intervention activities is available in the *AEPS Curriculum for Three to Six Years* (Bricker & Waddell, 1996). The curricular items correspond directly to AEPS Test items, clearly relating intervention activities to children's selected goals and objectives. The AEPS Curriculum follows an activity-based intervention philosophy that is described later in this chapter. Sample pages from the AEPS Curriculum are presented in Figure 5.4. For each AEPS Test item, the associated curricular page lists objective and concurrent goals and provides a series of intervention activities and suggestions.

Intervention Activities[1]

The intervention approach most consistent with the AEPS process and content is a naturalistic approach called activity-based intervention. Activity-based intervention is a child-directed, transactional approach that embeds children's individual goals and objectives in routine, planned, or child-initiated activities and uses logically occurring antecedents and consequences to develop functional and generalizable skills (Bricker & Cripe, 1989, 1992). Activity-based intervention consists of four major elements:

1.   A child-directed transactional approach
2.   Embedding training on children's goals and objectives in routine, planned, or child-initiated activities
3.   Using logically occurring antecedents and consequences
4.   Developing functional and generalizable skills

[1]This section was taken in part from Bricker, D., Janko, S., Bailey, E.J., & Kaminski, R. (1989). *Evaluation and programming system: For infants and young children.* Eugene: University of Oregon, Center on Human Development.

AEPS Social-Communication Domain

Social-Communication Domain

S = Scoring Key	Q = Qualifying Notes
2 = Pass consistently	A = Assistance provided
1 = Inconsistent	B = Behavior interfered
performance	R = Reported assessment
0 = Does not pass	M = Modification/adaptation
	D = Direct test

Name: **JOEY**

Test Period: **1**
Test Date: **5 / 95**
Examiner: **DB**

	IFSP	S	Q	S	Q	S	Q	S	Q
A. Social-communicative interactions									
1. Uses words, phrases, or sentences to inform, direct, ask questions, and express anticipation, imagination, affect, and emotions		2							
1.1 Uses words, phrases, or sentences to express anticipated outcomes		2							
1.2 Uses words, phrases, or sentences to describe pretend objects, events, or people		2							
1.3 Uses words, phrases, or sentences to label own or others' affect/emotions		2							
1.4 Uses words, phrases, or sentences to describe past events		2							
1.5 Uses words, phrases, or sentences to make commands to and requests of others		2							
1.6 Uses words, phrases, or sentences to obtain information		2							
1.7 Uses words, phrases, or sentences to inform		2							
2. Uses conversational rules	✓	0							
2.1 Alternates between speaker/listener role		0							
2.2 Responds to topic changes initiated by others		0							
2.3 Asks questions for clarification		0							
2.4 Responds to contingent questions		0							
2.5 Initiates context-relevant topics		1							
2.6 Responds to others' topic initiations		2							

(continued)

Figure 5.2. Completed sample of the AEPS Social-Communication Data Recording Form.

Figure 5.2. *(continued)*

AEPS   Social-Communication Domain

Social-Communication Domain

Name: **JOEY**

Test Period: **1**
Test Date: **5 /95**
Examiner: **DB**

	IFSP	S	Q	S	Q	S	Q	S	Q
3. Establishes and varies social-communicative roles		0							
3.1 Varies voice to impart meaning		0							
3.2 Uses socially appropriate physical orientation		0							
B. Production of words, phrases, and sentences									
1. Uses verbs		1							
1.1 Uses auxiliary verbs		1							
1.2 Uses copula verb "to be"		2							
1.3 Uses third person singular verb forms		1							
1.4 Uses irregular past tense verbs		1							
1.5 Uses regular past tense verbs		2							
1.6 Uses present progressive "ing"		2							
2. Uses noun inflections		0							
2.1 Uses possessive "s"		0							
2.2 Uses irregular plural nouns		0							
2.3 Uses regular plural nouns		1							
3. Asks questions		0							
3.1 Asks yes/no questions		0							
3.2 Asks questions with inverted auxiliary		0							
3.3 Asks when questions		0							
3.4 Asks why, who, and how questions		0							
3.5 Asks what and where questions		0							
3.6 Asks questions using rising inflection		0							
4. Uses pronouns		0							
4.1 Uses subject pronouns		0							
4.2 Uses object pronouns		0							

(continued)

Figure 5.2. *(continued)*

<u>**AEPS**</u>   Social-Communication Domain

Social-Communication Domain

	Test Period:	1							
Name: JOEY	Test Date:	5/95		/		/		/	
	Examiner:	DB							
	IFSP	S	Q	S	Q	S	Q	S	Q
4.3 Uses possessive pronouns		0							
4.4 Uses indefinite pronouns		0							
4.5 Uses demonstrative pronouns		1							
5. Uses descriptive words		0							
5.1 Uses adjectives		1							
5.2 Uses adjectives to make comparisons		0							
5.3 Uses adverbs		0							
5.4 Uses prepositions		0							
5.5 Uses conjunctions		0							
5.6 Uses articles		0							

A Total Domain Raw Score can be computed for the domain by adding all of the 2 and 1 scores entered in the S column for a specific test period. To determine the Domain Percent Score, divide the Total Domain Raw Score by the Total Domain Score Possible, then multiply by 100.

	RESULTS			
Test Date	5/95			
Total Domain Raw Score	32			
Total Domain Score Possible	98	98	98	98
Domain Percent Score	30%			

Two features of an activity-based approach should be emphasized. First, multiple targets (e.g., fine motor, gross motor, adaptive, cognitive, social-communication, social) can be addressed in single activities. For example, a water activity in which children are sailing boats can be used to promote communication ("Where is my boat?"), social skills (taking turns), adaptive skills (drying hands), fine motor skills (manipulating two hand-size objects at the same time), and cognitive skills (comparing boats of different materials, sizes, colors, and shapes). A second feature is the built-in reinforcement for children who are participating in fun and interesting activities. If they are well chosen or child selected, the activities will provide ample motivation for children, and the use of artificial contingencies may be eliminated.

An activity-based approach teaches skills by embedding targeted objectives into functional daily activities of interest to children. For example, rather than establishing special sessions for teaching counting, items are counted in the context of a relevant

Table 5.1. Example of correspondence between AEPS Test items and IEP/IFSP goal and objective statements for the Social-Communication Domain, Strand A: Social-communicative interactions

AEPS Test goal and objectives	IEP/IFSP goal and objective statements
Goal 2 — Uses conversational rules	The child will use conversational rules to initiate and maintain communicative exchanges for two or more consecutive exchanges. An exchange includes a response from both the child and another person.
Objective 2.1 — Alternates between speaker/listener role	The child will use appropriate responses in conversation to alternate between speaker and listener roles (e.g., the child pauses after making a comment and looks toward communicative partner).
Objective 2.2 — Responds to topic changes initiated by others	The child will respond to conversational topic changes initiated by others with comments, answers, or questions related to the new topic (e.g., the child says, "I want to play outside some more," and the adult says, "We need to go inside now to fix a snack"; the child responds, "What are we gonna eat?").
Objective 2.3 — Asks questions for clarification	The child will indicate a need for clarification (i.e., repetition, elaboration, or confirmation) by commenting or questioning during communicative exchanges (e.g., the child says, "What?" when the child does not understand what another person has said).
Objective 2.4 — Responds to contingent questions	The child will supply relevant information following another person's request for clarification, repetition, elaboration, or confirmation of the child's previous statement (e.g., the child says, "She threw it"; an adult asks, "Who?"; and the child answers, "Rachel").
Objective 2.5 — Initiates context-relevant topics	The child will initiate topics relevant to situations and/or communicative partners (e.g., the child sees a peer with crayons and asks, "Can I have a red one?").
Objective 2.6 — Responds to others' topic initiations	The child will respond to others' conversations with related topics, including acknowledgment of another's statement, an answer to a question, a request for clarification, or a related comment (e.g., an adult comments, "You have new shoes on today," and the child says, "My mommy got them at the store").

activity (e.g., counting the number of children at circle time, counting plates during snack time, counting the number of trees while on a nature walk). If threading and zipping a zipper is a targeted skill, the child can practice this skill while putting on his or her coat before going outside to play, while playing in the dress-up corner, or while dressing baby dolls.

There are many advantages to using an activity-based format with young children. First, incorporated into teaching functional skills in the child's usual environment is the notion of providing relevant antecedents and consequences within an activity. When the antecedents and consequences are relevant or a part of an activity, motivational and attentional problems tend to be less frequent. Second, activity-based intervention addresses the issues of generalization and maintenance. Teaching a particular skill is not limited to only one activity but, instead, is taught by a variety of interventionists and/or family members across a variety of materials and settings. Third, an activity-based approach also helps to keep targeted objectives functional for the child. If the skills targeted for intervention are those used in daily activities, they are useful to the child in adjusting to and coping with environmental demands. A fourth advantage is that, when skill training is embedded into daily activities, other people, such as caregivers

Child: Joey Williams _____   Interventionist: Ms. Ryan _____

Initiated: __6/95__   Expected completion: __12/95__

Domain: FM GM Adap Cog (SC) Soc

Type of setting: ___X___ Group ___X___ Individual ___X___ Home

Strand A

Goal 2.0   Uses conversational rules

Objective 2.4   Responds to contingent questions from adults or peers during classroom activities (e.g., Joey says, "These shoes"; adult asks, "Are those your shoes?" and Joey
nods affirmatively and says, "Uh-huh").

Intervention Activities:

Examples of questions that can be asked during free play:

1. Joey, tell me more about what you are making.
2. Where are the red and yellow blocks?
3. Are you and Ashley playing dress up?

Examples of questions that can be asked during snack time:

1. Did you bring lunch with you today?
2. What do you want to drink?
3. What happens after snack?

Examples of questions that can be asked during circle time:

1. Which song should we sing next, Joey?
2. Tell me about today's weather.
3. Could you tell me that again?

Child Progress Procedures: Teachers will record the frequency of Joey's responses to contingent questions during free play, snack, and circle activities each
day for 2 weeks.

Decision Rule: If Joey has not made progress by the end of 2 weeks, models of desired
responses or prompts may be provided.

Figure 5.3.   A completed program plan.

and peers, can be used as change agents and teaching resources. Fifth, activity-based
intervention can be used with a heterogeneous group of young children. Children can
act as peer models for one another and be involved in antecedent and consequent
events. For example, in a painting activity, children may be given different color paints
and will need to request various colors from one another to complete their paintings.
Sally's request for red paint may act as an antecedent event to which Paula responds.
Paula's response (e.g., looking, smiling, verbalizing, offering paint) may act as a positive
consequence to Sally. When all children actively participate, activities will be less
teacher directed and more child directed.

Planning an activity that incorporates many different individual goals for a group
of diverse young children can be challenging. Many of the goals of activity-based intervention can be met if the activities selected have more than one purpose. For example,
cutting paper, tissue, or cellophane during an art activity uses the fine motor skill of
cutting out shapes with straight or curved lines. The cutting activity may also include a
language component if the child is encouraged to inform others about what he or she is
cutting (e.g., "I'm cutting purple circles"), a cognitive component if the child groups the
paper according to size/shape, and a social component if the child shares or exchanges
objects (e.g., scissors, tissue).

GOAL 2.0 Uses conversational rules

Objective 2.1   Alternates between speaker/listener role
Objective 2.2   Responds to topic changes initiated by others
Objective 2.3   Asks questions for clarification
Objective 2.4   Responds to contingent questions
Objective 2.5   Initiates context-relevant topics
Objective 2.6   Responds to others' topic initiations

CONCURRENT GOALS

Cog A:2.0   Watches, listens, and participates during small group activities
Cog A:3.0   Watches, listens, and participates during large group activities
Cog D:3.0   Retells event in sequence
Cog E   Recalling Events (all goals)
Cog F:2.0   Makes statement and appropriately answers questions that require reasoning about objects, situations, or people
Cog G:2.0   Engages in games with rules
Soc A:1.0   Has play partners
Soc A:2.0   Initiates cooperative activity

DAILY ROUTINES

Routine events that provide opportunities for children to use conversational rules include the following:

Dressing	Snack time
Mealtime	Unstructured play time
Travel time	Transition time
Arrival and departure	Bathtime
Circle time at school	Bedtime

Example At breakfast, Joey's father says, "We're going to the zoo today!" If Joey does not respond, his father prompts him by saying, "We'll see tigers and elephants and…" *(SC A:2.6)*

Example Timmy has a goal to supply relevant information following another person's request for clarification, repetition, elaboration, or confirmation of his previous statement using sign language. When Timmy wakes up, he signs, WANT. His mother faces Timmy and speaks clearly: "What do you want?" Timmy responds, EAT. *(SC A:2.4, with adapted materials)*

(continued)

Figure 5.4.   Sample portion of the Social-Communication Domain of the AEPS Curriculum for Three to Six Years.

Figure 5.4.   *(continued)*

ENVIRONMENTAL ARRANGEMENTS

- Provide materials that promote communication and arrange the classroom into activity areas that include a dramatic play/house play activity center (see Environmental Arrangements in Section III and Dramatic Play Activities in Section V).

    Example   While playing in the "beauty salon," children alternate between speaker and listener roles during conversations between stylists and clients. For example, one child asks another, "You want your hair cut?" and waits for a response. *(SC A:2.1)*

    Example   Latifa speaks on the "telephone" to her friend Joey and says, "Hi. Who's this?" The interventionist who is close by looks expectantly at Joey and nods, but, when Joey does not respond, the interventionist gives him a more direct prompt by modeling, "It's Joey." Joey responds, "Joey." *(SC A:2.4)*

- Intervention strategies that involve environmental arrangements include the following:

Heterogeneous grouping	Piece by piece
Choices	Assistance
Forgetfulness	Sabotage
Visible but unreachable	Negotiation
Violation of expectations	

    Example (Choices)   During circle time, the interventionist lets children take turns choosing songs. For example, a child says, "I want a duck song!" *(SC A:2.5)*

    Example (Violation of expectations)   During snack time, the interventionist serves "blocks" for the children to eat. A child laughs and says, "Where snack?" *(SC A:2.3)*

PLANNED ACTIVITIES

Two examples of how to embed this goal and the associated objective within activities are presented here. For a complete set of activities that address goals and objectives across domains, see Section V.

Family Puppets (see Puppets in Section V)

Children make puppets of their family members and put on a "show" (a stage can be created from an old refrigerator box or by turning a table on its side). The interventionist models appropriate conversational rules (e.g., turn taking) by communicating through puppets. Opportunities for children to use conversational rules (e.g., respond to topic changes, respond to contingent questions) occur when children "talk" to each other through their puppets or can be prompted by the interventionist if necessary. Encouraging children to playact an event they are familiar with, such as eating dinner, helps them focus on conversational rules.

(continued)

Figure 5.4. *(continued)*

Example The interventionist plans an opportunity for children to converse by having two children at a time put on a show for the class. The interventionist may need to prompt the children (e.g., looking at them expectantly, modeling an exchange). *(SC A:2.0)*

Going to Grandma's

Children use conversational rules during a pretend visit to Grandma's house. They may dress up for their visit to play the role of "Grandma." The interventionist designs opportunities for a child to practice specific goals by playing the role of Grandma and planning opportunities for targeted skills. For example, the interventionist questions the child during role play to provide opportunities for the child to supply relevant information when responding. The interventionist should be in close proximity when children are playacting to provide prompts if necessary. This activity can be modified for any place children visit in their typical routines, such as a friend's house or a party.

Example Timmy's interventionist knows he enjoys making cookies with his grandmother, so when Timmy comes to "visit," his interventionist says, "I'm going to make cookies." The interventionist pauses to allow Timmy an opportunity to sign, Me HELP? *(SC A:2.6, with adaptation)*

PRESCHOOL CURRICULA WITH SIMILAR GOALS

The following preschool curricula provide information on this goal or similar goals. Interventionists whose programs have access to one or more of these curricula may refer to the referenced sections for additional programming strategies.

The Carolina Curriculum for Preschoolers with Special Needs
Conversational skills

High Scope—Young Children in ACTION
Language
- Expressing feelings in words
- Talking with other children and adults about personally meaningful experiences

Classification
- Using and describing objects in different ways

Portage Guide to Early Education
Language
- Changes word order appropriately to ask questions

Social
- Joins in conversation at mealtime
- Contributes to adult conversation

The following are additional considerations that may aid in developing interesting and motivating activities that incorporate individual children's goals. Interventionists should select activities that

1. Allow for grouping similar objectives of different children into one activity
2. Allow for grouping different goals of the same child into one activity
3. Are adaptable for varying ages and skill levels
4. Minimize the need for adult direction and assistance and focus on enhancing child-initiated activities
5. Are motivating because of built-in reinforcers

Targeting goals for different children and targeting a variety of goals for individual children within a single activity are challenging. To ensure that an activity-based approach is effective for the involved children, preplanning and organization are necessary. (For more details on the application of activity-based intervention, see Bricker & Cripe, 1989, 1992.)

Evaluating Child Progress[2]

Once intervention is initiated, it is essential for interventionists to monitor and evaluate child progress. Without the systematic documentation of child change, interventionists and caregivers cannot evaluate the effects of their intervention efforts.

It is particularly important that the activity-based approach be accompanied by the gathering of objective information to accurately assess the impact of the intervention. Measuring intervention impact and child progress can be challenging when intervention activities are embedded in the ongoing daily activities.

The type of child progress monitoring chosen will depend on the background of the professional staff and on program resources. The better trained the staff and the more resources that are available, the more elaborate the evaluation procedures can be; however, every program should conduct quarterly evaluations as well as weekly monitoring.

Quarterly Evaluation Readministration of the AEPS Test at 3- or 4-month intervals provides interventionists and caregivers with a systematic record of the child's progress in acquiring IEP/IFSP goals and objectives. Quarterly retests generally take significantly less time to administer because the interventionist is familiar with the child and can choose to test only those items that are currently being targeted. Results from quarterly administrations can be displayed on the graphs included on the AEPS Data Recording Forms. These forms have space to record outcomes from four separate test administrations.

Caregivers can be encouraged to complete the AEPS Family Report at quarterly or yearly intervals. Periodic use of the AEPS Family Report may assist in keeping caregivers involved in evaluation activities. Parents and caregivers can use the AEPS Child Progress Record to monitor their child's progress. Results from the AEPS Test or Family Report can be used to score the AEPS Child Progress Record on a quarterly or annual basis.

Weekly Monitoring Collecting information on children's weekly progress toward specific intervention targets is a requisite of quality intervention efforts. Data collection procedures should be selected to meet the needs of the child, family, interventionists, setting, and focus of intervention.

---

[2]A more extensive discussion on evaluating child progress can be found in Bricker and Cripe (1992).

Given adequate staff or caregiver time, we recommend the use of observational systems to collect weekly child progress data. The use of observation is consistent with the recommended procedures for administering the AEPS Test. In addition, observation permits obtaining information as children go about their daily activities. It provides information on whether the target response is used independently and is functional for the child. Other strategies, such as administering a few probe trials following or before beginning a specific intervention activity, can also be used. The type of weekly child monitoring strategy is less important than ensuring that child change is systematically evaluated.

If a probe system is used, one or two trials should be administered once a week, if possible, to determine the child's progress toward meeting an objective. For example, if a child is working on walking up and down stairs, he or she can be observed coming off the steps of a bus (e.g., no attempt to walk up or down, an unsuccessful or successful attempt) prior to introducing an activity that targets this objective.

Collection of data in center-based programs using probe techniques can be organized in a variety of formats to accommodate the program and individual child needs. The interventionist may choose to collect data on different children each day of the week as they participate in the group activities. For example, data could be collected on Carrie's and Jesse's IEP/IFSP targets on Monday, data on Denzel's and Joey's IEP/IFSP targets on Tuesday, and so forth. Another option is to collect data on each child during a limited number of activities designed to emphasize targets within a particular domain. Thus, gross motor data would be collected during outdoor play, and social-communication data would be collected during circle time for all children who have IEP/IFSP targets in those domains.

Data could be collected during a specified time within each activity, such as during the first or last 10 minutes of the activity, or as the opportunity arises. For example, data would be collected for motor skills as the children gather materials and set up the activity or during "outside" time, and data would be collected for social skills as the children work together at cleanup time. After skills are acquired (e.g., criteria are met), behaviors should be observed periodically to determine if target skills are used functionally and if skills are generalizing to other settings.

Weekly outcomes for children should be summarized in ways that are efficient and so that the outcomes are usable. Interventionists should work with caregivers to determine how to summarize results over time to make them most useful.

FAMILY PARTICIPATION

As indicated in Figure 5.1, family participation in assessment, IEP/IFSP development, intervention, and evaluation should be encouraged and promoted. This section discusses procedures for family involvement and participation in assessment, IEP/IFSP development, intervention, and evaluation.

Assessment

A three-phase process is recommended to promote family participation in assessment of the child's and family's strengths and needs: 1) an introductory interview, 2) a formal assessment, and 3) an outcome and intervention planning interview.

Introductory Interview   The first phase in the assessment process for families is holding the introductory interview. This interview has two purposes: 1) to provide information and clarification about the program and 2) to establish how the family chooses to participate in the assessment phase. The individuality of families requires flexibility in the approach. Some caregivers may choose to complete the assessment forms independently, whereas others may appreciate assistance. It is important during this meeting to convey to families that their values and choices will be respected.

Formal Assessment   The second phase, formal assessment, is focused on obtaining relevant information about the family and child from the parents. For families who have children whose developmental age ranges from 3 to 6 years, the AEPS provides two assessment tools to assist in obtaining this information: the AEPS Family Report and the AEPS Family Interest Survey.

The AEPS Family Report, described in Chapter 10, provides caregivers with an organizational guide for observing their child's behavioral repertoire and recording their observations. This tool was designed to be used in conjunction with the AEPS Test. Completion of the AEPS Family Report provides the interventionist with information about caregiver assessment of children's skills and abilities across major areas of development.

Families can also complete the AEPS Family Interest Survey, which is described in Chapter 9. The AEPS Family Interest Survey is a 30-item survey designed to determine a family's interests concerning their child, the family, and the community. Parents complete the Family Interest Survey by indicating whether each item is a priority or not a priority. For priority items, parents can indicate how they would like to receive the service or obtain the information.

It is important to emphasize that the assessment procedures used should not be seen as intrusive by parents. In addition, the focus should be on identifying strengths and interests rather than suggesting family limitations or pathology. Even when using tools with a positive focus, not all families will choose to complete formal assessment procedures. The interventionist's responsibility is to find means acceptable to families for gathering relevant information rather than insist that all families follow set guidelines.

Outcomes and Intervention Planning Interview   The third phase, outcomes and intervention planning interview, can be scheduled on completion of the family assessment activities. The purpose of this interview is to 1) identify priorities for developing IEP/IFSP goals and objectives or outcomes, 2) design intervention activities, and 3) determine an acceptable evaluation plan for each goal or outcome. In other words, this interview is designed to help prepare the family and interventionist for a productive IEP/IFSP meeting.

Family strengths and interests can be identified directly from the AEPS Family Interest Survey, whereas children's goals can come directly from the AEPS Family Report and the AEPS Test. Intervention priorities should be selected by the family with guidance from professional staff.

Once priorities are selected, it may be useful for the interventionist to have a set of interview questions to assist families in clarifying their goals and outcomes and their strategies for achieving them. The interviewer should be aware of the possible differences in values and priorities between the family and the professionals and seek not to impose his or her views on the family. Communication should be open, honest, and collaborative.

Either during or at the end of the interview, the family may choose to complete an IEP/IFSP Planning Guide. This guide permits listing pertinent information about the IEP/IFSP meeting, the child's and family's strengths, and the child's and family's goals and interests. A copy of an IEP/IFSP Planning Guide is shown in Chapter 4.

IEP/IFSP Development

A process similar to that described previously for the development of the child's IEP/IFSP goals and objectives can be used for developing family outcomes. Family outcomes are different from behavioral prescriptions written for children's IEP/IFSP goals and objectives. An outcome is a statement of what the family believes would help them facilitate their child's development. The outcome should be stated in candid language that identifies what is going to occur, the participants, and the anticipated results.

The development of children's IEP/IFSP goals and objectives and family outcomes should not be seen as separate activities. Rather, the IEP/IFSP meeting should combine these activities. Children's goals and objectives should be selected and written in concert with family outcomes.

More detail on the AEPS Family Report, Family Interest Survey, Child Progress Record, and interview process is contained in Section III of this volume; sample copies of the forms are located in Appendix D.

Intervention

Well-developed and carefully written child goals and family outcomes will specify families' involvement in intervention activities. Whenever possible, family members should be partners in the intervention efforts provided to their children. Again, it should be stressed that families will differ in the amount and type of participation they choose. Some families may choose to participate in a home-based program in which they share in daily intervention activities with their child. Other families may choose only minimal involvement with their child's intervention program. Interventionists should respect families' choices but should also encourage additional participation if it may benefit the child.

Evaluation

The importance of evaluation was discussed previously, as was the necessity of involving parents and caregivers in this process. Interventionists are likely to be more successful in getting parents to participate in evaluation efforts if formal procedures exist for doing so.

The AEPS Family Report can be used quarterly or annually by parents to monitor their child's progress toward IEP/IFSP goals and objectives. The child's progress can be tracked using the AEPS Child Progress Record. This form permits parents to indicate when their child has reached criteria on targeted goals and objectives.

SUMMARY

Too frequently in early intervention programs, the relationship between assessment outcomes and program planning is disconnected and remote. Often, individuals who will not work with the child or family conduct assessments employing tools that generate information that is not useful for developing IEPs/IFSPs or program plans. Using such approaches makes it extremely difficult for interventionists and caregivers to develop appropriate intervention targets and subsequent intervention plans. The AEPS offers an alternative.

Quality intervention services require the systematic and direct linking of assessment, intervention, and evaluation processes. The material contained in this chapter describes a set of practical procedures for forging direct links among assessment information, the development of IEPs/IFSPs, intervention, and evaluation activities.

REFERENCES

Bricker, D., & Waddell, M. (Eds.). (1996). *Assessment, evaluation, and programming system for infants and children: Vol. 4. AEPS curriculum for three to six years.* Baltimore: Paul H. Brookes Publishing Co.

Bricker, D., & Cripe, J. (1989). Activity-based intervention. In D. Bricker (Ed.), *Early intervention for at-risk and handicapped infants, toddlers and preschool children* (pp. 251–274). Palo Alto, CA: VORT Corp.

Bricker, D., & Cripe, J. (1992). *An activity-based approach to early intervention.* Baltimore: Paul H. Brookes Publishing Co.

Education for All Handicapped Children Act of 1975, PL 94-142. (August 23, 1977). 20 U.S.C. §1401 *et seq.*

Education of the Handicapped Act Amendments of 1986, PL 99-457. (October 8, 1986). 20 U.S.C. §1400 *et seq.*

Individuals with Disabilities Education Act (IDEA) of 1990, PL 101-476. (October 30, 1990). 20 U.S.C. §1400 *et seq.*

Individuals with Disabilities Education Act Amendments of 1991, PL 102-119. (October 7, 1991). 20 U.S.C. §1400 *et seq.*

Notari, A., & Bricker, D. (1990). The utility of a curriculum-based assessment instrument in the development of individualized education plans for infants and young children. *Journal of Early Intervention, 14*(2), 17–32.

Notari, A., & Drinkwater, S. (1991). Best practices for writing child outcomes: An evaluation of two methods. *Topics in Early Childhood Special Education, 11*(3), 92–106.

Notari-Syverson, A., & Shuster, S.L. (1995). Putting real-life skills into IEP/IFSPs for infants and young children. *Teaching Exceptional Children, 27*(2), 29–32.

AEPS Test Administration Guide

Users are encouraged to become familiar with the administration guidelines prior to using the AEPS Test. Test administrations that do not follow the guidelines are likely to be inefficient and may yield inaccurate child performance outcomes. This chapter contains the administration guidelines necessary for properly using the AEPS Test.

CONTENT AND ORGANIZATION

The content of the AEPS Test covers domains of behavior and specific skills thought to be essential for young children to develop independent functioning and cope with environmental demands. Six broad curricular areas called *domains* are included in the AEPS Test: Fine Motor, Gross Motor, Adaptive, Cognitive, Social-Communication, and Social. Each of the domains encompasses a particular set of developmentally related skills or behaviors. Categorization of behavior into domains often results in the somewhat arbitrary placement of skills into one domain rather than another (e.g., placing interaction skills while in a small/ large group in the Cognitive Domain rather than the Social Domain). In addition, some overlap occurs because the same or similar skills may be in more than one domain (e.g., fine motor responses such as tying and zipping in the Fine Motor Domain are necessary to demonstrate skills in dressing and undressing in the Adaptive Domain).

The six domains are divided into a series of *strands* that organize related groups of behaviors under a common category. For example, behaviors relating to large muscle movements used in play are grouped in the "play skills" strand in the Gross Motor Domain. Every strand contains a series of test items called *goals*. The goals were developed to be used as annual or semiannual goals on a child's IEP/ IFSP. The number of strands and goals varies for each domain. They are arranged from easiest to most difficult unless the strands or goals are of equal difficulty, in which case sequencing is arbitrary.

Associated with each goal is an accompanying set of test items called *objectives* that represent more discrete skills. The objectives enable the user to accurately pinpoint a child's level within a specific skill sequence. In addition, the objectives can serve as short-term or quarterly objectives on the child's IEP/IFSP. The objectives under each goal are arranged as hierarchical skills, with the most difficult occurring first; however, the sequencing is arbitrary if the skills have no distinction in difficulty.

The identification system associated with the strands (e.g., A, B, C), goals (e.g., G1, G2, G3), and objectives (e.g., 1.1, 1.2, 1.3) reflects a sequential arrangement designed to assist the test user in locating and referring to items. The organizational format of the strands, goals, and objectives is described in Chapter 3 of this volume. A complete list of domains, strands, and the number of goals and objectives in each strand is contained in Table 6.1.

ORDER OF TEST ADMINISTRATION

The user can choose to assess one domain at a time or assess across domains as items are observed. The latter procedure is clearly more efficient but requires greater familiarity with the test. Users of the AEPS Test may obtain more accurate results by observing

Table 6.1. AEPS Test domains, strands, and the number of goals and objectives in each strand

Domain	Strands	Number of goals	Number of objectives
Fine Motor	A: Manipulation of Objects	3	5
	B: Prewriting	2	4
		5	9
Gross Motor	A: Balance and Mobility in Standing and Walking	1	1
	B: Play Skills	5	11
		6	12
Adaptive	A: Dining	3	12
	B: Personal Hygiene	2	8
	C: Dressing and Undressing	3	11
		8	31
Cognitive	A: Participation	3	10
	B: Demonstrates Understanding of Concepts	7	16
	C: Categorizing	1	3
	D: Sequencing	3	3
	E: Recalling Events	2	3
	F: Problem Solving	2	5
	G: Play	2	5
	H: Premath	4	12
	I: Prereading	4	7
		28	64
Social-Communication	A: Social-Communicative Interactions	3	15
	B: Production of Words, Phrases, and Sentences	5	26
		8	41
Social	A: Interaction with Others	3	10
	B: Interaction with Environment	2	5
	C: Knowledge of Self and Others	3	10
		8	25
		63	182

and recording information by domain for the first few times. The user should begin with the first goal and attempt to observe whether the child meets criteria before moving to the next goal.

As familiarity with the AEPS Test increases, the user can shift to assessing children across domains. For example, clusters of skills can often be observed during the occurrence of daily activities in the classroom or at home. During large group time, the user may be able to observe cognitive skills (e.g., watching, listening, and participating in group activities; counting; rhyming of words); gross motor skills (e.g., running, jumping); social skills (e.g., following established rules); and social-communication skills (e.g., use of words and phrases to describe past events). During mealtime at home, the user may be able to observe fine motor skills (e.g., manipulating two small objects); adaptive skills (e.g., using a knife to spread food, assisting in clearing the table); cognitive skills (e.g., grouping objects on the basis of function); and social skills (e.g., seeking adult permission, meeting physical needs of hunger and thirst). Finally, the more experienced user may be able to assess several children simultaneously. For example, when three children are engaged in an outside activity, the user may be able to observe and record the social interactions, communication, and play skills of all three children. The AEPS Test does not require assessing the goals in a specific order.

Because the AEPS Test was designed to be used primarily as an observation tool, it is difficult to specify the time needed for administration. As indicated previously, familiarity with the instrument and with the child reduces administration time. Assessing across domains and across children also reduces administration time. Quarterly or yearly follow-up administrations generally take one quarter to one half the time of the initial assessment. Generally, young children take less time to assess than older children, who may have more extensive repertoires.

COLLECTING ASSESSMENT AND EVALUATION INFORMATION

The AEPS Test includes three methods of collecting assessment and evaluation information: observation, direct test, and report. Observation is the preferred method. Observation allows the user to view the topography, or form, of the behavior; when and how frequently the behavior is performed; and the environmental factors that may influence the child's performance (e.g., antecedents and consequences). Although observation is the preferred method of data collection, when a user does not have an opportunity to observe a behavior during a routine activity, a situation may be created to directly elicit the behavior (i.e., direct test). The third method of obtaining assessment and evaluation is through the use of report. Sources of reported information may be the parents, caregivers, therapists, or written documentation (e.g., medical reports).

RECORDING AND SCORING CHILD PERFORMANCE

The AEPS Test has a series of recording forms that can be used to record a child's performance on goals and objectives. There is a specific recording form for each of the six domains. Space is provided on the cover sheet that accompanies the recording forms to indicate the child's name, date of birth, the family's name, the name of the person completing the form, and the family's address. Directions for completing the forms precede the set of recording forms. An example of a portion of the recording form for the Gross Motor Domain of the AEPS Test is shown in Figure 6.1. The following is an explanation of the numbered items on this form.

AEPS   (1) Gross Motor Domain

(2) **S = Scoring Key**   **Q = Qualifying Notes** (3)

2 = Pass consistently	A = Assistance provided
1 = Inconsistent performance	B = Behavior interfered
	R = Reported assessment
0 = Does not pass	M = Modification/adaptation
	D = Direct test

(4)

Name: _____

Test Period: _____ _____ _____ _____
Test Date: ___/___ ___/___ ___/___ ___/___
Examiner: _____ _____ _____ _____

	IFSP	S	Q	S	Q	S	Q	S	Q
A. Balance and mobility in standing and walking									
(5) 1. Alternates feet walking up and down stairs									
1.1 Walks up and down stairs	(6)	(7)							
B. Play skills									
1. Jumps forward									
1.1 Jumps in place									
1.2 Jumps from platform									
1.3 Maintains balance in walking									
1.4 Balances on one foot									
2. Runs avoiding obstacles									
2.1 Runs									
3. Bounces, catches, kicks, and throws ball									
3.1 Bounces ball									
3.2 Catches ball									
3.3 Kicks ball									
3.4 Throws ball									
4. Skips									
4.1 Hops									
5. Rides and steers two-wheel bicycle									
5.1 Pedals and steers two-wheel bicycle with training wheels									

(continued)

Figure 6.1.   AEPS Data Recording Form for the Gross Motor Domain.

Figure 6.1. *(continued)*

A Total Domain Raw Score can be computed for the domain by adding all of the 2 and 1 scores entered in the S column for a specific test period. To determine the Domain Percent Score, divide the Total Domain Raw Score by the Total Domain Score Possible, then multiply by 100.

⑧ **RESULTS**

Test Date	_____	_____	_____	_____
Total Domain Raw Score	_____	_____	_____	_____
Total Domain Score Possible	36	36	36	36
Domain Percent Score	_____	_____	_____	_____

1. The *domain* is listed at the top of the recording form.
2. Scoring codes used to assess an item are indicated in the *scoring key*. These numbers are placed in the scoring boxes directly under the S on the recording form.
3. Codes used in the Q (*qualifying notes*) column are defined in this section.
4. The *test period* (1, 2, 3, or 4) is indicated here. Also, the date of assessment is recorded in the *test date* space and should include the month and year (e.g., 6/95). The examiner's initials are recorded below the testing date.
5. The *assessment items* are listed on the left of the data recording form and include the strands, goals, and objectives.
6. The IFSP column provides a place to check when goals and/or objectives have been selected as programming goals and/or objectives for a child.
7. *Performance data* and qualifying notes are recorded in the next four columns (one column per testing period). Performance data (i.e., 2, 1, 0) are recorded in the box under the S on the form and qualifying notes (e.g., A, B, M) are recorded in the space under the Q on the form.
8. *Assessment results* are recorded at the bottom of each data recording form for each domain.

Comments are recorded at the end of each recording form for each test period.

There are three options for scoring items on the AEPS Test: 2, 1, and 0. When the child consistently performs the item as specified in the criterion section, the item is scored 2 (i.e., pass). Scoring the item with a 2 indicates the child performed the behavior independently and the behavior is functional and used across settings and people. When the child's performance is inconsistent, the item is scored 1, indicating that the performance is situation specific (e.g., only performs the behavior with certain people or in certain settings) or the behavior is emerging (e.g., child does not have all components of the behavior). When a child cannot meet the criterion, the item is scored with a 0 (i.e., not observed or does not meet criterion), indicating the child was unable to perform the behavior or that complete, continuous assistance was needed. It is important to ensure that the child has had sufficient opportunities (e.g., three or more times when the behavior could be used) to demonstrate the response before scoring it as 0.

To determine whether the child's response should be scored 2, 1, or 0, specific criteria are provided for each goal and objective. Scoring criteria may differ for observation and direct test procedures. For example, when observing a child's ability to unzip a zipper (Adaptive Domain, Strand C, Objective 1.3), the child would receive a 2 if he or she is able to demonstrate the skill consistently and independently in a meaningful context. If the user must direct test the item, then the child must demonstrate the behavior on at least two out of three trials. It is essential to check each item's criteria and scoring guidelines before scoring the child's response. Table 6.2 presents a summary of the scoring criteria for observation and direct test.

In addition to the three-option scoring codes, qualifying notes are provided to allow users to record other information about a child's performance of a skill. For example, a child may use adaptive equipment such as a communication board to label objects and events. Because the child can demonstrate the concept of labeling, the item on the AEPS Test is scored 2, but it is also scored with a qualifying note (e.g., M in this case) so that this important information about the child's mode of communication is considered in the subsequent development of intervention programs as well as future evaluations. Adaptation of items for children with disabilities is encouraged; however, when such adaptations occur, they should be noted through the use of qualifying notes. Unless a program serves children with multiple or serious disabilities, qualifying notes are not usually required. The qualifying notes and associated scoring guidelines for their use are contained in Table 6.3. Figure 6.2 provides an example of a completed recording form using qualifying notes.

In addition to the standard recording form, the Social-Communication Domain has two supplementary forms called the Social-Communication Recording Form and the Social-Communication Summary Form, which are provided to sample the child's verbal, gestural, and conversational skills. These forms may be used to obtain initial assessment information that is transferred to the standard recording form. They may also be used to obtain more in-depth assessment information by systematically collecting, recording, and analyzing the child's social-communicative behavior. Instructions for using these forms are contained in the Social-Communication Domain of the AEPS Test. Copies of the data and supplemental recording forms are contained in Appendix D.

Table 6.2.   Scoring criteria for observation and direct test

Score	Criteria
Observation	
2 = Observed/Passed	Child consistently and independently meets stated item criterion. Behavior is functional and generalized (occurs in a variety of settings, with different people and/or different materials, and under varying conditions).
1 = Inconsistent	Child inconsistently meets stated item criterion. Behavior occurs, but it may be situation specific or just emerging in the child's repertoire.
0 = Not Observed/Not Passed	Child does not exhibit the behavior when given repeated opportunities to do so.
Direct Test	
2 = Observed/Passed	Child consistently and independently meets stated item criterion. Behavior is functional and generalized (occurs in a variety of settings, with different people and/or different materials, and under varying conditions). Behavior must occur on at least two out of three trials.
1 = Inconsistent	Child inconsistently meets stated item criterion. Behavior occurs, but it may be situation specific or just emerging in the child's repertoire. Behavior occurs on only one out of three trials.
0 = Not Observed/Not Passed	Child does not exhibit the behavior. Behavior occurs on zero out of three trials.

Table 6.3.   Qualifying notes and associated scoring guidelines used on the AEPS Data Recording Form

Qualifying note	Scoring guidelines
A	When a child is provided with some form of *assistance,* an A may be noted in the space next to the performance score box. If assistance is provided, the only scores allowed are 1 and 0, because a score of 2 indicates full independent performance. Assistance will include any direct verbal or physical prompt, cue, or model that assists the child in initiating or performing the desired behavior; however, a general direction given to the child to initiate the behavior is not considered assistance. For example, the directive "Put your coat on" is not considered assistance.
B	At times a child's *behavior* may interfere with the demonstration of the desired skill. In such cases, the item may be scored either 1 or 0, with a B noted next to the performance score. This qualifying note indicates that the child may have the skill, but disruptive or noncompliant behavior interfered with its demonstration.

R	When an item is assessed by *report,* an R is noted next to the performance score. Three report scoring options can be used.
	    1. When assessment information is collected by another person or a documented source, the item is scored either 2, 1, or 0, and an R is noted.
	    2. When the item is judged inappropriate because it assesses a primitive response (e.g., sucking on a nipple when the child is able to drink from a cup), the item is scored 2 and an R is noted.
	    3. When the item is judged inappropriate because it is too advanced (e.g., walking when the child is unable to stand), the item is scored 0 and an R is noted.

M	At times an examiner may need to modify the assessment directions (e.g., adaptive equipment) or the stated criteria (e.g., rate or mode of response) in order to assess children with sensory or motor disabilities. When *modifications* are made in assessment procedures, M is noted next to the performance score.
D	When an item is assessed by *direct test* (the examiner directly elicits a behavior), D is noted next to the performance score.

ADMINISTRATION PROCEDURES

Each of the six domains is composed of a series of test items designated as goals and their associated objectives. Each item contains the following information: domain; strand; goal (G1) or objective (1.1); criterion; and directions, including materials and procedure (observation or direct test). Although no specific sequence for administration is mandated, several rules should be followed when administering the AEPS Test.

Rule 1: All goals must be assessed and scored.   The user should eliminate items that are clearly below or above a child's developmental level. Such items may be scored without observing or directly testing the behavior(s); instead, the user may score the item and use the qualifying note R for report. Items below the child's developmental level are scored 2; however, the scores are qualified by noting R (reported assessment) in the qualifying notes (Q) column.

Likewise, items that are significantly above the child's developmental level can be scored with a 0 and an R in the Q column. However, because the behavioral repertoires of children with disabilities are often uneven, it may be advisable to administer all goal items that appear to be above the child's present level of functioning.

Rule 2: If a goal is assessed and scored as 1 or 0, all associated objectives must be assessed and scored.   If either the child's performance is inconsistent (indicated by a score of 1) or the behavior does not occur (indicated by a score of 0), it is necessary to determine the level at which the child is consistently performing the sequence of objectives. For

_____AEPS_____   Social Domain

S = Scoring Key	Q = Qualifying Notes
2 = Pass consistently	A = Assistance provided
1 = Inconsistent	B = Behavior interfered
performance	R = Reported assessment
0 = Does not pass	M = Modification/adaptation
	D = Direct test

Name: **ALEX**

Test Period:
Test Date: **5/95**
Examiner: **MB**

	IFSP	S	Q	S	Q	S	Q	S	Q
A. Interaction with others									
1. Has play partners		2							
1.1 Responds to peers in distress or need		2							
1.2 Establishes and maintains proximity to peers		2							
1.3 Initiates greetings to familiar peers		2							
1.4. Responds to affective initiations from peers		2							
2. Initiates cooperative activities		1							
2.1 Joins others in cooperative activity		2							
2.2 Maintains cooperative participation with others		2							
2.3 Shares or exchanges objects		2							
3. Resolves conflicts by selecting effective strategy		0							
3.1 Negotiates to resolve conflicts		0							
3.2 Uses simple strategies to resolve conflicts		1	A						
3.3 Claims and defends possessions		2							
B. Interaction with environment									
1. Meets physical needs in socially appropriate ways		2							
1.1 Meets physical needs when uncomfortable, sick, hurt, or tired		2							
1.2 Meets observable physical needs		2							
1.3 Meets physical needs of hunger and thirst		2							

(continued)

Figure 6.2.   The AEPS Test Social Domain Data Recording Form.

Figure 6.2. *(continued)*

	S									
2. Follows context-specific rules outside home and classroom	1	D								
2.1 Seeks adult permission	2									
2.2 Follows established rules at home and in classroom	2									
C. Knowledge of self and others										
1. Communicates personal likes and dislikes	2									
1.1 Initiates preferred activities	2									
1.2 Selects activities and/or objects	2									
2. Relates identifying information about self and others	1									
2.1 States address	1	D								
2.2 States telephone number	1	D								
2.3 Knows birthday	1									
2.4 Names siblings and gives full name of self	2									
2.5 Knows gender of self and others	2									
2.6 Knows name and age	2									
3. Accurately identifies affect/emotions in others and self consistent with demonstrated behaviors	1									
3.1 Accurately identifies affect/ emotions of others	1									
3.2 Accurately identifies own affect/emotions	1									

A Total Domain Raw Score can be computed for the domain by adding all of the 2 and 1 scores entered in the S column for a specific test period. To determine the Domain Percent Score, divide the Total Domain Raw Score by the Total Domain Score Possible, then multiply by 100.

RESULTS

Test Date	5/95			
Total Domain Raw Score	52			
Total Domain Score Possible	66	66	66	66
Domain Percent Score	72%			

example, if the child is not able to dress and undress, it is necessary to determine where in the dressing sequence the child is able to consistently perform (indicated by a score of 2). Failure to assess the objectives under a goal that has not been observed as a functional part of the child's repertoire does not give the child credit for mastering small increments of skills. As with goals that are clearly above or below a child's developmental level, objectives can also be scored 2 or 0 by report as long as this is indicated by the qualifying note R.

Although passing a goal will ensure for *most* children a satisfactory performance of all the associated objectives, this is not always the case. Consequently, when a goal is scored as 2, the user has the *option* of assessing the associated objectives or assuming the child has mastered the objective. Assessing all goals and their corresponding objectives is particularly advisable with children who may not follow typical developmental patterns.

Rule 3: The option coding system (2, 1, O) should be used with all scored items.   The three-option coding system considers performance consistency and is useful for developing intervention plans. When the test is completed, all tested items should be scored with a 2, 1, or 0, although many of the items may have been scored by report.

Rule 4: Any item assessed by direct test and/or report should be so noted on the Data Recording Form.   In order to discriminate among those items assessed through observation versus direct test or report, the user should add either D or R, when appropriate, under the Q column on the AEPS Data Recording Form. Most items should be assessed through observation and will not, therefore, have any accompanying qualifying note. At times, the use of two or more qualifying notes may be appropriate.

Assessment and Evaluation Modifications

Standardized tests require that items be presented following a specified format and that responses also meet specific criteria. The AEPS Test was designed to be used with children who are at risk for or who have disabilities, many of whom will not be able to respond to a standard presentation or produce a typical response. Rather than penalize children who are unable to respond as do typically developing children, the AEPS Test encourages modifications or adaptations to items that will increase the likelihood that the child will be successful. It is more important that the child communicates than that the child communicates in a specific manner. It is more important that the child develops mobility skills than that he or she learns to move following a set pattern that may be unattainable. In particular, children with sensory and motor disabilities may require modifications to successfully perform test items. The AEPS Test offers the user two ways to modify items for children with such disabilities: criterion modifications and direction modifications.

Criterion Modifications   Criterion adaptations modify the standard criteria for acceptable child performance (e.g., modification of the rate or manner of response). The objective "rides and steers two-wheel bicycle" may be adapted to "rides and adult steers two-wheel bicycle," therefore allowing a child with a visual disability the opportunity to pass the item.

Direction Modifications   Direction modifications allow the user to alter the materials, child position, or administration procedures of an item. For example, direction modifications may specify adaptive equipment (a built-up spoon handle), certain adaptive positions (positioned over a wedge), or special procedures (providing photographs for a child with autism to use when making choices of what to eat and drink for snack).

Although modifications are encouraged, it is important for the user to accurately record the types of modifications that are used. Recording this information is essential if future evaluations are to be valid. Without indicating the types of adaptations that occurred, accurately monitoring child progress is not possible. When an item is modified, the user should place the qualifying note M next to the performance score in the

Q column and note the modification used in the Comments section at the end of the recording form for each domain.

General modification guidelines are provided below for three types of disability: visual impairments, hearing impairments, and motor impairments.

Visual Impairments

1. When working with children with limited functional vision, the examiner should present each stimulus item within the child's field of vision (the visual field will need to be established for each child). It may be necessary to move objects close to the child; however, a large object placed too close may fill the child's entire visual field and obscure distinguishing features.
2. The examiner should attend to the background–foreground contrast of stimuli when evaluating a child with a visual impairment. For example, if working at a table with a dark surface, lighter color stimuli should be used.
3. Stimuli that provide more than one type of sensory feedback to the child, sound- or light-producing objects, and tactually interesting materials should be used. Objects that have high visual contrast (e.g., black, white, red, fluorescent orange) should be chosen to maximize the child's residual vision.
4. A child who cannot see certain materials should be made aware of all materials through physical contact with the objects. Guiding a child's hand over objects to be grasped, for example, may assist the child's performance of the task.
5. The child may not be aware of the desired behavior because there has been no prior visual experience with the object or task. Physical manipulation of the child through the movements will provide a model of the desired behavior and may give needed kinesthetic feedback to perform the task.

Hearing Impairments

1. Positioning the child is critical for optimal use of sensory information. The examiner should ensure that the child is facing the speaker and is in a proper position to see lips, gestures, or signs.
2. If the child wears a hearing aid, the examiner should make certain that the aid is operating at the optimal level.
3. The examiner must know the communication system of the child and be able to respond appropriately (e.g., understand and use signs).

Motor Impairments

1. The child with a motor impairment may have difficulty sequencing motor behaviors and may reverse steps in a sequence. For example, when requested to imitate a series of motor behaviors, the child may have difficulty either producing all of the actions or correctly sequencing the actions. The examiner may need to assist the child (through cues or prompts) to remember what behavior is next in the sequence.
2. The use of adaptive equipment or alterations in the types of objects used may be beneficial for the child. A physical or occupational therapist should be consulted when selecting adaptive equipment.
3. When attempting to complete a task, if the child's movements appear awkward, unstable, or uncoordinated, the child may benefit from positioning equipment (e.g., Mulholland chair, wedges, pillows).

4. The child's environment may require alteration to facilitate movement and allow the child to function more independently (e.g., stairs replaced by ramps, hand railing placed by toilets).

A maximally useful and accurate child assessment and evaluation will be obtained by employing a team of professionals whenever possible. It is particularly important to consult and involve a specialist when children have motor or sensory impairments. Specialists are mandatory when assessing and evaluating children with severe and multiple disabilities.

Assessment Activity Plans

To ensure that skills observed during the assessment session are representative, the AEPS Test should be administered in familiar settings and during activities that are typical for the child. For children in center-based settings and children who have more complex behavioral repertoires, individual observations during play and routine care activities may be difficult to arrange because of limited time and personnel resources. To allow efficient observation of groups of children in typical contexts, six Assessment Activity Plans have been developed and used successfully in classroom settings. (See Appendix C for a complete set of Assessment Activity Plans.) Each of the activity plans covers a range of AEPS items from several developmental domains that are likely to be observed during the activity. A sample Assessment Activity Plan is contained in Figure 6.3. On this plan, the name of the activity appears, the domains to be assessed are indicated, and the materials needed to conduct the activity are listed. This information is followed by a listing of goals and objectives that can be assessed during this activity and by directions for assessing these specific AEPS Test items.

Assessment Activity Plans have an associated recording form. AEPS Test items that are targeted in the activities can be listed on the left side of the Data Recording Form by domain, item number, and item description. On the right side of the form, the children's names can be listed. Below each name is space for recording responses. A copy of a completed Assessment Activity Plan Recording Form is contained in Figure 6.4.

Assessment Activity Plans present activities that are likely to occur in preschool classrooms. The activities may be embedded in the usual classroom schedule, creating minimal disruption for children and staff and increasing the likelihood that the assessment will yield an accurate and dynamic portrayal of the way children function during routine classroom activities. A sample daily classroom assessment schedule is presented in Figure 6.5.

As shown in Figure 6.6, groups of children can be assessed by organizing assessment stations in the classroom. A different scripted activity is conducted at each station, and small groups of children rotate from station to station across assessment sessions. Although items from the AEPS Test are likely to occur during play and routine activities, giving children multiple opportunities to perform skills with different people and materials and across a variety of situations is essential. Activity sessions can be used to increase the likelihood that skills will occur by arranging attractive and engaging physical and social environments. Most skills will be readily observed during the various activities, and the need to directly elicit items in test situations will be largely eliminated.

Assessment Activity Plans and recording forms may be attached to clipboards and positioned at assessment stations in the classroom. Whenever possible, activity sessions should be managed by one person who is familiar with the Assessment Activity Plan

Activity: **Snack:**

Domains Assessed:	Fine Motor, Cognitive, Adaptive, Social-Communication, Social
Materials:	Child-size cups, unbreakable bowls and plates, napkins, spoons, knives, forks
	Juice in pitchers
	Raisins, fruit, crackers, peanut butter, applesauce, yogurt
Preparation:	Cut fruit, such as bananas or apples, into large pieces. Place each type of food into a bowl. Pour a manageable amount of juice into small pitchers.
	During this activity, allow the children to serve themselves and to eat as independently as they are able. However, for health reasons, they should also be monitored to ensure that children handle only their own food and utensils.

Domain/Strand		Targeted Goals and/or Objectives	Description/Sequence
Cog H:	2.3	Demonstrate understanding of one-to-one correspondence	Encourage the children to prepare the table for snack time by having them distribute one dish, napkin, and so forth to each place.
Soc C:	1.0	Communicates personal likes and dislike	Ask the children to sit in their chairs and discuss what foods they like to eat.
Adap A:	2.3	Pours liquid into a variety of containers	Give the children the pitchers containing juice and allow them to pour some of the juice into their cups. Encourage each child to serve him- or herself.
Adap A:	2.4	Serves food with utensil	Allow the children to serve themselves applesauce with a spoon.
Adap A:	2.2	Uses knife to spread food	Give a child a plate of crackers and allow her to be in charge of passing them around the table. Let children use a knife to spread peanut butter onto their crackers.
Adap A:	2.0	Prepares and serves food	Present raisins to the children in small boxes. Observe each
	2.1	Prepares food for eating	child's ability to prepare and serve food for eating (i.e., they open the box and put raisins on a napkin or plate).
Soc A:	2.3	Shares and/or exchanges objects	Encourage the children to ask each other to pass food and other items.
Adap A:	1.0	Eats and drinks a variety of foods using appropriate utensils with little or no spilling	As the children are eating, observe each child's ability to eat and drink a variety of foods using appropriate utensils.
	1.1	Eats a variety of food textures	
	1.2	Selects and eats a variety of food types	
	1.3	Eats with fork and spoon	
Adap A:	3.0	Displays social dining skills	Observe each child's ability to demonstrate social dining skills.
	3.1	Puts proper amount of food in mouth, chews with mouth closed, swallows before taking another bite	
	3.2	Takes in proper amount of liquid and returns cup to surface	
	3.3	Remains seated during meal or until excused	
	3.4	Uses napkin to clean face and hands	
Cog E:	1.0	Recalls events that occurred on same day, without contextual cues	As the children are eating, discuss the day's events (i.e., "I enjoyed the stories," or "What have you been doing today?").
	1.1	Recalls events that occurred on same day, with contextual cues	

(continued)

Figure 6.3.   Sample AEPS Assessment Activity Plan.

Figure 6.3.   *(continued)*

Domain/Strand		Targeted Goals and/or Objectives	Description/Sequence
Cog B:	7.0	Demonstrates understanding of seven different temporal relations concepts	Observe the children's ability to use temporal concepts as they discuss these events (e.g., "Did we have story **before** or **after** circle time?" Spontaneously, the child says "My dad goes jogging in the morning," or "Tomorrow my grandpa is coming").
Cog D:	1.1	Follows directions of three or more related steps that are routinely given	When the children are finished eating, give them three-step directions while asking them to clear the table (e.g., "Put your cup in the sink, your napkin in the garbage, and push in your chair").
Adap A:	3.5	Assists in clearing table	Observe each child's ability to assist in clearing the table.

while a second person observes the child and records responses on the Assessment Activity Recording Form. Near the end of the activity, the recorder can ask the examiner to elicit particular AEPS Test items for a given child that were not observed during the activity session and items that were performed inconsistently. Because activities are designed to be flexible and open ended and to encourage children's independent behavior, the same activity plans can be used on multiple and consecutive days.

After assessment activities have been completed, scores are transferred from the Assessment Activity Recording Form to the individual AEPS Data Recording Form for each child. This is often an appropriate time for professionals from different disciplines to share their observations of children. Differences in observations among assessment team members can be discussed with consideration of the setting, time of day, and circumstances in which children performed skills. Parents can also join classroom personnel at this time and share observations and information about the skills their child uses in important settings outside the classroom such as home and child care.

AEPS Assessment Activity Plan Recording Form			
		Children's Names	
Activity: Snack	SUSIE	JOHN	MIKE
Date of Observation: _____			
Key: 2 = behavior observed 1 = inconsistent performance 0 = behavior not observed **Test items**			
Cog H: 2.3			

Figure 6.4.   Assessment Activity Plan Recording Form.

DAILY CLASSROOM ASSESSMENT SCHEDULE

Time	Activity	Targets
9:00–9:30	Arrival and Freeplay	(Observe children's greetings, interactions with people and objects—Social, Cognitive, Social-Communication)
9:30–9:50	Opening Circle Activity	(Observe children's familiarity with routines, ability to imitate motor and verbal responses, expressive and receptive communication, ability to engage in interactive games—Social, Cognitive, Social-Communication)
9:50–10:10	Activity Session I	(Set up three activity stations (1, 2, 3). Divide children into groups (A, B, C) and have them rotate from station to station across activity session (I, II, III) as shown in Figure 6.6
10:10–10:30	Activity Session II	
10:30–10:50	Activity Session III	
10:50–11:10	Snack	(Observe Adaptive, Cognitive, and Motor Skills)
11:10–11:40	Outdoor Play	(Observe Gross Motor skills)
11:40–12:00	Closing Circle	(Same as Opening Circle)

Figure 6.5.   Sample daily classroom assessment schedule.

SUMMARIZING ASSESSMENT INFORMATION

Using the assessment information obtained from the AEPS Test to develop an appropriate IEP/IFSP for a child is the most important activity to be accomplished prior to beginning intervention. The development of the IEP/IFSP from AEPS Test–generated assessment information is described in Chapter 5; however, before developing an

Assessment stations

		Corn-meal	Roads and bridges	Bathing dolls
Assessment sessions	I	Group A	Group B	Group C
	II	Group C	Group A	Group B
	III	Group B	Group C	Group A

Group A = Billy, Susie, and Amy
Group B = Ed, Kathleen, and Christopher
Group C = Tyler, Chrystal, and Gib

Figure 6.6.   Sample schedule for activity assessment sessions across three activity stations for three groups of children. (Corn-meal activities target Cognitive, Social-Communication, and Social test items; roads and bridges activities target Fine Motor, Gross Motor, Cognitive, and Social test items; and bathing dolls activities target Fine Motor, Gross Motor, Cognitive, Social-Communication, and Social test items.)

IEP/IFSP, a child's performance should be summarized following the administration of the AEPS Test.

The AEPS Test permits summarization in two ways. First, two numerical scores can be computed: the *Domain Percent Score* (by single domain) and the *Total Percent Score* (combining domains). Second, a narrative summary of the child's strengths and interests can be developed (i.e., domain-by-domain summary of the child's skills).

Numerical Summary

The most commonly computed score is a Domain Percent Score for each of the six domains. To obtain a Domain Percent Score, all of the items on which the child received a 2 and a 1 are summed. This total, which is the Domain Raw Score, is recorded at the end of each domain in the results section. The Domain Raw Score is then divided by the Total Domain Score Possible for the domain (provided in the results section). For example, if a child received a Domain Raw Score of 30 points on the Gross Motor Domain, his Domain Percent Score would be 83 (all scores of 2 and 1 are added together [30], then divided by the Total Domain Score Possible [36], and multiplied by 100[=83]). The Domain Percent Score can then be plotted on the graph at the end of the Data Recording Form. A Domain Percent Score can also be obtained separately for items scored with 2 and for items scored with 1.

Interventionists may want to calculate a child's Total Percent Score. A *Total Raw Score* is computed by counting all the scores of 2 and 1 the child received across all six domains. For example, if a child received a total of 330 when all the scores of 2 and 1 are added across domains, this would be the Total Raw Score. The Total Percent Score can be obtained by dividing the Total Raw Score by the total number of items in the test (490). Table 6.4 indicates the total number of items and the total score possible per domain. A Total Percent Score can also be calculated separately for items scored with 2 and items scored with 1 using the same procedure.

It is important that children's performances on the test be summarized so progress can be monitored over time. Children should be making steady progress toward their goals and objectives, which, in turn, should be reflected in the number of items scored with a 2 across test periods. The AEPS Test should be administered quarterly so assessment/evaluation information can be summarized and plotted three to four times per year. To assist in this task, a summary form is included with the AEPS Data Recording Form. An example of a summary form is contained in Figure 6.7. The Domain or Total Percent Score for each test period can be plotted to determine if the child's performance is improving over time.

Narrative Summary

A narrative summary can be written by examining a child's performance on the AEPS Test. The child's performance in each domain can be summarized by identifying those

Table 6.4. Number of items per domain and total score possible on the AEPS Test

Domain	Number of items	Total score possible
Fine Motor	14	28
Gross Motor	18	36
Adaptive	39	78
Cognitive	92	184
Social-Communication	49	98
Social	33	66
Total	**245**	**490**

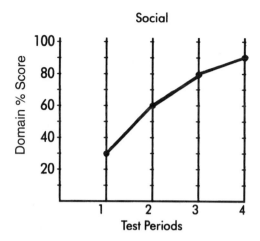

Figure 6.7. Sample summary form for the Social Domain with child's Domain Percent Scores plotted across four test periods.

items the child performs well (i.e., received a score of 2) and those items that are emerging (i.e., received a score of 1). The purpose of a narrative summary is to paint a picture of the child's strengths and interests by describing the child's functional skills using examples from the team's observations of the child.

Traditionally, test results are summarized from a deficit model, whereas a narrative summary written from the AEPS Test emphasizes the child's strengths, interests, and assets in selecting goals and objectives for the child's IEP/IFSP. A positively written summary of the child's skills does not ignore the areas in which the child may need intervention; it provides the team with an accurate picture of the child's current skill level and highlights those skills that are emerging and will be the target of intervention efforts.

SUMMARY

This chapter discusses AEPS Test administration guidelines with the goal of assisting the test user in the accurate and efficient application of the test. The use of the AEPS Test is governed by a set of general principles that should be followed; however, these principles provide only broad guidelines within which users are encouraged to individualize for children, particularly those with sensory or motor impairments.

Collection of educational and treatment-relevant assessment/evaluation data is critical to the development of functional IEPs/IFSPs and to monitoring children's important developmental progress. The AEPS Test is designed to provide information to the user about children's functional behavioral repertoire. The type of data generated by the AEPS Test is not appropriate to use for normative comparisons; rather, it provides data particularly appropriate for designing useful IEPs/IFSPs and intervention.

Assessment, Evaluation, and Programming System Test

AEPS Test Manual

This chapter contains the AEPS Test manual that covers the developmental period from 3 to 6 years and is generally appropriate for children whose chronological age is from 3 to 9 years. The test is composed of six domains; each domain encompasses a particular set of skills, behaviors, or information that is traditionally seen as comprising related developmental phenomena.

Fine Motor Domain

Items in the Fine Motor Domain assess fine motor behaviors by observation of specific arm and hand movements in activities, such as dressing, manipulating objects, and writing. Items in this domain measure the acquisition of the following skills:

- Manipulation of objects
- Prewriting

Gross Motor Domain

The development of gross motor skills is viewed as the continuous acquisition of behaviors culminating in the child's ability to maintain stability in various positions (balance) and to move from one position into another (positional change). Items in the Gross Motor Domain measure the acquisition of the following skills:

- Balance and mobility in standing and walking
- Play skills

Adaptive Domain

Items in the Adaptive Domain focus on dining skills such as drinking liquids and eating with a fork and spoon. This domain also measures skills used to maintain personal hygiene and dressing skills. Items in this domain measure the acquisition of the following skills:

- Dining
- Personal hygiene
- Dressing and undressing

Parental and cultural values have an effect on which skills a child learns and in what order the skills are learned.

Toilet training, the introduction of food and feeding utensils, and the degree of personal cleanliness are areas that may differ across cultures and families. While acknowledging these differences, the interventionist should help the child to acquire behaviors (e.g., eating with a fork rather than fingers, wiping nose on tissue rather than shirt sleeve) that are socially acceptable. The lack of socially acceptable skills often results in the exclusion of the child from certain environments.

Cognitive Domain

Items in the Cognitive Domain are designed to measure the child's group participation skills, use of various concepts, problem-solving skills, and recall skills. In addition, the child's ability to group and sequence objects and events is evaluated. Premath, prereading, and play skills are also measured in the Cognitive Domain. Items in this domain measure the acquisition of the following skills:

- Participation
- Demonstrates understanding of concepts
- Categorizing
- Sequencing
- Recalling events
- Problem solving
- Play
- Premath
- Prereading

The items in the Cognitive Domain were designed to assess the child's cognitive skills as they are used in daily activities. Some items in the Cognitive Domain are cross-referenced with items in the Social-Communication and Social Domains. It is important for several reasons to observe the child's behavior across domains. The first reason is that traditional developmental categories (e.g., social, cognitive, language) are somewhat arbitrary divisions. For example, a child's ability to engage in imaginary play or to participate in classroom activities can be viewed as both social and cognitive behavior. The ability to recall events and information can be viewed as social, cognitive, or communicative behavior.

The second reason to observe a child's behavior across domains is that behavior may be interdependent across domains. For example, a child's ability to follow directions in correct sequence (as in Strand D: Sequencing) is dependent on the child's understanding of verbal instructions. A child's ability to give a reason for an inference or to make a prediction about future events (as in Strand F: Problem Solving) is dependent on the child's expressive communication skills. If a child is unable to perform a given task, the interventionist should ask, "Is there some other behavior that is absent from the child's repertoire that prevents the child from demonstrating this behavior?"

Social-Communication Domain

Items in the Social-Communication Domain are based on the theoretical view that communication consists of three overlapping and interrelated developmental areas: 1) content (meaning expressed through language), 2) form (syntax and grammar of language), and 3) use (function of communication in social context).

The Social-Communication Domain was designed to assess the child's language and communication skills as they are used in classroom/home activities, conversations, and social interactions. Items in this domain evaluate social-communication interactions, such as the child's use of words and of conversational rules and grammatical structures. Items in this domain measure the acquisition of the following skills:

- Social-communicative interactions
- Production of words, phrases, and sentences

Two forms, the Social-Communication Recording Form and the Social Communication Summary Form (both forms are contained in Appendix D), are used for the purpose of collecting, recording, and analyzing the child's social-communication behavior. These forms, or similar forms, are recommended for use in scoring the Social-Communication Domain (see pages 203–205 for information on using these forms).

The user is reminded that items in the Social-Communication Domain are cross-referenced with items in the Cognitive and Social Domains. For example, a child's ability to name and identify colors (skills included in the Cognitive Domain) is dependent on the child's understanding of verbal instructions or questions such as, "Show me which one is green" or "What color is this?" A child may know the colors but not be able to say the appropriate word. If a child is unable to perform a given task, the interventionist should ask, "Is there another behavior absent from the child's repertoire that prevents the child from demonstrating this behavior?"

Social Domain

Items in the Social Domain are designed to assess children's interactions with peers, responses to the environment, and knowledge of self and others. Items in this domain measure the acquisition of the following skills:

- Interaction with others
- Interaction with environment
- Knowledge of self and others

The development of social skills is closely related to and interdependent on the development of cognitive, social-communication, and adaptive skills; therefore, data from all domains should be considered by the user when reviewing the Social Domain assessment data. The influence of cultural values on children's social behavior should also be considered during administration of the Social Domain.

ORGANIZATION OF THE TEST MANUAL

Each test domain begins with a list of the strands, goals, and associated objectives, with their indexing numbers. Each strand is defined, followed by a list of the test items (called goals and objectives) included in the strand.

Strands are identified with capital letters (e.g., strand A, B, C). Goals are identified with a capital G followed by a number (e.g., G1, G2, G3) and are listed under their respective strand. Objectives are listed under their respective goal and are identified with a decimal number (e.g., 1.1, 1.2, 1.3) that reflects the associated goal number. For example, objectives associated with G3 (goal 3) are indexed as 3.1, 3.2, and 3.3.

A consistent presentation format is followed for each item. The strand is indicated, as is the goal, for each objective. The item criterion is given, followed by directions for its administration. When appropriate, notes regarding cross-references to other goals and/or objectives are included.

Scoring Criteria

The scoring criteria are consistent across items. When using *observation*, the following criteria are to be employed:

2 = Child consistently and independently meets stated item criterion. Behavior is functional and generalized (occurs in a variety of settings, with different people or
materials, and under varying conditions).

1 = Child inconsistently meets stated item criterion. Behavior occurs, but it may be situation specific or emerging in the child's repertoire.

0 = Child does not exhibit the behavior when given repeated opportunities to do so.

When employing *direct test*, the following criteria are to be employed:

2 = Child consistently and independently meets stated item criterion. Behavior is functional and generalized (occurs in a variety of settings, with different people or
materials, and under varying conditions). Behavior must occur on at least two out
of three trials.

1 = Child inconsistently meets stated item criterion. Behavior occurs, but it may be situation specific or emerging in the child's repertoire. Behavior occurs on only one
out of three trials.

0 = Child does not exhibit the behavior. Behavior occurs on zero out of three trials.

AEPS TEST

FINE MOTOR DOMAIN

The Fine Motor Domain assesses fine motor behaviors by observation of specific arm and hand movement in skills such as dressing, manipulating objects, and writing. Items in this domain measure the acquisition of the following skills:

- Manipulation of objects
- Prewriting

Strand A Manipulation of Objects
> G1 Manipulates two small objects at same time
>> 1.1 Manipulates two hand-size objects at same time
>
> G2 Cuts out shapes with curved lines
>> 2.1 Cuts out shapes with straight lines
>> 2.2 Cuts paper in two
>
> G3 Ties string-type fastener
>> 3.1 Fastens buttons
>> 3.2 Threads and zips zipper

Strand B Prewriting
> G1 Copies complex shapes
>> 1.1 Copies simple shapes
>
> G2 Prints first name
>> 2.1 Prints three letters
>> 2.2 Copies first name
>> 2.3 Copies three letters

Strand A   Manipulation of Objects

GOAL 1   Manipulates two small objects at same time

CRITERION   Child uses two hands to manipulate two small objects at the same time in order to build or put things together (e.g., strings small beads; builds with Lego toys; puts key in padlock, caps on markers, or button through buttonhole).

DIRECTIONS

Materials   Small objects that can be put together.

Procedure   *Observation:* Observe child's ability to manipulate two small objects at the same time in order to build or put things together (e.g., strings beads, combines Tinkertoys, puts caps on markers/pens, puts large button through buttonhole).
Direct Test: Present small objects that can be put together (e.g., key and padlock, beads on a string, marking pens and caps). Observe child's ability to manipulate two small objects at the same time in order to build or put things together.

Objective 1.1   Manipulates two hand-size objects at same time

CRITERION   Child uses two hands to manipulate two hand-size objects at the same time in order to build or put things together (e.g., strings small beads, puts pop beads together, puts lid on a jar, puts soap on a washcloth).

DIRECTIONS

Materials   Hand-size objects that can be put together.

Procedure   *Observation:* Observe child's ability to manipulate two hand-size objects at the same time in order to build or put things together (e.g., string large beads, put lid on a jar).
Direct Test: Present hand-size objects that can be put together (e.g., bar of soap and a washcloth, giant Lego toys). Observe child's ability to manipulate two hand-size objects at the same time in order to build or put things together.

GOAL 2   Cuts out shapes with curved lines

CRITERION   Child uses scissors to cut out simple shapes with curved lines (e.g., circles, ovals). Child uses paper with printed shapes (at least 3 inches in
diameter) and cuts within ¼ inch of line. Ideally, child holds scissors
between thumb and first two fingers of one hand and holds paper
with other hand.

DIRECTIONS

Materials   Scissors, paper with printed shapes.

Procedure   *Observation:* Observe child's ability to use scissors to cut out simple
shapes with curved lines.
Direct Test: Present scissors and paper with printed shapes. Observe
child's ability to use scissors to cut out simple shapes with curved lines.

Objective 2.1   Cuts out shapes with straight lines

CRITERION   Child uses scissors to cut out simple shapes with straight lines (e.g.,
squares, rectangles, triangles). Child uses paper with printed shapes
(at least 3 inches in diameter) and cuts within ¼ inch of the lines.
Ideally, child holds scissors between thumb and first two fingers of one
hand and holds paper with other hand.

DIRECTIONS

Materials   Scissors, paper with printed shapes.

Procedure   *Observation:* Observe child's ability to use scissors to cut out simple
shapes with straight lines.
Direct Test: Present scissors and paper with printed shapes. Observe
child's ability to use scissors to cut out simple shapes with straight
lines.

Objective 2.2   Cuts paper in two

CRITERION   Child uses scissors to cut paper in two. Edge may be jagged. Ideally,
child holds scissors between thumb and first two fingers of one hand
and holds paper with other hand.

DIRECTIONS

Materials   Scissors, paper.

Procedure   *Observation:* Observe child's ability to use scissors to cut paper in two.
Direct Test: Present scissors and paper. Observe child's ability to use scissors to cut paper in two.

GOAL 3   Ties string-type fastener

CRITERION   Child uses functional means to tie string-type fastener (e.g., shoelace, ribbon, string). Fastener may be any size and does not need to be on child's own clothing.

DIRECTIONS

Materials   Shoelace, string.

Procedure   *Observation:* Observe child's ability to use any functional means to tie string-type fastener. *Example:* Child ties shoes.
Direct Test: Present string-type fastener and encourage child to tie. Observe child's ability to use any functional means to tie the fastener. *Example:* After activity, adult asks child to help tie string around a box.

Note: This item is cross-referenced with Adaptive Domain, Strand C, Objective 3.1.

Objective 3.1   Fastens buttons

CRITERION   Child uses any functional means to fasten buttons. Buttons may be any size and do not need to be on child's own clothing.

DIRECTIONS

Materials   Clothing with buttons, toys with buttons (e.g., doll, book).

Procedure   *Observation:* Observe child's ability to use any functional means to fasten buttons. *Example:* Child buttons coat.
Direct Test: Present object with unfastened buttons (e.g., clothing, doll, book) and encourage child to button. Observe child's ability to use any functional means to fasten buttons. *Example:* During dress-up activity, adult asks child to help button garment.

Note: This item is cross-referenced with Adaptive Domain, Strand C, Objective 3.2.

Objective 3.2   Threads and zips zipper

CRITERION   Child uses functional means to thread and zip zipper. Zipper may be any size and does not need to be on child's own clothing.

DIRECTIONS

Materials   Clothing and objects with zipper (e.g., coat, doll).

Procedure   *Observation:* Observe child's ability to use any functional means to thread and zip zipper. *Example:* Child zips coat.
Direct Test: Present object with unfastened zipper. Encourage child to thread and zip zipper. Observe child's ability to thread and zip zipper *Example:* During doll play, adult asks child to help zip doll's coat.

Note: This item is cross-referenced with Adaptive Domain, Strand C, Objective 3.3.

Strand B   Prewriting

GOAL 1   Copies complex shapes

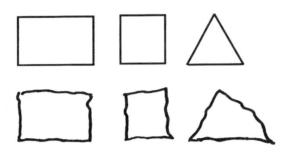

CRITERION   Child copies shapes with angular contours (e.g., rectangle, square, triangle) from a drawn model.

DIRECTIONS

Materials   Complex shapes drawn on cards or paper, blank paper, chalkboard, chalk, pencil, crayon, felt pen.

Procedure   *Observation:* Observe child's ability to copy shapes with angular contours (e.g., rectangle, square, triangle) from a drawn model.
Direct Test: Present model of shape and writing materials and ask child to draw one like it. Observe child's ability to copy shapes with angular contours.

Objective 1.1   Copies simple shapes

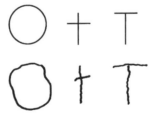

CRITERION   Child copies shapes with circular contours or lines (e.g., circle, cross, T) from a drawn model.

DIRECTIONS

Materials   Simple shapes (e.g., circle, cross, T) drawn on cards or paper, blank paper, chalkboard, chalk, pencil, crayon, felt pen.

Procedure   *Observation:* Observe child's ability to copy shapes with circular contours or lines (e.g., circle, cross, T) from a drawn model.
Direct Test: Present model of shape and writing materials and ask child to draw one like it. Observe child's ability to copy shapes with circular contours from a drawn model.

GOAL 2   Prints first name

CRITERION   Child prints own first name without model. Letters must be in correct order, but printing errors are permissible (e.g., letter printed backward); however, name should be recognizable.

DIRECTIONS

Materials   Paper, writing implement.

Procedure   *Observation:* Observe child's ability to print own first name without model.
Direct Test: Present child with writing materials and ask child to print first name. Observe child's ability to print own first name without a model.

Objective 2.1   Prints three letters

CRITERION   Child prints three upper- or lowercase letters without model. Printing errors are permissible (e.g., letter printed backward); however, individual letters should be recognizable. Verbal cues may be provided (e.g., "Can you write some letters?"; "Make an E").

DIRECTIONS

Materials   Paper, writing implement.

Procedure   *Observation:* Observe child's ability to print three upper- or lowercase letters.
Direct Test: Present child with writing materials and ask child to print letters. Observe child's ability to print three upper- or lowercase letters.

Notes: This item is cross-referenced with Cognitive Domain, Strand I, Objective 4.1.

If verbal cues are given (e.g., "Draw an S"), letter names presented should be those with which the child is familiar.

Objective 2.2   Copies first name

CRITERION   Child copies own first name from model. Letters should be in correct order. Printing errors are permissible (e.g., letter printed backward); however, name should be recognizable.

DIRECTIONS

Materials   Paper on which child's own first name is printed, writing implement.

Procedure   *Observation:* Observe child's ability to copy own first name from model.
Direct Test: Present writing implement and paper on which child's own first name is printed. Observe child's ability to copy first name from model.

Objective 2.3   Copies three letters

CRITERION   Child copies three upper- or lowercase letters from model. Printing errors are permissible (e.g., letter printed backward); however, individual letters should be recognizable.

DIRECTIONS

Materials   Paper with printed letters, writing implements.

Procedure   *Observation:* Observe child's ability to copy three upper- or lowercase letters from model.
Direct Test: Present writing implements and paper with printed letters. Observe child's ability to copy three upper- or lowercase letters from model.

Note: V, H, and T are generally the easiest letters for children to copy. If child can copy these letters, score the item 2.

GROSS MOTOR DOMAIN

The development of gross motor skills is viewed as the continuous acquisition of behaviors culminating in the child's ability to maintain stability in various positions (balance) and to move from one position to another (positional change). Items in this domain measure the acquisition of the following skills:

- Balance and mobility in standing and walking
- Play skills

Strand A   Balance and Mobility in Standing and Walking

     G1   Alternates feet walking up and down stairs

        1.1   Walks up and down stairs

Strand B   Play Skills

     G1   Jumps forward

        1.1   Jumps in place

        1.2   Jumps from platform

        1.3   Maintains balance in walking

        1.4   Balances on one foot

     G2   Runs avoiding obstacles

        2.1   Runs

     G3   Bounces, catches, kicks, and throws ball

        3.1   Bounces ball

        3.2   Catches ball

        3.3   Kicks ball

        3.4   Throws ball

     G4   Skips

        4.1   Hops

     G5   Rides and steers two-wheel bicycle

        5.1   Pedals and steers two-wheel bicycle with training wheels

Strand A   Balance and Mobility in Standing and Walking

GOAL 1   Alternates feet walking up and down stairs

CRITERION   Child walks up and down stairs, alternating feet without holding handrail or wall.

DIRECTIONS

Materials   Stairs, objects interesting to the child.

Procedure   *Observation:* Observe child's ability to walk up and down stairs, alternating feet without holding onto rail or wall.
Direct Test: Present an object several steps up or down in front of child and encourage child to obtain object. Observe child's ability to walk up and down stairs, alternating feet without holding onto rail or wall.

Objective 1.1   Walks up and down stairs

CRITERION   Child walks up and down stairs without alternating feet. Child may hold handrail or wall with one hand for support.

DIRECTIONS

Materials   Stairs, objects interesting to the child.

Procedure   *Observation:* Observe child's ability to walk up and down stairs without alternating feet. Child may hold onto rail or wall with one hand for support.
Direct Test: Present an object several steps up or down in front of child and encourage child to obtain object. Observe child's ability to walk up and down stairs without alternating feet. Child may hold onto rail or wall with one hand for support.

Strand B   Play Skills

GOAL 1   Jumps forward

CRITERION   Child jumps forward with feet together. Ideally, hips, knees, and ankles are flexed, and body is crouched on takeoff and landing. Arms lead with a vigorous forward and upward thrust, and body is fully extended as it becomes airborne. Child lands on two feet without falling. Adult may model action.

DIRECTIONS

Materials   Long, thin object (e.g., rope, tape, chalkline, stick).

Procedure   *Observation:* Observe child's ability to jump forward with feet together and land without falling. Adult may model action.

Direct Test: Place long, thin object (e.g., rope, tape, chalkline, stick) on ground in front of child and encourage child to jump over it. Observe child's ability to jump forward (over object) with feet together and land on feet without falling. Adult may model action.

Objective 1.1   Jumps in place

CRITERION   Child jumps up and down in place. Ideally, hips, knees, and ankles are flexed on takeoff and landing. Arms lead with a vigorous forward and upward thrust, and body extends as it becomes airborne. Child lands on two feet without falling. Adult may model action.

DIRECTIONS

Materials   Object interesting to the child.

Procedure   *Observation:* Observe child's ability to jump up and down in one place and land on two feet without falling. Adult may model action.

Direct Test: Present an object above child and encourage child to jump up to touch or get the object. Observe child's ability to jump up and down in one place and land on feet without falling. Adult may model action.

Objective 1.2   Jumps from platform

CRITERION   Child jumps from a low platform (e.g., curb, low step, raised platform) to the supporting surface. Child lands on two feet without falling. Adult may model action.

DIRECTIONS

Materials   Low, stable structure (e.g., curb, low step, raised platform).

Procedure   *Observation:* Observe child's ability to jump from a low platform (e.g., curb, low step, raised platform) to a supporting surface and land on two feet without falling. Adult may model action.

Direct Test: When child is standing on a low platform (e.g., curb, low step, raised platform), encourage child to jump off. Observe child's ability to jump to the supporting surface and land on two feet without falling. Adult may model action.

Objective 1.3   Maintains balance in walking

CRITERION   Child maintains balance during at least two of the following walking activities:

- Walks 6 feet on 4-inch–wide balance beam
- Walks 10 feet on line
- Walks 10 feet on tiptoe
- Walks 10 feet backward
- Walks 6 feet on heels

Adult may model action.

DIRECTIONS

Materials   4-inch–wide balance beam, chalkline, tape.

Procedure   *Observation:* Observe child's ability to maintain balance in at least two of the walking activities listed in the criterion. Adult may model action.

Direct Test: Set up an obstacle course game with a leader and observe child's ability to maintain balance in at least two of the walking activities listed in the criterion.

Objective 1.4   Balances on one foot

CRITERION   Child balances on one foot for at least 5 seconds. Adult may model action.

DIRECTIONS

Materials   No materials are required.

Procedure   *Observation:* Observe child's ability to balance on one foot for at least 5 seconds. Adult may model action.
Direct Test: During play activity, encourage child to balance on one foot. Observe child's ability to balance on one foot for at least 5 seconds. Adult may model action.

GOAL 2   Runs avoiding obstacles

CRITERION   Child avoids obstacles while running by controlling starts, stops, and sudden changes in direction.

DIRECTIONS

Materials   Usual obstacles in the environment (e.g., chair, table, toys) or an obstacle course.

Procedure   *Observation:* Observe child's ability to avoid obstacles while running by controlling starts, stops, and sudden changes in direction.
Direct Test: Set up an obstacle course and take turns running through it. Observe child's ability to avoid obstacles while running by controlling starts, stops, and sudden changes in direction.

Objective 2.1   Runs

CRITERION   Child runs. Ideally, trunk is inclined slightly forward, arms swing freely, legs alternately flex and extend, and there is a period of no support by either leg.

GM B

DIRECTIONS

Materials   Objects interesting to the child.

Procedure   *Observation:* Observe child's ability to run.

Direct Test: During play activities, encourage child to run toward an object or person. Observe child's ability to run.

GOAL 3   Bounces, catches, kicks, and throws ball

CRITERION   Child performs the following ball activities:

- Bounces
- Catches
- Kicks
- Throws

DIRECTIONS   (See Objectives 3.1–3.4 for specific directions.)

Note: If a child's performance on *all* objectives was scored with a 2, the goal is scored 2. If a child's performance on the objectives was scored with *any* combination of a 0, 1, or 2, the goal is scored 1. If a child's performance on *all* objectives was scored with a 0, the goal is scored 0.

Objective 3.1   Bounces ball

CRITERION   Child bounces a large ball (i.e., at least 8 inches in diameter) at least twice, using the palm of one hand. Ideally, child contacts the ball with fingers spread and pushes the ball to the floor by extending elbow.

DIRECTIONS

Materials   Ball at least 8 inches in diameter.

Procedure   *Observation:* Observe child's ability to bounce a large ball using the palm of one hand.

Direct Test: Present a large ball and encourage child to bounce it. If necessary, demonstrate the skill. Observe child's ability to bounce ball using the palm of one hand.

Objective 3.2 Catches ball

CRITERION   Child catches ball at least 6 inches in diameter using palms of two hands. Ball is thrown underhand from a distance of 6–10 feet.

DIRECTIONS

Materials   Ball at least 6 inches in diameter.

Procedure   *Observation:* When ball is thrown to child, observe child's ability to catch it using palms of two hands.
Direct Test: Throw ball and encourage child to catch it. Observe child's ability to catch ball using palms of two hands.

GM B

Objective 3.3 Kicks ball

CRITERION   Child kicks stationary ball with one foot while maintaining balance. Ideally, support leg is flexed while kicking leg swings backward and forward and follows through in direction of kick. Trunk is inclined slightly backward, and ball contact is made with toes or foot.

DIRECTIONS

Materials   Large ball.

Procedure   *Observation:* When large ball is placed in front of child, observe child's ability to kick ball with one foot while maintaining balance.
Direct Test: Place a large ball in front of child and encourage child to kick it. If necessary, demonstrate the skill for child. Observe child's ability to kick stationary ball with one foot while maintaining balance.

Objective 3.4 Throws ball

CRITERION   Child throws ball forward with one hand, using overhand throw. Ideally, throwing arm is moved backward in preparation, and child uses shoulder and elbow to throw.

DIRECTIONS

Materials   Hand-size ball.

Procedure   *Observation:* Observe child's ability to throw ball with one hand using overhand throw.

Direct Test: Present a ball and encourage child to throw it at a target (e.g., person ready to catch, target board, bucket). If necessary, demonstrate the skill. Observe child's ability to throw ball with one hand using overhand throw.

GOAL 4   Skips

CRITERION   Child skips at least 15 feet, using alternating step–hop pattern.

DIRECTIONS

Materials   No specific materials are required, objects of interest to the child.

Procedure   *Observation:* Observe child's ability to skip at least 15 feet using alternating step–hop pattern.

Direct Test: Encourage child to skip toward an object or person. If necessary, demonstrate the skill. Observe child's ability to skip at least 15 feet using alternating step–hop pattern.

Objective 4.1   Hops

CRITERION   Child hops forward with five or more consecutive hops on one foot.

DIRECTIONS

Materials   No specific materials are required, objects of interest to the child.

Procedure   *Observation:* Observe child's ability to hop forward with five or more consecutive hops on one foot.

Direct Test: Encourage child to hop toward an object or person. If necessary, demonstrate the skill. Observe child's ability to hop forward with five or more consecutive hops on one foot.

GOAL 5   Rides and steers two-wheel bicycle

CRITERION   While sitting on a two-wheel bicycle, child pedals forward and steers bicycle at least 20 feet.

DIRECTIONS

Materials   Two-wheel bicycle (child's feet must reach the ground).

Procedure   *Observation:* When child is sitting on a two-wheel bicycle, observe
                     child's ability to pedal and steer bicycle forward for at least 20 feet.
                     Direct Test: Seat child on two-wheel bicycle. Stand next to bicycle and
                     encourage child to pedal forward. Observe child's ability to pedal and
                     steer bicycle forward for at least 20 feet.

Objective 5.1   Pedals and steers two-wheel bicycle with training wheels

---

CRITERION   While sitting on a two-wheel bicycle with training wheels with both
                     feet on pedals, child pedals bicycle forward and steers for at least
                     10 feet.

DIRECTIONS

Materials   Two-wheel bicycle with training wheels (child's feet must reach the
                     ground).

Procedure   *Observation:* When child is sitting on a two-wheel bicycle with training
                     wheels, observe child's ability to pedal and steer bicycle forward for at
                     least 10 feet.
                     Direct Test: Seat child on a two-wheel bicycle with training wheels.
                     Stand next to bicycle and encourage child to pedal forward. Observe
                     child's ability to pedal and steer bicycle forward for at least 10 feet.

GM B

ADAPTIVE DOMAIN

Items in the Adaptive Domain focus on dining skills such as drinking liquids and eating with a fork and spoon. This domain also measures skills used to maintain personal hygiene and dressing skills. Items in this domain measure the acquisition of the following skills:

- Dining
- Personal hygiene
- Dressing and undressing

Parental and cultural values have an effect on what skills a child learns and in what order the skills are learned. Toilet training, the introduction of food and feeding utensils, and personal cleanliness are areas that may differ across cultures and families. While acknowledging these differences, the interventionist should help the child to acquire behaviors (e.g., eating with a fork rather than fingers, wiping nose on tissue rather than shirt sleeve) that are socially acceptable. The lack of socially acceptable skills often results in the exclusion of the child from certain environments.

Strand A   Dining

G1   Eats and drinks a variety of foods using appropriate utensils with little or no spilling
   1.1   Eats a variety of food textures
   1.2   Selects and eats a variety of food types
   1.3   Eats with fork and spoon

G2   Prepares and serves food
   2.1   Prepares food for eating
   2.2   Uses knife to spread food
   2.3   Pours liquid into a variety of containers
   2.4   Serves food with utensil

G3   Displays social dining skills
   3.1   Puts proper amount of food in mouth, chews with mouth closed, swallows before taking another bite
   3.2   Takes in proper amount of liquid and returns cup to surface
   3.3   Remains seated during meal or until excused
   3.4   Uses napkin to clean face and hands
   3.5   Assists in clearing table

Strand B   Personal Hygiene

G1   Carries out all toileting functions
   1.1   Uses toilet paper, flushes toilet, washes hands after using toilet
   1.2   Uses toilet

          1.3   Indicates need to use toilet

G2   Washes and grooms self

          2.1   Uses tissue to clean nose

          2.2   Brushes teeth

          2.3   Bathes and dries self

          2.4   Brushes or combs hair

          2.5   Washes and dries face

Strand C   Dressing and Undressing

G1   Unfastens fasteners on garments

          1.1   Unfastens buttons/snaps/Velcro fasteners on garments

          1.2   Unties string-type fastener

          1.3   Unzips zipper

G2   Selects appropriate clothing and dresses self at designated times

          2.1   Puts on long pants

          2.2   Puts on front-opening garment

          2.3   Puts on pullover garment

          2.4   Puts on shoes

          2.5   Puts on underpants, shorts, or skirt

G3   Fastens fasteners on garments

          3.1   Ties string-type fastener

          3.2   Fastens buttons, snaps, and Velcro fasteners

          3.3   Threads and zips zipper

Adap

Strand A   Dining

GOAL 1   Eats and drinks a variety of foods using appropriate utensils with little or no spilling

CRITERION   Child performs all of the following activities:

- Eats a variety of food textures
- Selects and eats a variety of food types
- Eats with fork and spoon

DIRECTIONS   (See Objectives 1.1–1.3 for specific directions.)

Note: If a child's performance on *all* objectives was scored with a 2, the goal is scored 2. If a child's performance on the objectives was scored with *any* combination of a 0, 1, or 2, the goal is scored 1. If a child's performance on *all* objectives was scored with a 0, the goal is scored 0.

Objective 1.1   Eats a variety of food textures

CRITERION   Child eats food of different textures (e.g., soft, chewy).

DIRECTIONS

Materials   Variety of foods that includes

- Semisolid foods (applesauce, yogurt)
- Chewy foods (meats, dried fruits)
- Hard foods (apples, raw vegetables, pretzels)
- Soft foods (bananas, cooked vegetables, macaroni)

Procedure   *Observation:* When child is eating, observe child's ability to eat foods of different textures (e.g., soft, chewy).
Direct Test: Present a variety of food textures (e.g., soft, chewy) and encourage child to feed self. Observe child's ability to eat food of different textures.

Objective 1.2   Selects and eats a variety of food types

CRITERION   Child selects and eats a variety of foods from different food groups (e.g., dairy, meat, fruit).

DIRECTIONS

Materials   Variety of foods (e.g., applesauce, vegetables, meat, breads, fruits, cheese, yogurt).

Procedure   *Observation:* When child is eating, observe child's ability to select and eat a variety of foods from different food groups (e.g., dairy, meat, fruit, vegetables, breads).
Direct Test: Present a variety of foods from different food groups (e.g., dairy, meat, fruit, vegetables, breads) and encourage child to feed self. Observe child's ability to select and eat a variety of food types.

Objective 1.3   Eats with fork and spoon

CRITERION   The child eats by spearing with fork and scooping with spoon, bringing food to mouth with minimal spilling. Child chooses appropriate utensil (e.g., spoon for soup, fork for meat).

DIRECTIONS

Materials   Foods that can be speared (e.g., meat, vegetables, pieces of fruit); foods that can be scooped (e.g., soup, cereal, applesauce); utensils (e.g., fork, spoon, dish).

Procedure   *Observation:* When child is eating, observe child's ability to choose the appropriate utensil (e.g., spoon for soup, fork for meat) and to spear with fork and scoop with spoon, bringing utensil to mouth with minimal spilling.
Direct Test: Present food to be speared in one dish and food to be scooped in another; present fork and spoon and encourage child to feed self. Observe child's ability to choose the appropriate utensil (e.g., spoon for soup, fork for meat) and to spear with a fork and scoop with a spoon, bringing utensil to mouth with minimal spilling.

Adap A

GOAL 2 Prepares and serves food

CRITERION Child performs the following activities prior to eating:

- Prepares food for eating
- Uses knife to spread food
- Pours liquid into a variety of containers
- Serves food with utensil

DIRECTIONS (See Objectives 2.1–2.4 for specific directions.)

Note: If a child's performance on *all* objectives was scored with a 2, the goal is scored 2. If a child's performance on the objectives was scored with *any* combination of a 0, 1, or 2, the goal is scored 1. If a child's performance on *all* objectives was scored with a 0, the goal is scored 0.

Objective 2.1 Prepares food for eating

CRITERION Child prepares food for eating by removing inedible parts (e.g., peels skin or shell from food, removes paper wrapping, pulls tab on soft drink can).

DIRECTIONS

Materials Foods that need inedible parts removed prior to eating (e.g., banana, hard-boiled egg, candy in wrapper, crackers in box).

Procedure *Observation:* Observe child's ability to prepare food for eating by removing inedible parts (e.g., peels banana, peels hard-boiled egg, unwraps candy) or by gaining access to food (e.g., pulls tab on soft drink can, opens cracker box).

Direct Test: Present foods that require inedible parts be removed prior to eating (e.g., banana, hard-boiled egg, candy in wrapper) and encourage child to prepare food to eat. Observe child's ability to prepare food for eating by removing inedible parts (e.g., peels banana, peels hard-boiled egg, unwraps candy) or by gaining access to food (e.g., pulls tab on soft drink can, opens cracker box).

Adap A

Objective 2.2   Uses knife to spread food

CRITERION   Child uses a knife to spread soft, spreadable foods (e.g., margarine, cream cheese, jam) on bread or cracker. The bread or cracker should be covered by the food and be intact after child spreads the food. The food does not have to be spread smoothly.

DIRECTIONS

Materials   A blunt-edged knife; soft, spreadable foods (e.g., peanut butter, cream cheese, jam); bread or crackers.

Procedure   *Observation:* Observe child's ability to use a blunt-edged knife to spread soft, spreadable food (e.g., margarine, cream cheese, jam) on bread or cracker. The bread or cracker should be covered by the food and be intact after child spreads the food. The food does not have to be spread smoothly.
Direct Test: Present soft, spreadable foods (e.g., margarine, cream cheese, jam), bread or cracker, and a blunt-edged knife. Observe child's ability to use a knife to spread soft, spreadable food on bread or cracker. The bread or cracker should be covered by the food and be intact after child spreads the food. The food does not have to be spread smoothly.

Objective 2.3   Pours liquid into a variety of containers

CRITERION   Child pours liquid from one container (e.g., pitcher, bottle) into another container (e.g., cup, bowl, glass). Child does not spill liquid and stops pouring at the appropriate time to avoid overfilling container.

DIRECTIONS

Materials   Liquids (e.g., milk, juice, water); containers for pouring (e.g., pitcher, bottle); containers for filling (e.g., cup, bowl, glass).

Procedure   *Observation:* Observe child's ability to pour liquid from one container into another without spilling or overfilling the container.
Direct Test: Present container of liquid (e.g., pitcher of juice, bottle of water) and containers for filling (e.g., cup, bowl, glass) and encourage child to pour. Observe child's ability to pour liquid from one container into another without spilling or overfilling the container.

Objective 2.4   Serves food with utensil

CRITERION   Child uses a utensil to transfer food from one container to another.

DIRECTIONS

Materials   Bowl filled with food, a second container, utensils.

Procedure   *Observation:* Observe child's ability to use a utensil to transfer food from one container to another.

Direct Test: Present bowl filled with food, utensil, and second container. Observe child's ability to use a utensil to transfer food from one container to another.

GOAL 3   Displays social dining skills

CRITERION   Child displays social dining skills by performing the following activities:

- Puts proper amount of food in mouth, chews with mouth closed, swallows before taking another bite
- Takes in proper amount of liquid and returns cup to surface
- Remains seated during meal or until excused
- Uses napkin to clean face and hands
- Assists in clearing table

DIRECTIONS   (See Objectives 3.1–3.5 for specific directions.)

Note: If a child's performance on *all* objectives was scored with a 2, the goal is scored 2. If a child's performance on the objectives was scored with *any* combination of a 0, 1, or 2, the goal is scored 1. If a child's performance on *all* objectives was scored with a 0, the goal is scored 0.

Objective 3.1   Puts proper amount of food in mouth, chews with mouth closed, swallows before taking another bite

CRITERION   Child puts appropriate amount of food in mouth (i.e., does not overfill mouth), chews with mouth closed, and swallows before taking another bite.

Adap A

DIRECTIONS

Materials	Food, eating utensils.
Procedure	*Observation:* When child is eating, observe child's ability to put appropriate amount of food in mouth (i.e., does not overfill mouth), chew with mouth closed, and swallow before taking another bite.
	Direct Test: Present eating utensils and food in dishes and encourage child to feed self. Observe child's ability to put appropriate amount of food in mouth (i.e., does not overfill mouth), chew with mouth closed, and swallow before taking another bite.

Objective 3.2   Takes in proper amount of liquid and returns cup to surface

---

CRITERION	Child takes in appropriate amount of liquid from child-size cup without spilling and returns cup to table at least once before emptying cup.

DIRECTIONS

Materials	Cup or glass; liquid (e.g., milk, juice, water).
Procedure	*Observation:* While child is drinking, observe child's ability to take in appropriate amount of liquid from cup without spilling, swallow liquid, and return cup to table at least once before emptying cup.
	Direct Test: Present a cup or glass of liquid and encourage child to drink. Observe child's ability to take in proper amount of liquid without spilling, swallow liquid, and return cup to table at least once before emptying cup.

Objective 3.3   Remains seated during meal or until excused

CRITERION	Child remains seated during meal or until excused from table.

DIRECTIONS

Materials	No materials are required.
Procedure	*Observation:* While child is eating at a table, observe child's ability to remain seated for meal or until excused.
	Direct Test: Present child with eating situation (e.g., snack time) at a table. Observe child's ability to remain seated for meal or until excused.

Adap A

Objective 3.4 Uses napkin to clean face and hands

CRITERION   Child uses napkin to clean food from face and hands. Child may be given assistance to thoroughly clean face and hands.

DIRECTIONS

Materials   Napkins, paper towels.

Procedure   *Observation:* When child is eating, observe child's ability to use napkin to clean food from face and hands when necessary. Child may be given assistance to thoroughly clean face and hands.
Direct Test: Present child with napkin when child is eating. Observe child's ability to use napkin to clean food from face and hands when necessary. Child may be given assistance to thoroughly clean face and hands.

Objective 3.5 Assists in clearing table

CRITERION   After eating, child removes own dishes and silverware from table and puts them in an appropriate place (e.g., sink, counter, dishwasher).

DIRECTIONS

Materials   Bowls, cups, glasses, plates, and silverware.

Procedure   *Observation:* After child has finished at table, observe child's ability to remove own dishes and silverware and put in appropriate place (e.g., sink, counter, dishwasher).
Direct Test: Present eating situation (e.g., snack time) at a table. After the child has finished eating, encourage child to clear the dishes. Observe child's ability to remove own dishes and silverware and put in appropriate place (e.g., sink, counter, dishwasher).

Adap A

Strand B   Personal Hygiene

GOAL 1   Carries out all toileting functions

CRITERION   Child initiates trip to bathroom, pulls down pants, uses toilet paper, flushes toilet, pulls up pants, washes hands, and remains dry and unsoiled between trips to the bathroom. Reminders are acceptable.

DIRECTIONS

Materials   Toilet or potty chair, sink.

Procedure   *Observation:* Observe child's ability to initiate trips to bathroom. Child pulls pants down, uses toilet paper, flushes toilet, pulls pants up, washes hands after using the toilet. Child remains dry and unsoiled between self-initiated trips to the bathroom. Reminders are acceptable.
Direct Test: Direct test is not appropriate for this item.

Objective 1.1   Uses toilet paper, flushes toilet, washes hands after using toilet

CRITERION   Child completes the following toileting routine: pulls down pants, uses toilet paper after using the toilet, pulls up pants, flushes toilet, and washes hands.

DIRECTIONS

Materials   Toilet or potty chair, sink.

Procedure   *Observation:* Observe child's ability to complete the toileting routine of pulling down pants, using toilet and toilet paper, pulling up pants, flushing toilet, and washing hands.
Direct Test: Direct test is not appropriate for this item.

Objective 1.2   Uses toilet

CRITERION   Child initiates a trip to the bathroom and uses the toilet for urination and bowel movement. Child remains dry and unsoiled between trips to the bathroom. Occasional reminders are acceptable. Child may have assistance with other toileting skills (e.g., pulling pants down and up, washing hands).

DIRECTIONS

Materials   Toilet or potty chair, sink.

Procedure   *Observation:* Observe child's ability to initiate toileting and use the toilet for urination or bowel movement. Child remains dry and unsoiled between self-initiated trips to the bathroom. Occasional reminders are acceptable, and child may have assistance with other toileting skills (e.g., pulling pants down and up, washing hands).
Direct Test: Direct test is not appropriate for this item.

Objective 1.3   Indicates need to use toilet

CRITERION   Child accurately indicates (e.g., tells, signs, gestures) to an adult the need to use the toilet for urination and bowel movement.

DIRECTIONS

Materials   Toilet or potty chair.

Procedure   *Observation:* Observe child's ability to accurately indicate (e.g., tell, sign, gesture) to adult the need to use the toilet.
Direct Test: Direct test is not appropriate for this item.

GOAL 2   Washes and grooms self

CRITERION   Child performs the following washing and grooming activities:

- Uses tissue to clean nose
- Brushes teeth
- Bathes and dries self
- Brushes or combs hair
- Washes and dries face

Adap B

DIRECTIONS   (See Objectives 2.1–2.5 for specific directions.)

Note: If a child's performance on *all* objectives was scored with a 2, the goal is scored 2. If a child's performance on the objectives was scored with *any* combination of a 0, 1, or 2, the goal is scored 1. If a child's performance on *all* objectives was scored with a 0, the goal is scored 0.

Objective 2.1   Uses tissue to clean nose

CRITERION   Child uses a tissue to blow or wipe nose. Child may be given assistance to thoroughly clean nose.

DIRECTIONS

Materials   Tissue.

Procedure   *Observation:* Observe child's ability to blow or wipe nose. Child may be given assistance to thoroughly clean nose.
Direct Test: Direct test is not appropriate for this item.

Objective 2.2   Brushes teeth

CRITERION   Child puts toothpaste on toothbrush, brushes teeth, and rinses mouth. Reminders are acceptable (e.g., "What should you do next?").

DIRECTIONS

Materials   Toothbrush, toothpaste, sink.

Procedure   *Observation:* Observe child's ability to put toothpaste on toothbrush, brush teeth, and rinse mouth. Reminders are acceptable.
Direct Test: When child's teeth need brushing, encourage child to begin brushing routine. Observe child's ability to put toothpaste on toothbrush, brush teeth, and rinse mouth. Reminders are acceptable.

Objective 2.3   Bathes and dries self

CRITERION   Child performs the following bathing routine: removes clothing, gets into tub or shower, uses soap to clean body, rinses off, obtains towel, dries body, returns towel to towel rack. Reminders are acceptable, and child may be given assistance to thoroughly clean and dry self.

Adap B

DIRECTIONS

Materials Soap, water, towel, tub or shower.

Procedure *Observation:* Observe child's ability to perform bathing and drying routine of removing clothes, getting into tub or shower, using soap to clean body, rinsing off, obtaining towel, drying body, and returning towel to towel rack. Reminders are acceptable, and child may be given assistance to thoroughly clean and dry self.

Direct Test: When child needs bathing, encourage child to begin bathing routine. Observe child's ability to perform bathing and drying routine of removing clothing, getting into tub or shower, using soap to clean body, rinsing off, obtaining towel, drying body, and returning towel to towel rack. Reminders are acceptable, and child may be given assistance to thoroughly clean and dry self.

Objective 2.4 Brushes or combs hair

CRITERION Child uses a brush to brush hair or a comb to comb hair.

DIRECTIONS

Materials Brush, comb.

Procedure *Observation:* Observe child's ability to use a brush to brush hair or a comb to comb hair.

Direct Test: When the child's hair needs to be brushed or combed, encourage the child to use a brush to brush hair or a comb to comb hair.

Objective 2.5 Washes and dries face

CRITERION Child completes face washing and drying routine by turning faucet on, washing face with soap, rinsing face, turning faucet off, drying face with towel, and returning towel to towel rack.

DIRECTIONS

Materials Soap, water, towel, sink or wash basin.

Procedure *Observation:* Observe child's ability to complete face washing and drying routine of turning faucet on, washing face with soap, rinsing face, turning faucet off, drying face with towel, and returning towel to towel rack.

Adap B

Direct Test: When child's face needs washing, encourage child to begin face washing routine. Observe child's ability to complete face washing routine of turning faucet on, washing face with soap, rinsing face, turning faucet off, drying face with towel, and returning towel to towel rack.

Strand C Dressing and Undressing

GOAL 1   Unfastens fasteners on garments

CRITERION   Child uses any functional means to perform all of the following unfastening activities:

- Unfastens buttons/snaps/Velcro fasteners on garments
- Unties string-type fastener
- Unzips zipper

DIRECTIONS   (See Objectives 1.1–1.3 for specific directions.)

Note: If a child's performance on *all* objectives was scored with a 2, the goal is scored 2. If a child's performance on the objectives was scored with *any* combination of a 0, 1, or 2, the goal is scored 1. If a child's performance on *all* objectives was scored with a 0, the goal is scored 0.

Objective 1.1   Unfastens buttons/snaps/Velcro fasteners on garments

CRITERION   Child unfastens buttons/snaps/Velcro fasteners on garments (e.g., shirt, dress, pants) when undressing, using any functional means that does not damage clothing or fastener.

DIRECTIONS

Materials   Shoes, shirt, pants, dress that fastens with buttons/snaps/Velcro fasteners.

Procedure   *Observation:* Observe child's ability to use any functional means to unfasten buttons/snaps/Velcro fasteners on garments (e.g., shoes, shirt, dress, pants) without damaging clothing or fastener.
Direct Test: When child is wearing garment with buttons/snaps/Velcro fasteners (e.g., shoes, shirt, pants, dress), encourage child to take garment off at appropriate time (e.g., when pants are muddy from playing outside). Observe child's ability to use any functional means to unfasten buttons/snaps/Velcro fasteners on garments without damaging clothing or fasteners.

Objective 1.2   Unties string-type fastener

CRITERION   Child unties string-type fastener (e.g., shoelace, hood string) when undressing, using any functional means that does not damage clothing or fastener.

DIRECTIONS

Materials   Shoe with shoelace, hood with string.

Procedure   *Observation:* Observe child's ability to use any functional means to untie string-type fastener (e.g., shoelace, hood string) without damaging clothing or fastener.
Direct Test: When child is wearing garment with string-type fastener (e.g., shoe, hood), encourage child to take it off at appropriate time (e.g., when child comes in from outside). Observe child's ability to use any functional means to untie string-type fastener without damaging clothing or fastener.

Objective 1.3   Unzips zipper

CRITERION   Child unzips and detaches zipper when undressing, using any functional means that does not damage clothing or zipper.

DIRECTIONS

Materials   Coat, jacket, sweater that fastens with zipper.

Procedure   *Observation:* Observe child's ability to use any functional means to unzip and detach zipper without damaging clothing or zipper.
Direct Test: When child is wearing garment with zipper (e.g., coat, sweater), encourage child to take it off at appropriate time (e.g., when child comes in from playing outside). Observe child's ability to use any functional means to unzip and detach zipper without damaging clothing or zipper.

GOAL 2   Selects appropriate clothing and dresses self at designated times

CRITERION   Child selects appropriate clothing (i.e., shorts in summer, sweater in winter, nightgown at bedtime) and dresses self at designated time (e.g., after breakfast). Reminders are acceptable.

DIRECTIONS

Materials   Child's clothing.

Procedure   *Observation:* Observe child's ability to select appropriate clothing (i.e., shorts in summer, sweater in winter, nightgown at bedtime) and dress self at designated time (e.g., after breakfast). Reminders are acceptable.

Direct Test: Direct test is not appropriate for this item.

Objective 2.1   Puts on long pants

CRITERION   Child uses any functional means to put long pants over both feet and pull them up to the waist. Adult may fasten fasteners.

DIRECTIONS

Materials   Long pants.

Procedure   *Observation:* Observe child's ability to use any functional means to put long pants over both feet and pull up to the waist. Assistance with fasteners is acceptable.

Direct Test: When child needs to change pants (e.g., pants are muddy from playing outside), encourage child to undress and put on another pair of long pants. Observe child's ability to use any functional means to put long pants over both feet and pull up to waist. Child may be given assistance to fasten fastener.

Objective 2.2   Puts on front-opening garment

CRITERION   Child uses any functional means to put on front-opening garment (e.g., blouse, shirt, coat). *Example:* Child puts arm in one sleeve, puts garment around back, and puts other arm in second sleeve. Adult may fasten fasteners.

DIRECTIONS

Materials   Front-opening garment (e.g., blouse, shirt, coat).

Procedure   *Observation:* Observe child's ability to use any functional means to put on front-opening garment (e.g., blouse, shirt, coat). *Example:* Child puts arm in one sleeve, puts garment around back, and puts other arm in second sleeve.

Direct Test: When child needs to change shirt (e.g., shirt is wet from water play), encourage child to undress and put on another shirt. When child goes outside, encourage child to put on coat. Observe

Adap C

child's ability to use any functional means to put on front-opening garment (e.g., blouse, shirt, coat). *Example:* Child puts arm in one sleeve, puts garment around back, and puts other arm in second sleeve.

Objective 2.3   Puts on pullover garment

CRITERION   Child uses any functional means to put on pullover garment (e.g., T-shirt, dress, sweater).

DIRECTIONS

Materials   Pullover garment (e.g., T-shirt, dress, sweater).

Procedure   *Observation:* Observe child's ability to use any functional means to put on pullover garment (e.g., T-shirt, dress, sweater).
Direct Test: When child needs to change T-shirt or sweater (e.g., T-shirt or sweater is dirty), encourage child to undress and put on another T-shirt or sweater. Observe child's ability to use any functional means to put on pullover garment (e.g., T-shirt, dress, sweater).

Objective 2.4   Puts on shoes

CRITERION   Child uses any functional means to put shoes on both feet. Adult may tie shoes.

DIRECTIONS

Materials   Shoes, sandals, slippers.

Procedure   *Observation:* Observe child's ability to use any functional means to put shoes on both feet. Adult may tie shoes.
Direct Test: Encourage child to put on shoes at appropriate times (e.g., when dressing in the morning, to go outside). Observe child's ability to use any functional means to put shoes on both feet. Adult may tie shoes.

Objective 2.5   Puts on underpants, shorts, or skirt

CRITERION   Child uses any functional means to pull garment over feet and up to waist. Adult may fasten fasteners.

Adap C

DIRECTIONS

Materials   Underpants, shorts, skirt.

Procedure   *Observation:* Observe child's ability to use any functional means to pull garment over feet and up to waist. Adult may fasten fastener.
Direct Test: Encourage child to put on underpants, shorts, or skirt at appropriate times (e.g., after bath, when dressing in the morning). Observe child's ability to use any functional means to pull garment over feet and up to waist. Adult may fasten fastener.

GOAL 3   Fastens fasteners on garments

CRITERION   Child uses any functional means to perform the following:

- Tie string-type fastener
- Fasten buttons, snaps, and Velcro fasteners
- Thread and zip zipper

DIRECTIONS   (See Objectives 3.1–3.3 for specific directions.)

Note: If a child's performance on *all* objectives was scored with a 2, the goal is scored 2. If a child's performance on the objectives was scored with *any* combination of a 0, 1, or 2, the goal is scored 1. If a child's performance on *all* objectives was scored with a 0, the goal is scored 0.

Objective 3.1   Ties string-type fastener

CRITERION   Child uses any functional means to tie string-type fastener (e.g., shoelace) when dressing.

DIRECTIONS

Materials   Shoelace, string.

Procedure   *Observation:* Observe child's ability to use any functional means to tie string-type fastener.
Direct Test: Encourage child to tie string-type fastener at appropriate times (e.g., when putting on shoes). Observe child's ability to use any functional means to tie string-type fastener (e.g., shoelace).

Note: This item is cross-referenced with Fine Motor Domain, Strand A, Goal 3.

Adap C

Objective 3.2   Fastens buttons, snaps, and Velcro fasteners

CRITERION   Child uses any functional means to fasten buttons, snaps, and Velcro fasteners when dressing.

DIRECTIONS

Materials   Coat, shirt, or pants with buttons; shoes with Velcro fasteners.

Procedure   *Observation:* Observe child's ability to use any functional means to fasten buttons, snaps, and Velcro fasteners.
Direct Test: Encourage child to fasten buttons, snaps, and Velcro fasteners at appropriate times (e.g., when putting on shirt with buttons or snaps, when putting on shoes with Velcro fasteners). Observe child's ability to use any functional means to fasten buttons, snaps, and Velcro fasteners.

Note: This item is cross-referenced with Fine Motor Domain, Strand A, Objective 3.1.

Objective 3.3   Threads and zips zipper

CRITERION   Child uses any functional means to thread and zip zipper when dressing.

DIRECTIONS

Materials   Coat with zipper.

Procedure   *Observation:* Observe child's ability to use any functional means to thread and zip zipper.
Direct Test: Encourage child to thread and zip zipper at appropriate times (e.g., when putting on coat to go outside). Observe child's ability to use any functional means to thread and zip zipper.

Note: This item is cross-referenced with Fine Motor Domain, Strand A, Objective 3.2.

COGNITIVE DOMAIN

Items in the Cognitive Domain are designed to measure the child's group participation skills, use of various concepts, problem-solving skills, and recall skills. In addition, the child's ability to group and sequence objects and events is evaluated. Premath, prereading, and play skills are also measured in the Cognitive Domain. Items in this domain measure the acquisition of the following skills:

- Participation
- Demonstrates understanding of concepts
- Categorizing
- Sequencing
- Recalling events
- Problem solving
- Play
- Premath
- Prereading

The items in the Cognitive Domain were designed to assess the child's cognitive skills as they are used in daily activities. Some items in the Cognitive Domain are cross-referenced with items in the Social-Communication and Social Domains. It is important for several reasons to observe the child's behavior across domains. The first is that traditional developmental categories, such as social, cognitive, and language, are somewhat arbitrary divisions. For example, a child's ability to engage in imaginary play or to participate in classroom activities can be viewed as both social and cognitive behavior. The ability to recall events and information can be viewed as social, cognitive, or communicative behavior.

The second reason to observe a child's behavior across domains is that behavior may be interdependent across domains. For example, a child's ability to follow directions in correct sequence (as in Strand D: Sequencing) is dependent on the child's understanding of verbal instructions. A child's ability to give a reason for an inference or to make a prediction about future events (as in Strand F: Problem Solving) is dependent on the child's expressive communication skills. If a child is unable to perform a given task, the interventionist should ask, "Is there some other behavior that is absent from the child's repertoire that prevents the child from demonstrating this behavior?"

Strand A Participation
G1 Initiates and completes age-appropriate activities
   1.1 Responds to request to finish activity
   1.2 Responds to request to begin activity

G2 Watches, listens, and participates during small group activities
    2.1 Interacts appropriately with materials during small group activities
    2.2 Responds appropriately to directions during small group activities
    2.3 Looks at appropriate object, person, or event during small group activities
    2.4 Remains with group during small group activities
G3 Watches, listens, and participates during large group activities
    3.1 Interacts appropriately with materials during large group activities
    3.2 Responds appropriately to directions during large group activities
    3.3 Looks at appropriate object, person, or event during large group activities
    3.4 Remains with group during large group activities

Strand B **Demonstrates Understanding of Concepts**
G1 Demonstrates understanding of eight different colors
    1.1 Demonstrates understanding of six different colors
    1.2 Demonstrates understanding of three different colors
G2 Demonstrates understanding of five different shapes
    2.1 Demonstrates understanding of three different shapes
    2.2 Demonstrates understanding of one shape
G3 Demonstrates understanding of six different size concepts
    3.1 Demonstrates understanding of four different size concepts
    3.2 Demonstrates understanding of two different size concepts
G4 Demonstrates understanding of 10 different qualitative concepts
    4.1 Demonstrates understanding of six different qualitative concepts
    4.2 Demonstrates understanding of four different qualitative concepts
    4.3 Demonstrates understanding of two different qualitative concepts
G5 Demonstrates understanding of eight different quantitative concepts
    5.1 Demonstrates understanding of five different quantitative concepts
    5.2 Demonstrates understanding of two different quantitative concepts
G6 Demonstrates understanding of 12 different spatial relations concepts
    6.1 Demonstrates understanding of nine different spatial relations concepts
    6.2 Demonstrates understanding of six different spatial relations concepts
    6.3 Demonstrates understanding of three different spatial relations concepts
G7 Demonstrates understanding of seven different temporal relations concepts
    7.1 Demonstrates understanding of five different temporal relations concepts

Cog

  7.2 Demonstrates understanding of three different temporal relations concepts

Strand C Categorizing

  G1 Groups objects, people, or events on the basis of specified criteria
    1.1 Groups objects, people, or events on the basis of category
    1.2 Groups objects on the basis of function
    1.3 Groups objects on the basis of physical attribute

Strand D Sequencing

  G1 Follows directions of three or more related steps that are not routinely given
    1.1 Follows directions of three or more related steps that are routinely given
  G2 Places objects in series according to length or size
    2.1 Fits one ordered set of objects to another
  G3 Retells event in sequence
    3.1 Completes sequence of familiar story or event

Strand E Recalling Events

  G1 Recalls events that occurred on same day, without contextual cues
    1.1 Recalls events that occurred on same day, with contextual cues
    1.2 Recalls events immediately after they occur
  G2 Recalls verbal sequences
    2.1 Recalls verbal information about self

Strand F Problem Solving

  G1 Evaluates solutions to problems
    1.1 Suggests acceptable solutions to problems
    1.2 Identifies means to goal
  G2 Makes statements and appropriately answers questions that require reasoning about objects, situations, or people
    2.1 Gives reason for inference
    2.2 Makes prediction about future or hypothetical events
    2.3 Gives possible cause for some event

Strand G Play

  G1 Engages in imaginary play
    1.1 Enacts roles or identities
    1.2 Plans and acts out recognizable event, theme, or story line
    1.3 Uses imaginary props
  G2 Engages in games with rules
    2.1 Maintains participation
    2.2 Conforms to game rules

Strand H Premath

  G1 Recites numbers from 1 to 20
    1.1 Recites numbers from 1 to 10
    1.2 Recites numbers from 1 to 5
    1.3 Recites numbers from 1 to 3
  G2 Counts 10 objects
    2.1 Counts five objects

Cog

  2.2 Counts two objects
  2.3 Demonstrates understanding of one-to-one correspondence
 G3 Identifies printed numerals 1–10
  3.1 Identifies printed numerals 1–8
  3.2 Identifies printed numerals 1–5
  3.3 Identifies printed numerals 1–3
 G4 Matches printed numerals to sets of 1–10 object(s)
  4.1 Matches printed numerals to sets of 1–8 object(s)
  4.2 Matches printed numerals to sets of 1–5 object(s)
  4.3 Matches printed numerals to sets of 1–3 object(s)

Strand I **Prereading**
 G1 Demonstrates prereading skills
  1.1 Demonstrates functional use of books
  1.2 Tells about pictures in book
  1.3 Participates actively in storytelling
 G2 Demonstrates prereading auditory skills
  2.1 Blends sounds
  2.2 Rhymes words
 G3 Sounds out words
  3.1 Produces phonetic sounds for letters
 G4 Reads words by sight
  4.1 Identifies letters

Cog

Strand A   Participation

GOAL 1   Initiates and completes age-appropriate activities

CRITERION   Child initiates and completes age-appropriate activities without adult prompting. *Examples:* During free play, child gets out puzzle, puts it together, then puts it away. During free play, child goes to easel, paints picture, then hangs picture to dry.

DIRECTIONS

Materials   A variety of objects that are age appropriate and interesting to the child (e.g., puzzles, paints, blocks, paper and crayons, puppets).

Procedure   *Observation:* Observe child's ability to initiate and complete age-appropriate activity without adult prompting. *Example:* During free play, child gets out block set, builds a house, then puts blocks away. *Direct Test:* Present a variety of age-appropriate materials and observe child's ability to initiate and complete an activity without adult prompting.

Objective 1.1   Responds to request to finish activity

CRITERION   Child responds to first request to finish an activity. *Example:* Child carries out adult's request to pick up all the blocks or to finish putting together a puzzle.

DIRECTIONS

Materials   A variety of objects that are age appropriate and interesting to the child.

Procedure   *Observation:* Observe child's ability to finish an activity after adult's first request.
Direct Test: When child begins to leave unfinished activity, direct child to complete the activity. Observe child's ability to finish an activity after adult's first request.

Note: This item is cross-referenced with Social-Communication Domain, Strand A, Objective 2.6.

Cog A

Objective 1.2   Responds to request to begin activity

CRITERION   Child responds to first request to begin an activity. *Example:* Child is sitting at table watching peers draw with crayons. Child begins to draw with paper and crayons in response to adult's first request to do so.

DIRECTIONS

Materials   A variety of objects that are age appropriate and interesting to the child.

Procedure   *Observation:* Observe child's ability to begin an activity after adult's first request. *Example:* Child watches a peer work a puzzle. Child begins to put puzzle together in response to adult's request, "Put one of these puzzles together."
Direct Test: Present a variety of age-appropriate materials and ask child to begin an activity. Observe child's ability to begin activity after adult's first request. *Example:* Child gets paper and crayons and begins to draw in response to adult's request, "Get a piece of paper and crayons and draw a picture."

Note: This item is cross-referenced with Social-Communication Domain, Strand A, Objective 2.6.

GOAL 2   Watches, listens, and participates during small group activities

---

CRITERION   Child engages in the following behaviors during structured small group activities (i.e., group of five or fewer children):

- Interacts appropriately with materials
- Responds appropriately to directions
- Looks at appropriate object, person, or event
- Remains with group

Adult may provide group directions to help the child.

DIRECTIONS   (See Objectives 2.1–2.4 for specific directions.)

Notes: If a child's performance on *all* objectives was scored with a 2, the goal is scored 2. If a child's performance on the objectives was scored with *any* combination of a 0, 1, or 2, the goal is scored 1. If a child's performance on *all* objectives was scored with a 0, the goal is scored 0.

This item is cross-referenced with Social Domain, Strand A, Objectives 2.1 and 2.2.

Objective 2.1   Interacts appropriately with materials during small group activities

---

CRITERION   Child interacts with materials in functional or demonstrated fashion during structured small group activities (i.e., group of five or fewer children). Adult may provide group directions. *Examples:* Child uses cookie cutters to make shapes from Play-Doh. Child uses hammer to pound pegs into pegboard.

DIRECTIONS

Materials   Any age-appropriate activity.

Procedure   *Observation:* During structured small group activities, observe child's ability to interact with materials in a functional or demonstrated fashion. Adult may provide directions and model how materials will be used. *Example:* Child dips a paintbrush in a jar of paint and brushes it across a piece of paper during painting activity.
Direct Test: Direct test is not appropriate for this item.

Objective 2.2   Responds appropriately to directions during small group activities

---

CRITERION   Child responds with appropriate verbal or motor action to group directions provided by adult during structured small group activities (i.e., group of five or fewer children). *Example:* During painting activity, child follows directions to dip paintbrush in paint and brush it across paper.

DIRECTIONS

Materials   Any age-appropriate activity.

Procedure   *Observation:* During structured small group activities, observe child's ability to carry out an adult's request or direction. *Example:* During gross motor activity, child follows directions to go through obstacle course.
Direct Test: Direct test is not appropriate for this item.

Note: This item is cross-referenced with Social-Communication Domain, Strand A, Objective 2.6.

Cog A

Objective 2.3   Looks at appropriate object, person, or event during small group activities

CRITERION   Child looks at object, person, or event that is focus of activity during structured small group activities (i.e., group of five or fewer children). Adult may provide group directions. *Examples:* Child looks at adult while adult is talking. Child looks at toy train that is topic of adult's conversation.

DIRECTIONS

Materials   Any age-appropriate activity.

Procedure   *Observation:* During structured small group activities, observe child's ability to look at an object, person, or event that is the focus of the activity. *Example:* Child looks at each musical instrument as adult talks about it and plays it.
        Direct Test: Direct test is not appropriate for this item.

Note: This item is cross-referenced with Social-Communication Domain, Strand A, Objective 3.2.

Objective 2.4   Remains with group during small group activities

CRITERION   Child stays in seat or in indicated area for duration of an activity during structured small group activities (i.e., group of five or fewer children). Adult may provide group directions. *Example:* Child remains in seat at table during table activity.

DIRECTIONS

Materials   Any age-appropriate activity.

Procedure   *Observation:* During structured small group activities, observe child's ability to stay in seat or in indicated area for duration of the activity. Group directions may be provided by adult. Length of time of activities will vary depending on class structure and child's developmental level.
        Direct Test: Direct test is not appropriate for this item.

Cog A

GOAL 3   Watches, listens, and participates during large group activities

CRITERION   Child engages in the following behaviors during large group activities (i.e., group of six or more children):

- Interacts appropriately with materials
- Responds appropriately to directions
- Looks at appropriate object, person, or event
- Remains with group

Adult may provide group directions to help the child.

DIRECTIONS   (See Objectives 3.1–3.4 for specific directions.)

Notes: If a child's performance on *all* objectives was scored with a 2, the goal is scored 2. If a child's performance on the objectives was scored with *any* combination of a 0, 1, or 2, the goal is scored 1. If a child's performance on *all* objectives was scored with a 0, the goal is scored 0.

This item is cross-referenced with Social-Communication Domain, Strand A, Objective 2.6.

Objective 3.1   Interacts appropriately with materials during large group activities

CRITERION   Child interacts with materials in functional or demonstrated fashion during structured large group activities (i.e., group of six or more children). Adult may provide group directions. *Example:* Child passes ball to next child during group game.

DIRECTIONS

Materials   Any age-appropriate activity.

Procedure   *Observation:* During structured large group activities, observe child's ability to interact with materials in a functional or demonstrated fashion. Adult may provide directions and model how materials are used. *Example:* During opening circle, child plays musical instrument during the parade song.
Direct Test: Direct test is not appropriate for this item.

Cog A

Objective 3.2   Responds appropriately to directions during large group activities

CRITERION   Child responds with appropriate verbal or motor action to group directions provided by adult during structured large group activities (i.e., group of six or more children). *Example:* During music activity, child selects instrument and follows directions to play instrument while marching to music.

DIRECTIONS

Materials   Any age-appropriate activity.

Procedure   *Observation:* During structured large group activities, observe child's ability to carry out adult's request or directions. *Example:* During a music activity, child stands up to begin the game "Follow the Leader" and follows through with appropriate actions.
Direct Test: Direct test is not appropriate for this item.

Note: This item is cross-referenced with Social-Communication Domain, Strand A, Objective 2.6.

Objective 3.3   Looks at appropriate object, person, or event during large group activities

CRITERION   Child looks at object, person, or event that is focus of activity during structured large group activities (i.e., group of six or more children). Adult may provide group directions. *Example:* During show-and-tell activity, child looks at person who is talking and showing toy boat.

DIRECTIONS

Materials   Any age-appropriate activity.

Procedure   *Observation:* During structured large group activities, observe child's ability to look at an object, person, or event that is the focus of the activity. *Example:* Child looks at peer's toy truck as peer holds up truck and talks about it.
Direct Test: Direct test is not appropriate for this item.

Note: This item is cross-referenced with Social-Communication Domain, Strand A, Objective 3.2.

Cog A

Objective 3.4 Remains with group during large group activities

CRITERION   Child stays in seat or in indicated area for duration of an activity during large group activities (i.e., group of six or more children). Adult may provide group directions. *Examples:* Child remains seated in place on floor or in chair during circle time. Child remains in seat at table during snack time.

DIRECTIONS

Materials   Any age-appropriate activity.

Procedure   *Observation:* During structured large group activities, observe child's ability to stay in seat or in indicated area for duration of the activity. Group directions may be provided by adult. Length of activities will vary depending on class structure and child's developmental level.
Direct Test: Direct test is not appropriate for this item.

Cog A

Strand B　Demonstrates Understanding of Concepts

GOAL 1　Demonstrates understanding of eight different colors

CRITERION　Child follows directions, answers questions, or identifies objects, people, or events using at least eight different terms that describe color. Terms may include, but are not limited to, the following:

red	blue	orange	pink
yellow	black	purple	gray
green	white	brown	

Examples: Child selects a red crayon and begins coloring in response to adult's directions to "Color the car red." Child gives peer a yellow block in response to peer's request to "Give me some yellow ones." While painting with green paint, child says, "I am painting the house green."

DIRECTIONS

Materials　Objects interesting to the child that are of identifiable colors (e.g., red, yellow, green, orange, purple, brown, blue, black, white, pink, gray).

Procedure　*Observation:* Observe child's ability to identify objects on the basis of color. Child may identify colors by correctly following directions that involve color terms (e.g., child gives adult red crayon in response to adult's request to "Give me the red one") or by correctly using color names (e.g., child selects blue paint and says, "I want blue"). Child must correctly identify eight different colors.

Direct Test: Present at least four different-color objects and ask child to select a specific color (e.g., "Give me the orange block"), or present object and have child identify the color (e.g., "What color is this?"). Observe child's ability to correctly select or name eight colors.

Note:　This item is cross-referenced with Social-Communication Domain, Strand B, Objective 5.1.

Objective 1.1   Demonstrates understanding of six different colors

---

CRITERION   Child follows directions, answers questions, or identifies objects, people, or events using at least six different terms that describe color. Terms may include, but are not limited to, the following:

red	blue	orange	pink
yellow	black	purple	gray
green	white	brown	

Examples: Child selects a blue cup at snack time and says, "I want the blue cup." Child says, "Look at my purple coat," when getting coat to go outside. Child selects the red paint in response to direction to "Get the red paint."

DIRECTIONS

Materials   Objects interesting to the child that are of identifiable colors (e.g., red, yellow, green, blue, black, white, orange, purple, brown, pink, gray).

Procedure   *Observation:* Observe child's ability to identify objects on the basis of color. Child may identify colors by correctly following directions that involve color terms (e.g., child gets yellow chair in response to adult's direction to "Put the yellow chair at the table") or by correctly using color names (e.g., child points to peer in a pink coat and says, "I like your pink coat"). Child must correctly identify six different colors.
Direct Test: Present at least four different-color objects and ask child to select a specific color (e.g., "Give me the orange block"), or present object and have child identify the color (e.g., "What color is this?"). Observe child's ability to correctly select or name six different colors.

Cog B

Objective 1.2   Demonstrates understanding of three different colors

---

CRITERION   Child follows directions, answers questions, or identifies objects, people, or events using at least three different terms that describe color. Terms may include, but are not limited to, the following:

red	blue	orange	pink
yellow	black	purple	gray
green	white	brown	

Examples: Child points to the yellow bird and says, "That's a yellow bird." Child selects the green car in response to direction to "Put the green car away." Child says, "Look at my black picture," while painting with black paint.

DIRECTIONS

Materials   Objects interesting to the child that are of identifiable colors (e.g., red, yellow, green, blue, black, white, orange, purple, brown, pink, gray).

Procedure   *Observation:* Observe child's ability to identify objects on the basis of color. Child may identify colors by correctly following directions that involve color terms (e.g., child puts orange blocks in container in response to adult's direction to "Put the orange blocks in here") or by correctly using color names (e.g., child collects purple pegs and says, "Look at all the purple ones"). Child must correctly identify three different colors.

Direct Test: Present at least four different-colored objects and ask child to select a specific color (e.g., "Give me the orange block"), or present object and have child identify the color (e.g. "What color is this?"). Observe child's ability to correctly select or name three different colors.

GOAL 2   Demonstrates understanding of five different shapes

CRITERION   Child follows directions, answers questions, or identifies objects using at least five different terms that describe shape. Terms may include, but are not limited to, the following:

circle   triangle   diamond
square   rectangle   star

Examples: While playing with form boards, child finds circle and gives it to adult in response to adult's request to "Find a circle." While gluing triangles on paper, child says, "This triangle goes here."

DIRECTIONS

Materials   Objects interesting to the child that have an identifiable shape (e.g., circle, square, triangle, rectangle, diamond, star).

Procedure   *Observation:* Observe child's ability to identify objects on the basis of shape. Child may identify shapes by correctly following directions that involve shape terms (e.g., child gives adult triangular block in response to adult's request to "Give me the triangle") or by correctly using shape names (e.g., child selects a square puzzle piece and says, "I put the square in"). Child must correctly identify five different shapes.

Direct Test: Present at least three objects of different shapes and ask child to select a specific shape (e.g., "Give me the circle"), or present object and ask child to identify the shape (e.g., "What shape is this?"). Observe child's ability to correctly select or name five different shapes.

Note: This item is cross-referenced with Social-Communication Domain, Strand B, Objective 5.1.

Objective 2.1 Demonstrates understanding of three different shapes

CRITERION Child follows directions, answers questions, or identifies objects using at least three different terms that describe shape. Terms may include, but are not limited to, the following:

circle   triangle   diamond
square   rectangle   star

Examples: Child puts the circle shape in the shape sorter and says, "I put the circle in." While pasting shapes, child finds the star and pastes it in response to the adult's direction to "Put a star on now."

DIRECTIONS

Materials Objects interesting to the child that have an identifiable shape (e.g., circle, square, triangle, rectangle, diamond, star).

Procedure *Observation:* Observe child's ability to identify objects on the basis of shape. Child may identify shapes by correctly following directions that involve shape names (e.g., child gives coins and buttons in response to adult's request to "Give me the ones shaped like a circle") or by correctly using shape names (e.g., child says, "Look, a triangle," on seeing a "Yield" sign). Child must correctly identify three different shapes.
Direct Test: Present at least three objects of different shapes and ask child to select a specific shape (e.g., "Give me the circle"), or present object and ask child to identify the shape (e.g., "What shape is this?"). Observe child's ability to correctly select or name three different shapes.

Objective 2.2 Demonstrates understanding of one shape

CRITERION Child follows directions, answers questions, or identifies objects using at least one term that describes shape. Terms may include, but are not limited to, the following:

circle   triangle   diamond
square   rectangle   star

Examples: Child gives the rectangular puzzle piece to adult in response to adult's question "Where's the rectangle?" While playing with Play-Doh, child says, "I have a diamond," after using a diamond-shaped cookie cutter.

Cog B

DIRECTIONS

Materials   Objects interesting to the child that have an identifiable shape (e.g., circle, square, triangle, rectangle, diamond, star).

Procedure   *Observation:* Observe child's ability to identify objects on the basis of shape. Child may identify shapes by correctly following directions that involve shapes (e.g., child points to a tricycle wheel in response to adult's request to "Find an object that is shaped like a circle") or by correctly using shape names (e.g., child selects a square block and says, "The square goes on the bottom"). Child must correctly identify one of the shapes.

Direct Test: Present at least three objects of different shapes and ask child to select a specific shape (e.g., "Give me the circle"), or present object and ask child to identify the shape (e.g., "What shape is this?"). Observe child's ability to correctly select or name one shape.

GOAL 3   Demonstrates understanding of six different size concepts

---

CRITERION   Child follows directions, answers questions, or identifies objects or people using at least six different terms that describe size. Terms may include, but are not limited to, the following:

big	thick	small	skinny	chubby
tall	thin	short	tiny	itsy bitsy
little	fat	large	gigantic	long

Examples: While building with blocks of various sizes, child hands adult a small block in response to adult's request to "Give me a small one." Child selects a large car from a group of cars, places a doll in the car, and says, "He wants to ride in the big car."

DIRECTIONS

Materials   Objects interesting to the child in various sizes (e.g., small and big blocks and cars, short and tall dolls).

Procedure   *Observation:* Observe child's ability to identify objects or people on the basis of size. Child may identify size by correctly following directions that involve size terms (e.g., child gives adult a big ball in response to adult's request to "Give me the big ball") or by correctly using size names (e.g., child selects a small piece of cake and says, "I want the small piece"). Child must correctly select or name objects using six different terms that describe size.

Direct Test: Present different-size objects and ask child to select a specific object (e.g., "Give me the large paintbrush"), or present object and ask child to identify the size (e.g., "What size is this ball?"). Observe child's ability to correctly select or name objects using six different terms that describe size.

Cog B

Note: This item is cross-referenced with Social-Communication Domain, Strand B, Objective 5.1.

Objective 3.1   Demonstrates understanding of four different size concepts

---

CRITERION   Child follows directions, answers questions, or identifies objects or people using at least four different terms that describe size. Terms may include, but are not limited to, the following:

big	thick	small	skinny	chubby
tall	thin	short	tiny	itsy bitsy
little	fat	large	gigantic	long

Examples: Child points to an adult when adult asks, "Where is a tall person?" While combing a doll's hair with a toy brush, the child says, "She needs the little brush."

DIRECTIONS

Materials   Objects interesting to the child in various sizes (e.g., small and big blocks and cars, short and tall dolls).

Procedure   *Observation:* Observe child's ability to identify objects or people on the basis of size. Child may identify size by correctly following directions that involve size terms (e.g., child pours juice from the small pitcher in response to adult's directions to "Pour your juice from the small pitcher") or by correctly using size names (e.g., child says, "I drew a long line," when drawing with chalk). Child must correctly select or name objects using four different terms that describe size.
Direct Test: Present different-size objects and ask child to select a specific object (e.g., "Give me the large paintbrush"), or present object and ask child to identify the size (e.g., "What size is this ball?"). Observe child's ability to correctly select or name objects using four different terms that describe size.

Objective 3.2   Demonstrates understanding of two different size concepts

---

CRITERION   Child follows directions, answers questions, or identifies objects or people using at least two different terms that describe size. Terms may include, but are not limited to, the following:

Cog B

big	thick	small	skinny	chubby
tall	thin	short	tiny	itsy bitsy
little	fat	large	gigantic	long

Examples: While coloring, child selects "chubby" crayon and says, "My red crayon is fat." Child takes a big ball to an adult in response to adult's request to "Bring me the big ball."

DIRECTIONS

Materials   Objects interesting to the child in various sizes (e.g., small and big blocks and cars, short and tall dolls).

Procedure   *Observation:* Observe child's ability to identify objects or people on the basis of size. Child may identify size by correctly following directions that involve size terms (e.g., child puts small blocks into container when instructed to "Put the little blocks in here") or by correctly using size names (e.g., child selects a cut piece of drinking straw and says, "This is short"). Child must correctly select or name objects using two different terms that describe size.

Direct Test: Present different-size objects and ask child to select a specific object (e.g., "Give me the large paintbrush?"), or present object and ask child to identify the size (e.g., "What size is this ball?"). Observe child's ability to correctly select or name objects using two different terms that describe size.

GOAL 4   **Demonstrates understanding of 10 different qualitative concepts**

CRITERION   Child follows directions, answers questions, or identifies objects, people, or events using at least 10 different terms that describe quality. Terms may include, but are not limited to, the following:

hot	hard	light	cold	different
soft	same	loud	sour	quiet
good	rough	heavy	wet	slow
bad	smooth	dry	sweet	fast

Examples: During art activity, child selects smooth paper from paper of a variety of textures in response to adult's direction to "Put the glue on the smooth piece of paper." Child pushes truck across floor and says, "The truck can drive fast."

DIRECTIONS

Materials   Objects interesting to the child that can be identified by qualitative characteristics.

Procedure
Observation: Observe child's ability to identify objects, people, or events on the basis of qualitative terms. Child may identify by correctly following directions that involve qualitative terms (e.g., during art activity, child selects cotton from materials of various textures in response to request to "Pick something soft to make the snowman") or by correctly using qualitative terms (e.g., child turns on water and says, "It's too cold," and adjusts water temperature). Child must correctly select or name objects using 10 different terms that describe quality.

Direct Test: Present a variety of objects that can be identified by qualitative characteristics and ask child to select a specific item (e.g., "Give me the rough one"), or present object and ask child to identify qualitative characteristics (e.g., "How does the rock feel?", "How does the ice cream taste?"). Observe child's ability to correctly select and describe objects using 10 different terms that describe quality.

Note: This item is cross-referenced with Social-Communication Domain, Strand B, Objective 5.1.

Objective 4.1   Demonstrates understanding of six different qualitative concepts

---

CRITERION
Child follows directions, answers questions, or identifies objects, people, or events using at least six different terms that describe quality. Terms may include, but are not limited to, the following:

hot	hard	light	cold	different
soft	same	loud	sour	quiet
good	rough	heavy	wet	slow
bad	smooth	dry	sweet	fast

Examples: While carrying a full basket of toys, the child says, "This is heavy." Child selects the red block from a group of yellow blocks in response to adult's direction to "Find the one that is different."

DIRECTIONS

Materials
Objects interesting to the child that can be identified by qualitative characteristics.

Procedure
Observation: Observe child's ability to identify objects, people, or events on the basis of qualitative terms. Child may identify by correctly following directions that involve qualitative terms (e.g., during music, child increases voice volume in response to adult's request to "Sing this part loudly") or by correctly using qualitative terms (e.g., child chooses the sandpaper from a group of textured squares and says, "This one is rough"). Child must correctly select or name objects using six different terms that describe quality.

Cog B

Direct Test: Present a variety of objects that can be identified by qualitative characteristics and ask child to select a specific item (e.g., "Give me the one that is rough"), or present object and ask child to identify qualitative characteristics (e.g., "How does the rock feel?", "How does the ice cream taste?"). Observe child's ability to correctly select and describe objects using six different terms that describe quality.

Objective 4.2   Demonstrates understanding of four different qualitative concepts

---

CRITERION   Child follows directions, answers questions, or identifies objects, people, or events using at least four different terms that describe quality. Terms may include, but are not limited to, the following:

hot	hard	light	cold	different
soft	same	loud	sour	quiet
good	rough	heavy	wet	slow
bad	smooth	dry	sweet	fast

Examples: Child touches bath water and says, "It's hot." Child indicates correctly by saying, "My pants are dry."

DIRECTIONS

Materials   Objects interesting to the child that can be identified by qualitative characteristics.

Procedure   *Observation:* Observe child's ability to identify objects, people, or events on the basis of qualitative terms. Child may identify by correctly following directions that involve qualitative terms (e.g., during a movement activity, child walks slowly when the music says, "An elephant moves very slowly") or by correctly using qualitative terms (e.g., child says, "I am going fast," when swinging on a swing). Child must correctly select or name objects using four different terms that describe quality.

Direct Test: Present a variety of objects that can be identified by qualitative characteristics and ask child to select a specific item (e.g., "Give me the one that is rough"), or present object and ask child to identify qualitative characteristics (e.g., "How does the rock feel?", "How does the ice cream taste?"). Observe child's ability to correctly select and describe objects using four different terms that describe quality.

> # Objective 4.3 Demonstrates understanding of two different qualitative concepts

CRITERION Child follows directions, answers questions, or identifies objects, people, or events using at least two different terms that describe quality. Terms may include, but are not limited to, the following:

hot	hard	light	cold	different
soft	same	loud	sour	quiet
good	rough	heavy	wet	slow
bad	smooth	dry	sweet	fast

Examples: During art activity, child selects cotton from materials of various textures in response to adult's direction to "Choose something soft for making the clouds." Child takes hands out of fingerpaint and says, "My hands are wet."

DIRECTIONS

Materials Objects interesting to the child that can be identified by qualitative characteristics.

Procedure *Observation:* Observe child's ability to identify objects, people, or events on the basis of qualitative terms. Child is able to follow directions that involve qualitative terms (e.g., child selects the "heavy" block in response to adult's direction to "Pick up the heavy block") or by correctly using qualitative terms (e.g., child takes off coat and says, "I'm too hot with my coat on"). Child must correctly select or name objects using two different terms that describe quality.
Direct Test: Present a variety of objects that can be identified by qualitative characteristics and ask child to select a specific item (e.g., "Give me the one that is rough"), or present object and ask child to identify qualitative characteristics (e.g., "How does the rock feel?", "How does the ice cream taste?"). Observe child's ability to correctly select and describe objects using two different terms that describe quality.

> # GOAL 5 Demonstrates understanding of eight different quantitative concepts

CRITERION Child follows directions, answers questions, or identifies objects or events using at least eight different terms that describe quantity. Terms may include, but are not limited to, the following:

Cog B

all	many	none	full	more	few
each	less	empty	lots	some	any

Examples: During cleanup after snack, child gathers empty cups in response to adult's request to "Bring me the empty cups." While playing at the sand table, child holds up a large bucket filled with sand, points to a peer's small container of sand, and says, "I have more sand."

DIRECTIONS

Materials   Objects interesting to the child that can be identified by quantitative characteristics.

Procedure   *Observation:* Observe child's ability to identify objects or events on the basis of quantitative terms. Child may identify by correctly following directions that involve quantitative terms (e.g., child gives the empty crayon box in response to adult's request to "Give me the box that is empty") or by correctly using quantitative terms (e.g., after child receives cup of juice, child tells adult, "I have a full cup of juice"). Child must correctly identify eight different terms that describe quantity.

Direct Test: Present objects that can be identified or described in quantitative terms and ask child to select a specific object (e.g., "Give me all the blue ones"), or present object and ask child to identify quantity in relation to other objects (e.g., "Do you have more or less marbles than Emilio?"). Observe child's ability to correctly select and describe objects using eight different terms that describe quantity.

Note: This item is cross-referenced with Social-Communication Domain, Strand B, Objective 5.1.

Objective 5.1   **Demonstrates understanding of five different quantitative concepts**

CRITERION   Child follows directions, answers questions, or identifies objects or events using at least five different terms that describe quantity. Terms may include, but are not limited to, the following:

all	many	none	full	more	few
each	less	empty	lots	some	any

Examples: At snack time, child takes several raisins and says, "I have many raisins." On direction to put away all the blocks, child puts all the blocks in the storage bin.

DIRECTIONS

Materials   Objects interesting to the child that can be identified by quantitative characteristics.

Procedure   *Observation:* Observe child's ability to identify objects or events on the basis of quantitative terms. Child may identify by correctly following directions that involve quantitative terms (e.g., child gives one cup to each child in response to direction to "Give one cup to each child") or by correctly using quantitative terms (e.g., during sand play, child fills a bucket with sand and says, "My bucket is full"). Child must correctly identify five different terms that describe quantity.

Direct Test: Present objects that can be identified or described in quantitative terms and ask child to select specific objects (e.g., "Give me all the blue ones"), or present object and ask child to identify quantity in relation to other objects (e.g., "Do you have more or less blocks than Jenny?"). Observe child's ability to correctly select and describe objects using five different terms that describe quantity.

Objective 5.2   Demonstrates understanding of two different quantitative concepts

---

CRITERION   Child follows directions, answers questions, or identifies objects or events using at least two different terms that describe quantity. Terms may include, but are not limited to, the following:

all	many	none	full	more	few
each	less	empty	lots	some	any

Examples: Child points to peer with no toy animals in response to adult's question, "Which child has none?" Child with two crackers says to peer with four crackers, "You have more."

DIRECTIONS

Materials   Objects interesting to the child that can be identified by quantitative characteristics.

Procedure   *Observation:* Observe child's ability to identify objects or events on the basis of quantitative terms. Child may identify by correctly following directions that involve quantitative terms (e.g., child puts empty cups in the garbage in response to adult's direction to "Throw away the empty cups") or by correctly using quantitative terms (e.g., child says, "I have been to the coast many times. My grandparents live there"). Child must correctly identify two different terms that describe quantity.

Direct Test: Present objects that can be identified or described in quantitative terms and ask child to select a specific object (e.g., "Give me all

Cog B

the blue ones"), or present object and ask child to identify the quantity in relation to other objects (e.g., "Do you have more or less cars than Tom?"). Observe child's ability to correctly select and describe objects using two different terms that describe quantity.

GOAL 6   Demonstrates understanding of 12 different spatial relations concepts

---

CRITERION   Child follows directions, answers questions, or identifies objects, people, or events using at least 12 different terms that describe spatial relations. Terms may include, but are not limited to, the following:

in	to	back	front	behind
under	here	middle	last	in back of
bottom	beside	down	up	in front of
on	next to	between	there	first

Examples: At cleanup time, child puts doll beside dollhouse in response to adult's direction. Child lines up dolls and, while placing the last one, says, "This baby is last."

DIRECTIONS

Materials   Objects interesting to the child.

Procedure   *Observation:* Observe child's ability to identify objects on the basis of spatial relations. Child may correctly follow directions that involve spatial relations (e.g., child puts truck under table in response to adult's request) or by correctly using spatial relations (e.g., child throws ball and says, "Look, it went over the fence"). Child must correctly identify 12 different terms that describe spatial relations.
Direct Test: Present objects to child and ask child to place objects in different positions (e.g., "Put the ball on the table," "Put the truck under the bed"), or place objects in different positions relative to other objects and ask child to describe position of objects (e.g., place doll in box and ask, "Where is the doll?"). Observe child's ability to follow directions or describe objects using 12 different terms that describe spatial relations.

Note: This item is cross-referenced with Social-Communication Domain, Strand B, Objectives 5.1 and 5.4.

Objective 6.1   Demonstrates understanding of nine different spatial relations concepts

CRITERION   Child follows directions, answers questions, or identifies objects, people, or events using at least nine different terms that describe spatial relations. Terms may include, but are not limited to, the following:

in	to	back	front	behind
under	here	middle	last	in back of
bottom	beside	down	up	in front of
on	next to	between	there	first

Examples: When lining up to go for a walk, the line leader says, "I am first." Child puts crayons in box in response to adult's direction to "Put the crayons in the box."

DIRECTIONS

Materials   Objects interesting to the child.

Procedure   *Observation:* Observe child's ability to identify objects on the basis of spatial relations. Child may correctly follow directions that involve spatial relations (e.g., child comes to peer in response to peer's request to "Come here") or by correctly using spatial relations terms (e.g., during music time, child says, "I'm sitting next to my friend"). Child must correctly identify nine different terms that describe spatial relations. *Direct Test:* Present objects to child and ask child to place objects in different positions (e.g., "Put the ball on the table," "Put the truck under the bed"), or place objects in different positions relative to other objects and ask child to describe position of objects (e.g., place doll in box and ask, "Where is the doll?"). Observe child's ability to follow directions or describe objects using nine different terms that describe spatial relations.

Objective 6.2   Demonstrates understanding of six different spatial relations concepts

CRITERION   Child follows directions, answers questions, or identifies objects, people, or events using at least six different terms that describe spatial relations. Terms may include, but are not limited to, the following:

Cog B

in	to	back	front	behind
under	here	middle	last	in back of
bottom	beside	down	up	in front of
on	next to	between	there	first

Examples: During cleanup, child puts beads on the shelf in response to adult's direction. When helping a peer find a lost ball, child says, "The ball is behind the tree."

DIRECTIONS

Materials   Objects interesting to the child.

Procedure   *Observation:* Observe child's ability to identify objects on the basis of spatial relations. Child may correctly follow directions that involve spatial relations (e.g., child locates blocks on the bottom shelf in the cupboard in response to adult's direction) or by correctly using spatial relations terms (e.g., child points to tree and says, "There's a cat up there"). Child must correctly identify six different terms that describe spatial relations.
Direct Test: Present objects to child and ask child to place objects in different positions (e.g., "Put the ball on the table," "Put the truck under the bed"), or place objects in different positions relative to other objects and ask child to describe position of objects (e.g., place doll in box and ask, "Where is the doll?"). Observe child's ability to follow directions or describe objects using six different terms that describe spatial relations.

Objective 6.3   Demonstrates understanding of three different spatial relations concepts

---

CRITERION   Child follows directions, answers questions, or identifies objects, people, or events using at least three different terms that describe spatial relations. Terms may include, but are not limited to, the following:

in	to	back	front	behind
under	here	middle	last	in back of
bottom	beside	down	up	in front of
on	next to	between	there	first

Examples: When playing a game, child moves back in response to adult's direction to "Get behind the children in line." When going down the slide, child says, "I'm sliding down."

DIRECTIONS

Materials   Objects interesting to the child.

Procedure   *Observation:* Observe child's ability to position objects on the basis of spatial relations. Child may identify by correctly following directions that involve spatial relations terms (e.g., child puts red block in the middle of two blue blocks in response to direction to "Put the red blocks between the blue blocks") or by correctly using spatial relations terms (e.g., child finds place in line and says, "I'm in back of Kelly"). Child must correctly use three different terms that describe spatial relations.

Direct Test: Present objects to child and ask child to place objects in different positions (e.g., "Put the ball on the table," "Put the truck under the bed"), or place objects in different positions relative to other objects and ask child to describe position of objects (e.g., place doll in box and ask, "Where is the doll?"). Observe child's ability to follow directions or describe objects using three different terms that describe spatial relations.

GOAL 7   Demonstrates understanding of seven different temporal relations concepts

---

CRITERION   Child follows directions, answers questions, or identifies events using at least seven different terms that describe temporal relations. Terms may include, but are not limited to, the following:

yesterday	early	before	if–then	today
later	after	tomorrow	last	first

Examples: Child gives appropriate response to adult's question, "What do we do before we have lunch?" (e.g., "We wash our hands"). While building tower of blocks, child says, "After this is big, I'll knock it down." Child builds tower, then knocks it down.

DIRECTIONS

Materials   Objects interesting to the child.

Procedure   *Observation:* Observe child's ability to identify events on the basis of temporal relations. Child may identify by correctly responding to questions that involve temporal relations terms (e.g., child says, "Wash hands," in response to adult's question, "What do we do before snack?") or by correctly using temporal relations (e.g., during circle time, child talks about a planned trip, "Tomorrow we go to the zoo"). Child must correctly identify seven different terms that describe temporal relations.

Direct Test: Ask child to follow directions or identify pictures, objects, or events on the basis of temporal relations (e.g., show child series of three pictures that depict a simple sequence and ask child, "Which one do you do first?"). Observe child's ability to follow directions or identify pictures, objects, or events on the basis of temporal relations using seven different terms that describe temporal relations.

Note: This item is cross-referenced with Social-Communication Domain, Strand A, Objectives 1.1 and 1.4, and Strand B, Objectives 1.4, 1.5, and 3.3.

Objective 7.1   Demonstrates understanding of five different temporal relations concepts

---

CRITERION   Child follows directions, answers questions, or identifies events using at least five different terms that describe temporal relations. Terms may include, but are not limited to, the following:

yesterday	early	before	if–then	today
later	after	tomorrow	last	first

Examples: Child gives appropriate response to adult's question, "When are we going swimming?" (e.g., "today," "tomorrow"). Child says, "If we make the bridge taller, then the cars can go under." Child adds blocks to the bridge to make it taller.

DIRECTIONS

Materials   Objects interesting to the child.

Procedure   *Observation:* Observe child's ability to identify events on the basis of temporal relations. Child may correctly respond to questions that involve temporal relations terms (e.g., child says, "Brush teeth" in response to adult's question, "What do you do after you eat?") or by correctly using temporal relations terms (e.g., child says, "I woke up early today, before my mom"). Child must correctly use five different terms that describe temporal relations.

Direct Test: Ask child to follow directions or identify pictures, objects, or events on the basis of temporal relations (e.g., show child series of three pictures that depict a simple sequence and ask child, "Which one do you do first?"). Observe child's ability to follow directions or identify pictures, objects, or events on the basis of temporal relations using five different terms that describe temporal relations.

Objective 7.2   Demonstrates understanding of three different temporal relations concepts

CRITERION   Child follows directions, answers questions, or identifies events using at least three different terms that describe temporal relations. Terms may include, but are not limited to, the following:

yesterday	early	before	if–then	today
later	after	tomorrow	last	first

Examples: Child gives appropriate response to adult's question, "When was your birthday?" (e.g., "Yesterday"). Before participating in cooking activity, child says, "First I need to wash my hands."

DIRECTIONS

Materials   Objects interesting to the child.

Procedure   *Observation:* Observe child's ability to identify events on the basis of temporal relations. Child may correctly respond to questions that involve temporal relations terms (e.g., child says, "Have circle," in response to adult's question, "What do we do after free play and cleanup?") or correctly use temporal relations terms (e.g., child says, "We will go home later"). Child must correctly identify three different terms that describe temporal relations.

Direct Test: Ask child to follow directions or identify pictures, objects, or events on the basis of temporal relations (e.g., show child series of three pictures that depict a simple sequence and ask child, "Which one do you do first?"). Observe child's ability to follow directions or identify pictures, objects, or events on the basis of temporal relations using three different terms that describe temporal relations.

Cog B

Strand C   Categorizing

GOAL 1   Groups objects, people, or events on the basis of specified criteria

CRITERION   Child specifies a criterion and sorts all objects into groups according to that criterion (e.g., category, function, attribute). Adult may provide general cue (e.g., "Put all the ones together that go together"). *Example:* When playing with group of miniature objects, child separates objects into groups of people, animals, and vehicles; or child separates objects according to color.

DIRECTIONS

Materials   Three sets of objects that can be grouped in different ways (e.g., category, function, attribute).

Procedure   *Observation:* When playing with a variety of objects or when it is time to pick up toys, observe child's ability to devise a criterion and group objects according to that criterion (e.g., category, function, attribute). *Example:* When cleaning up a variety of toys, child puts them away into groups of vehicles, animals, and people (on the basis of category); or child puts all big toys on one shelf and small toys on another (on the basis of physical attribute).

Direct Test: Present three sets of objects that can be grouped different ways (e.g., category, function, attribute) and ask child to group them. Observe child's ability to devise a criterion and group objects according to that criterion. *Example:* Adult presents a group of vehicles and big and small animals and asks child, "Which ones go together?" Child puts all vehicles together and all animals together; or child puts all big objects together and all small objects together; or child puts all things that go in the water together (e.g., sailboat, motorboat, fish) and all things that go on land together (e.g., truck, car, dog, cat).

Objective 1.1   Groups objects, people, or events on the basis of category

CRITERION   Child sorts all objects into groups according to some categorical criterion (e.g., food, animals, clothing). Adult may provide categories (e.g., "Put the food on the table and the clothing in the box").

144

DIRECTIONS

Materials Three sets of objects that can be grouped into categories.

Procedure *Observation:* When playing with a variety of objects or when it is time to pick up toys, observe child's ability to group objects according to category (e.g., people, vehicles, animals). *Example:* Child selects all animals from a group of miniature objects that includes animals, people, and food and places the animals in toy barn. Child then selects all vehicles and places them in garage.

Direct Test: Present three sets of objects that can be grouped into categories and ask child to group objects according to category. Provide a demonstration if necessary. Observe child's ability to group objects according to category (e.g., people, vehicles, animals). *Example:* Adult presents a group of toy animals and vehicles and tells child to "Put all the vehicles in this box and all the animals in this box." Child does so.

Objective 1.2 Groups objects on the basis of function

CRITERION Child sorts all objects from a group according to function (e.g., things to eat with, things that go in water). *Example:* Before water play activity, child chooses from a group of objects all those appropriate for water play.

DIRECTIONS

Materials At least two sets of objects that can be grouped according to function (e.g., things to eat, things to wear, things to ride on).

Procedure *Observation:* When playing with a variety of objects or when it is time to pick up toys, observe child's ability to group objects according to function. *Example:* Before painting activity, child chooses from a group of art supplies all objects needed for painting.

Direct Test: Present a variety of objects that can be grouped according to function and ask child to group them that way. Provide a demonstration if necessary. Observe child's ability to group objects according to function. *Example:* Adult presents a box of clothing and a box of eating utensils and asks child to "Put all the things you wear in this box and all the things you eat with in this box." Child does so.

Cog C

Objective 1.3 Groups objects on the basis of physical attribute

---

CRITERION Child sorts all objects from a group according to some physical attribute (e.g., color, shape, size, texture). *Examples:* When playing with colored blocks, child separates them into groups according to color. After playing with toy vehicles, child puts large vehicles on one shelf and small vehicles on another.

DIRECTIONS

Materials   At least two sets of objects that can be grouped according to physical attribute.

Procedure   *Observation:* When playing with a variety of objects or when it is time to pick up toys, observe child's ability to group objects according to physical attributes. *Example:* When playing with a variety of form boards, child separates form board pieces according to shape.

Direct Test: Present a group of objects that can be identified on the basis of physical attributes and ask child to group them that way. Provide a demonstration if necessary. Observe child's ability to group objects according to physical attributes. *Example:* Adult presents different colored blocks and asks child to "Put all of the blue ones (or all the ones like this) in this can and all of the yellow ones (or all the ones like this) in this can." Child does so.

Cog C

Strand D Sequencing

GOAL 1 Follows directions of three or more related steps that are not routinely given

CRITERION Child responds with actions in correct sequence to a functional three-step direction (i.e., within context) that is not routinely given. Contextual cues such as gestures may be given. *Example:* During gross motor activity, adult gestures and tells child to "Run to the bench, pick up the ball, and then run to the slide." Child follows directions in correct sequence.

DIRECTIONS

Materials Objects interesting to the child.

Procedure *Observation:* During daily activities, observe child's ability to respond with actions in correct sequence to a three-step direction that relates to child's immediate environment or activity and is not routinely given. Contextual cues such as gestures may be given. *Example:* During art activity, adult demonstrates steps to make paper chain and tells child to "Put glue on paper, place end of paper through hole, and glue ends of paper together." Child follows directions in correct sequence. *Direct Test:* Present a three-step direction to child that relates to child's immediate environment or activity and is not routinely given. Observe child's ability to carry out the direction by performing the appropriate motor response in correct sequence. Contextual cues such as gestures may be given. *Example:* At cleanup time, adult tells child to "Put the blocks in the can, put the doll on the shelf, and then come here." Child follows directions in correct sequence.

Objective 1.1 Follows directions of three or more related steps that are routinely given

CRITERION Child responds with actions in correct sequence to a functional three-step direction (i.e., within context) that is routinely given. Contextual cues such as gestures may be given. *Example:* After being outside, adult gestures and tells child to "Take off your coat, hang it up, and then wash your hands." Child follows directions in correct sequence.

Cog D

DIRECTIONS

Materials   Objects interesting to the child.

Procedure   *Observation:* Observe child's ability to respond with actions in correct sequence to a three-step direction that relates to child's immediate environment or activity and is routinely given. Contextual cues such as gestures may be given. *Example:* After snack, adult gestures and tells child to "Throw away your napkin, put your cup in the sink, and then get a book." Child follows directions in correct sequence.

Direct Test: Present a three-step direction that relates to child's immediate environment or activity and is routinely given. Observe child's ability to carry out the direction by performing the appropriate motor response in correct sequence. Contextual cues such as gestures may be given. *Example:* Before snack, adult gestures and tells child to "Wash your hands, get your placemat, and sit down at the table." Child follows directions in correct sequence.

GOAL 2   Places objects in series according to length or size

---

CRITERION   Child places three or more objects in a series according to length or size. Child may correct self. *Examples:* Child puts books on shelf in order of height. Child stacks dishes with largest on bottom and others progressively smaller.

DIRECTIONS

Materials   Several sets of objects that can be arranged in a series according to length or size.

Procedure   *Observation:* When playing with a variety of objects or when it is time to pick up toys, observe child's ability to place three or more objects in a series according to length or size. Child may correct self. *Example:* Child lines up measuring cups with largest first and others progressively smaller.

Direct Test: Present three or more objects that can be placed in a series according to length or size. Observe child's ability to place the objects in a series according to length or size. Child may correct self. *Example:* Adult presents child with four different-size bowls and asks child to "Put these in order." Child lines up or stacks the bowls from largest to smallest.

Objective 2.1 Fits one ordered set of objects to another

CRITERION Child matches two related sets of two or more objects by assigning each object from one set to its matching object from the other set. Child may correct self. *Examples:* Child fits a set of two different-size lids to correct bowls. Child fits a set of three different bolts to correct nuts.

DIRECTIONS

Materials Two related sets of two or more objects that can be arranged in a series according to length, size, or color.

Procedure *Observation:* When playing with a variety of objects or when it is time to pick up toys, observe child's ability to fit one ordered set of two or more objects to another by assigning each object to its matching object. Child may correct self. *Example:* When playing with toy tools, child matches different-size bolts to corresponding nuts.

Direct Test: Present two ordered sets of two or more objects to child. Ask child to assign each object to its matching object. Observe the child's ability to match objects. Child may correct self. *Example:* Adult presents two different-size bears and two different-size beds and asks child to match each bear to the appropriate-size beds (beds can be made of shoe boxes, tissue boxes, and so forth). Child matches bears to correct beds.

GOAL 3 Retells event in sequence

CRITERION Child retells a sequence of at least three events verbally, through gestures and demonstration, or by arranging pictures in correct sequence. *Example:* Adult tells three-part story and asks child to retell story. Child gestures, tells story verbally, or arranges story pictures in correct sequence to retell story.

DIRECTIONS

Materials Age-appropriate activities or a series of at least three sequential pictures that depict a story or event.

Procedure *Observation:* Observe child's ability to retell a sequence of at least three parts verbally or through gestures and demonstration. *Example:* Adult describes three-step activity to child (e.g., "First we will make starch, next we will paint with the starch, and then we will use chalk to color

Cog D

the pictures") and asks child to explain activity to peer. Child correctly explains activity.

Direct Test: Tell story consisting of three events to child. Ask child to retell story. Child may retell story verbally, through gestures and demonstration, or by arranging pictures in correct sequence. *Example:* Adult tells three-part story and asks child to retell story. Child gestures, tells story verbally, or arranges pictures that depict story in correct sequence.

Objective 3.1   Completes sequence of familiar story or event

---

CRITERION   Child responds appropriately to question about sequence of story or event verbally, through gestures and demonstration, or by arranging pictures in correct sequence. *Examples:* When telling story, child responds appropriately to adult's question, "Then what happened?" Child responds with appropriate motor action to adult's question, "What do you do next?" Child chooses correct picture to complete sequence in response to adult's request to "Pick the one that goes here."

DIRECTIONS

Materials   Age-appropriate activities or series of at least three pictures depicting routine events.

Procedure   *Observation:* Observe child's ability to respond appropriately to questions about sequence of story or events verbally or through gestures and demonstration. *Example:* As children line up to go indoors after outside play, adult asks child, "What do we do when we go inside?" Child correctly answers, "We have snack."

Direct Test: Ask child question about sequence of story or events and observe the child's ability to respond appropriately verbally, through gestures and demonstration, or by selecting the correct picture to complete a sequence. *Example:* After telling story of "The Three Bears," adult asks child, "What did Goldilocks do when she tasted Baby Bear's porridge?" Child answers, "She ate it all up," or child selects correct picture.

Strand E Recalling Events

GOAL 1 Recalls events that occurred on same day, without contextual cues

CRITERION Without contextual cues and at least 30 minutes after occurrence of event, child spontaneously and accurately relates (e.g., tells, demonstrates) an event that occurred on the same day. *Example:* At end of school day, adult asks, "What did you make in art today?" when art project and materials are not present in environment. Child responds by accurately telling what was made during art activity (e.g., child says, "I painted a picture of a dog" or pantomimes making a hat and putting it on).

DIRECTIONS

Materials No materials are necessary.

Procedure *Observation:* Observe child's ability without contextual cues to accurately relate, at least 30 minutes after occurrence of event, an event that occurred on the same day. *Example:* At end of school day when food item is not present in environment, child accurately tells adult what child ate during snack time (e.g., "We ate popcorn").

Direct Test: At least 30 minutes after occurrence of event and without the presence of contextual cues, ask child question about an event that occurred on the same day. *Example:* At end of school day, adult asks, "What did you do outside today?" Child responds by accurately telling what was done outside (e.g., "I climbed on an obstacle course," or pantomimes going down a slide).

Note: This item is cross-referenced with Social-Communication Domain, Strand A, Objective 1.4, and Strand B, Objectives 1.4 and 1.5.

Objective 1.1 Recalls events that occurred on same day, with contextual cues

CRITERION With contextual cues (e.g., being in same setting or with same object) and at least 30 minutes after occurrence of event, child spontaneously and accurately relates (e.g., tells, demonstrates) an event that occurred on the same day. *Example:* During circle time in classroom, adult asks, with toys present in the environment, "Did you have fun today?"

Child responds by saying, "I played with the dolls," which had occurred prior to circle time.

DIRECTIONS

Materials   No materials are necessary.

Procedure   *Observation:* Observe child's ability with contextual cues to accurately relate, at least 30 minutes after occurrence of event, an event that occurred on the same day. *Example:* During close circle, child says, "I drew a picture of a train" and points to picture hanging on wall.
Direct Test: At least 30 minutes after occurrence of event and in the presence of contextual cues, ask child question about event that occurred on the same day. *Example:* At end of day, with toys present in environment, adult asks, "What did you play in music today?" Child responds by accurately telling what child played (e.g., child says, "I played a drum," or points to bells).

Objective 1.2   Recalls events immediately after they occur

CRITERION   Spontaneously or on request, child accurately relates (e.g., tells, demonstrates) events that occurred immediately before. *Example:* Child washes hands, walks out of bathroom, and tells adult, "I washed my hands."

DIRECTIONS

Materials   No materials are necessary.

Procedure   *Observation:* Observe child's ability to accurately recall events immediately after they occur. *Example:* Child comes in from outside and tells peer, "I went down the big slide."
Direct Test: Ask child question about event immediately after it occurs. *Example:* When child is playing with dolls and has performed a specific behavior, adults asks, "What did you do with the baby?" Child says, "I gave her a drink of water because she was thirsty."

GOAL 2   Recalls verbal sequences

CRITERION   Spontaneously or on request, child recites two of the following verbal sequences:

- Telephone number
- Alphabet
- Numbers from 1 to 20

Cog E

- Spelling of name
- Days of week

DIRECTIONS

Materials   No materials are necessary.

Procedure   *Observation:* Observe child's ability to recite two of the verbal sequences listed in the criterion.
Direct Test: Ask child to recite several of the verbal sequences listed in criterion. Observe child's ability to correctly recite two of the verbal sequences listed in the criterion.

Note: This item is cross-referenced with Social Domain, Strand C, Objective 2.1.

Objective 2.1   Recalls verbal information about self

CRITERION   Spontaneously or on request, child tells two of the following:

- First and last name
- Birthday
- Age
- First name(s) of sibling(s)
- First name(s) of parent(s)

DIRECTIONS

Materials   No materials are necessary.

Procedure   *Observation:* Observe child's ability to relate information about self. Child must correctly relate two of the pieces of information listed in criterion.
Direct Test: Ask child about self. Observe child's ability to relate information about self. Child must correctly relate two of the pieces of information listed in the criterion.

Note: This item is cross-referenced with Social Domain, Strand C, Objectives 2.3, 2.4, and 2.6.

Cog E

Strand F   Problem Solving

GOAL 1   Evaluates solutions to problems

CRITERION   Spontaneously or on request, child indicates (e.g., tells, demonstrates) why a particular solution to a problem within context would or would not work. *Examples:* Child responds with reason when asked, "Why couldn't we glue these on with water? (e.g., "Water isn't sticky"). Child stands on chair to reach toys on shelf and says to adult, "This chair is too small. I can't reach." Child finds taller chair.

DIRECTIONS

Materials   Objects and activities interesting to the child.

Procedure   *Observation:* Observe child's ability to indicate why a particular solution to a problem within context of immediate activity would or would not work. *Example:* When cleaning up blocks, child says, "We can't put the blocks in this can because the blocks are too big."
Direct Test: Present a problem and observe child's ability to indicate why a particular solution would or would not work. *Example:* Child is given a box of watercolors, paper, and a brush and is asked, "Can you make a picture with these things?" Child says, "No, we need some water first."

Objective 1.1   Suggests acceptable solutions to problems

CRITERION   Spontaneously or on request, child indicates (e.g., tells, demonstrates) acceptable solutions to problems. General cues may be given by adult (e.g., "What can we do?" "What can you try?"). *Example:* Child who is having difficulty cutting says, "You hold the paper for me," or points to a different pair of scissors when asked, "What can we try?"

DIRECTIONS

Materials   Objects and activities interesting to the child.

Procedure   *Observation:* Observe child's ability to suggest acceptable solutions to problem. General cues may be given by adult (e.g., "What can we do?", "What can you try?"). *Example:* Child who cannot reach ball under chair says, "I need something long to reach it."

154

Direct Test: Present a problem and observe child's ability to suggest acceptable solutions to the problem. General cues may be given by adult (e.g., "What can we do?", "What can you try?"). *Example:* Adult is stringing beads that keep sliding off the string. Adult asks child, "What can we do?" Child suggests tying a knot at the end of the string.

Objective 1.2   Identifies means to goal

CRITERION   Spontaneously or on request, child names or selects appropriate/functional means to goal when problem and solution have been identified. *Examples:* Child brings a large empty container in response to adult's request to "Find something for carrying the blocks." Child points to chair in response to adult's request to "Find something to stand on that will help you reach the toy."

DIRECTIONS

Materials   Objects and activities interesting to the child.

Procedure   *Observation:* Observe child's ability to name or select means to goal when problem and goal have been identified. *Example:* Child gets a pitcher off the counter in response to adult's request to "Find a container to put the juice in."

Direct Test: Identify problem and goal and observe child's ability to name or select means to goal. *Example:* Adult says, "I can't reach the truck behind the toy box. I need something to reach it and push it out." Child hands broom to adult.

GOAL 2   Makes statements and appropriately answers questions that require reasoning about objects, situations, or people

---

CRITERION   Child makes statements and appropriately answers questions that require the child to do the following:

● Give a reason for some inference
● Make a prediction about a future or hypothetical event
● Determine a possible cause of some event

DIRECTIONS   (See Objectives 2.1–2.3 for specific directions.)

Note: If a child's performance on *all* objectives was scored with a 2, the goal is scored 2. If a child's performance on the objectives was scored with *any* combination of a 0, 1, or 2, the goal is scored 1. If a child's performance on *all* objectives was scored with a 0, the goal is scored 0.

Cog F

Objective 2.1   Gives reason for inference

CRITERION   Spontaneously or on request, child gives plausible reason for making inference. *Examples:* Child says, "She is sad," and adult asks, "How do you know that the girl is sad?"; child answers, "She is crying." Child looks out the window and says, "I think it's raining, because he has an umbrella."

DIRECTIONS

Materials   Objects and activities interesting to the child.

Procedure   *Observation:* Observe child's ability to give a plausible reason for inference child makes. *Example:* Child is playing with doll and says, "I think baby is sick, because she feels hot."
Direct Test: After child makes inferential statement, ask child to give reason for the inference. *Example:* Child says, "Mommy happy," and adult asks, "How do you know that your mommy is happy?" Child answers, "She's laughing."

Objective 2.2   Makes prediction about future or hypothetical events

CRITERION   Spontaneously or on request, child makes a plausible prediction about future or hypothetical events that take place within context. *Example:* Adult who is reading unfamiliar story pauses and asks child, "What do you think will happen?" Child tells possible event.

DIRECTIONS

Materials   Objects and activities interesting to the child.

Procedure   *Observation:* Observe child's ability to make a prediction about future or hypothetical events that take place within context. *Example:* Child pushes train around track. When child notices the track is broken, child says, "Uh-oh, the train is going to fall off the track."
Direct Test: Within context of activity child is engaged in, ask child to make a prediction about future or hypothetical events. *Example:* Child is playing with ball outside. Adult points to doghouse and asks, "What would happen if I rolled the ball over there?" Child says, "The dog would chase it and chew it up."

Note: This item is cross-referenced with Social-Communication Domain, Strand A, Objective 1.1.

Objective 2.3 Gives possible cause for some event

CRITERION Spontaneously or on request, child tells possible cause for observed event. *Example:* Child tells possible cause for event in response to adult's question, "Why do you think she is crying?" (e.g., "Because she fell down," "Maybe somebody broke her doll").

DIRECTIONS

Materials Objects and activities interesting to the child.

Procedure *Observation:* Observe child's ability to tell possible cause for event. *Example:* When playing, child picks up broken toy car and says, "I think somebody stepped on it."
Direct Test: Within context of activity child is engaged in, ask child to tell possible cause for event. *Example:* When child is playing with toy people, adult points to man with bandage on arm and asks, "How do you think he got hurt?" Child says, "I think he fell off of his horse."

Cog F

Strand G   Play

GOAL 1   Engages in imaginary play

CRITERION   Child engages in the following play behaviors:

- Takes on roles or identities
- Enacts out a recognizable event, theme, or story line
- Uses imaginary props

DIRECTIONS   (See Objectives 1.1–1.3 for specific directions.)

Notes: If a child's performance on *all* objectives was scored with a 2, the goal is scored 2. If a child's performance on the objectives was scored with *any* combination of a 0, 1, or 2, the goal is scored 1. If a child's performance on *all* objectives was scored with a 0, the goal is scored 0.

This item is cross-referenced with Social-Communication Domain, Strand A, Objective 1.2.

Objective 1.1   Enacts roles or identities

CRITERION   Child assumes recognizable roles or identities by announcing the role or by changing voice, manner, or behavior to indicate an identity. *Example:* Child says, "I'll be the bus driver," sits in front seat of pretend bus, and tells children in an adult voice, "Sit down and be quiet while I'm driving."

DIRECTIONS

Materials   Toys that encourage imaginary play.

Procedure   *Observation:* Observe child's ability when playing to assume recognizable roles by announcing the role or by changing voice, manner, or behaviors to indicate an identity. *Example:* Child says, "I'm going to be He-man, and you will be my transformers," and points to peers.
Direct Test: Present materials or props in a play activity in which a role can be taken. Observe child's ability to assume recognizable roles by announcing the role or changing voice, manner, or behaviors to indicate an identity. *Example:* Child says, "I'll be the mother," and begins to feed the doll, saying, "Here, baby, Mommy has your breakfast."

Objective 1.2   Plans and acts out recognizable event, theme, or story line

CRITERION   Child plans and enacts a recognizable event, theme, or story line. *Example:* Child says, "I'll be the mommy, and I'm going to the store." Child puts on hat and takes purse, pretends to go to the store, comes home, and cooks dinner.

DIRECTIONS

Materials   Toys that encourage imaginary play.

Procedure   *Observation:* When playing, observe child's ability to plan and enact a recognizable theme or story line. *Example:* Child puts on a cape, says, "I'm Superman," pretends to fly through the room to save a peer, comes back to the play area, and changes roles.
Direct Test: Present materials or props in a play activity and observe child's ability to plan and enact a recognizable theme or story line. *Example:* Child puts on fire hat and says, "I'm going to fight the fire" and pretends to climb on the fire truck and drive away.

Objective 1.3   Uses imaginary props

CRITERION   Child plays using imaginary props. *Examples:* Child gallops around room pretending to hold reins and says, "Giddyup, horsie, go fast." Child pretends to feed doll with imaginary spoon.

DIRECTIONS

Materials   No materials are required.

Procedure   *Observation:* Observe child's ability to play using imaginary props. *Example:* Child gets ready for work by pretending to wash face and brush hair.
Direct Test: Direct test is not appropriate for this item.

GOAL 2   Engages in games with rules

CRITERION   Child engages in games with rules by

- Maintaining participation
- Conforming to game rules

Cog G

DIRECTIONS   (See Objectives 2.1 and 2.2 for specific directions.)

Note: If a child's performance on *all* objectives was scored with a 2, the goal is scored 2. If a child's performance on the objectives was scored with *any* combination of a 0, 1, or 2, the goal is scored 1. If a child's performance on *all* objectives was scored with a 0, the goal is scored 0.

Objective 2.1   Maintains participation

CRITERION   Child continues to participate in organized game until completion of game. Group directions may be provided by adult. *Example:* Child rolls ball back and forth to adult until adult says, "It's time for snack."

DIRECTIONS

Materials   Toys and/or objects used in games with rules.

Procedure   *Observation:* Observe child's ability to continue participation in organized game until the completion of game. Adult may provide group directions. *Example:* Child plays musical chairs from beginning to end. *Direct Test:* Direct organized game. Observe child's ability to continue participation in organized game until the completion of game. Adult may provide group directions.

Objective 2.2   Conforms to game rules

CRITERION   Child follows rules in organized games. Group directions may be provided by adult. *Example:* Child waits for turn, follows appropriate sequence of steps in game, knows beginning and end of game.

DIRECTIONS

Materials   Toys and/or objects used in games with rules.

Procedure   *Observation:* Observe child's ability to follow rules in organized games. Adult may provide group directions. *Example:* Child spins the spinner before moving marker on board game. *Direct Test:* Present the rules of organized game and observe child's ability to follow the rules. Adult may provide group directions. *Example:* Child waits turn during "Duck, Duck, Goose" in response to adult's directions.

Strand H   Premath

GOAL 1   Recites numbers from 1 to 20

CRITERION   Spontaneously or on request, child recites numbers from 1 to 20 in correct order.

DIRECTIONS

Materials   No materials are necessary.

Procedure   *Observation:* Observe child's ability to recite numbers from 1 to 20 in correct order. *Example:* While playing "Hide-and-Seek," child correctly counts from 1 to 20.
Direct Test: Ask child to count to 20. Observe child's ability to recite numbers from 1 to 20 in correct order.

Objective 1.1   Recites numbers from 1 to 10

CRITERION   Spontaneously or on request, child recites numbers from 1 to 10 in correct order.

DIRECTIONS

Materials   No materials are necessary.

Procedure   *Observation:* Observe child's ability to recite numbers from 1 to 10 in correct order. *Example:* While waiting for turn in game, child correctly counts from 1 to 10.
Direct Test: Ask child to count to 10. Observe child's ability to recite numbers from 1 to 10 in correct order.

Objective 1.2   Recites numbers from 1 to 5

CRITERION   Spontaneously or on request, child recites numbers from 1 to 5 in correct order.

DIRECTIONS

Materials   No materials are necessary.

Procedure   *Observation:* Observe child's ability to recite numbers from 1 to 5 in correct order. *Example:* When playing hiding game, child closes eyes and correctly counts to 5.
Direct Test: Ask child to count. Observe child's ability to recite numbers from 1 to 5 in correct order.

Objective 1.3   Recites numbers from 1 to 3

CRITERION   Spontaneously or on request, child recites numbers from 1 to 3 in correct order.

DIRECTIONS

Materials   No materials are necessary.

Procedure   *Observation:* Observe child's ability to recite numbers from 1 to 3 in correct order. *Example:* While pretending to perform magic trick, child counts, "One, two, three."
Direct Test: Ask child to count. Observe child's ability to recite numbers from 1 to 3 in correct order.

GOAL 2   Counts 10 objects

CRITERION   When presented with a set of 10 objects, child correctly counts objects.

DIRECTIONS

Materials   A set of 10 objects.

Procedure   *Observation:* Observe child's ability to accurately count 10 objects. *Example:* At circle time, child correctly counts number of children present.
Direct Test: Present child with 10 objects. Ask child to count the objects. Observe child's ability to accurately count 10 objects.

Objective 2.1   Counts five objects

CRITERION   When presented with a set of five objects, child correctly counts objects.

DIRECTIONS

Materials   A set of five objects.

Procedure   *Observation:* Observe child's ability to accurately count five objects. *Example:* At snack time, child correctly counts five cups. *Direct Test:* Present child with five objects. Ask child to count the objects. Observe child's ability to accurately count five objects.

Objective 2.2   Counts two objects

CRITERION   When presented with a set of two objects, child correctly counts objects.

DIRECTIONS

Materials   A set of two objects.

Procedure   *Observation:* Observe child's ability to accurately count two objects. *Example:* At snack time, child correctly counts two crackers. *Direct Test:* Present child with two objects. Observe child's ability to accurately count two objects.

Objective 2.3   Demonstrates understanding of one-to-one correspondence

CRITERION   Spontaneously or on request, child demonstrates one-to-one correspondence by assigning one object to each of four or more objects or people. *Example:* Child places one fork next to each plate. Child gives one paintbrush to each child.

DIRECTIONS

Materials   Enough objects to assign to people involved (e.g., five paintbrushes for five children).

Cog H

Procedure *Observation:* During play or during preparation of activity, observe child's ability to assign one object to each of four or more objects or people. *Example:* Child gives one napkin to each of four children.
Direct Test: Present objects and ask child to pass items to other children (e.g., give each person a crayon) or to place items at each setting (e.g., place one napkin next to each plate). Observe child's ability to assign one object to each of four or more objects or people.

GOAL 3   Identifies printed numerals 1–10

CRITERION Spontaneously or on request, child identifies printed numerals 1–10. *Examples:* Adult shows child printed numerals and asks, "What number is this?" Child correctly names number. As child looks at number book, child points to and correctly identifies numbers from 1 to 10.

DIRECTIONS

Materials Cards, books, or other materials with printed numerals from 1 to 10.

Procedure *Observation:* Observe child's ability to name numerals 1–10. *Example:* When child is working on number puzzle, adult points to number and asks, "What number is this?" Child correctly identifies number.
Direct Test: Present cards with printed numerals. Ask child to identify numbers. Observe child's ability to name/identify numbers from 1 to 10.

Objective 3.1   Identifies printed numerals 1–8

CRITERION Spontaneously or on request, child identifies printed numerals 1–8. *Examples:* Adult shows child printed numerals and asks, "What number is this?" Child correctly names number. As child looks at number book, child points to and correctly identifies numbers from 1 to 8.

DIRECTIONS

Materials Cards, books, or other materials with printed numerals from 1 to 8.

Procedure *Observation:* Observe child's ability to name numerals 1–8. *Example:* When child is working on number puzzle, adult points to number and asks, "What number is this?" Child correctly identifies number.
Direct Test: Present cards with printed numerals. Ask child to identify numbers. Observe child's ability to name/identify numbers from 1 to 8.

Cog H

Objective 3.2 Identifies printed numerals 1–5

CRITERION Spontaneously or on request, child identifies printed numerals 1–5. *Examples:* Adult shows child printed numerals and asks, "What number is this?" Child correctly names number. As child looks at number book, child points to and correctly identifies numbers from 1 to 5.

DIRECTIONS

Materials Cards, books, or other materials with printed numerals from 1 to 5.

Procedure *Observation:* Observe child's ability to name numerals 1–5. *Example:* When child is working on number puzzle, adult points to number and asks, "What number is this?" Child correctly identifies number.
Direct Test: Present cards with printed numerals. Ask child to identify numbers. Observe child's ability to name/identify numbers from 1 to 5.

Objective 3.3 Identifies printed numerals 1–3

CRITERION Spontaneously or on request, child identifies printed numerals 1–3. *Examples:* Adult shows child printed numerals and asks, "What number is this?" Child correctly names number. As child looks at number book, child points to and correctly identifies numbers from 1 to 3.

DIRECTIONS

Materials Cards, books, or other materials with printed numerals from 1 to 3.

Procedure *Observation:* Observe child's ability to name numerals 1–3. *Example:* When child is working on number puzzle, adult points to number and asks, "What number is this?" Child correctly identifies number.
Direct Test: Present cards with printed numerals. Ask child to identify numbers. Observe child's ability to name/identify numbers from 1 to 3.

GOAL 4 Matches printed numerals to sets of 1–10 object(s)

CRITERION On request, child selects printed numerals that correspond to sets of 1–10 object(s).

Cog H

DIRECTIONS

Materials   Cards or other materials with printed numerals from 1 to 10 and groups of 10 similar objects.

Procedure   *Observation:* It may be necessary to direct test this item.
Direct Test: Present cards with printed numerals. Present objects in sets of 1, 2, 3, 4, 5, 6, 7, 8, 9, and 10. Ask child to select printed numerals that correspond to sets of 1–10 object(s).

Objective 4.1   Matches printed numerals to sets of 1–8 object(s)

CRITERION   On request, child selects printed numerals that correspond to sets of 1 to 8 object(s).

DIRECTIONS

Materials   Cards or other materials with printed numerals from 1 to 8 and groups of 8 similar object(s).

Procedure   *Observation:* It may be necessary to direct test this item.
Direct Test: Present cards with printed numerals. Present objects in sets of 1, 2, 3, 4, 5, 6, 7, and 8. Ask child to select printed numerals that correspond to sets of 1–8 object(s).

Objective 4.2   Matches printed numerals to sets of 1–5 object(s)

CRITERION   On request, child selects printed numerals that correspond to sets of 1–5 object(s).

DIRECTIONS

Materials   Cards or other materials with printed numerals from 1 to 5 and groups of 5 similar object(s).

Procedure   *Observation:* It may be necessary to direct test this item.
Direct Test: Present cards with printed numerals. Present objects in sets of 1, 2, 3, 4, and 5. Ask child to select printed numerals that correspond to sets of 1–5 object(s).

Cog H

Objective 4.3   Matches printed numerals to sets of 1–3 object(s)

CRITERION   On request, child selects printed numerals that correspond to sets of 1–3 object(s).

DIRECTIONS

Materials   Cards or other materials with printed numerals from 1 to 3 and groups of 3 similar objects.

Procedure   *Observation:* It may be necessary to direct test this item.
Direct Test: Present cards with printed numerals. Present objects in sets of 1, 2, and 3. Ask child to select printed numerals that correspond to sets of 1–3 object(s).

Strand I Prereading

GOAL 1 Demonstrates prereading skills

CRITERION Child demonstrates understanding of purpose, function, and use of books by performing the following prereading tasks:

- Demonstrates functional use of books
- Tells about pictures in book
- Participates actively in storytelling

DIRECTIONS (See Objectives 1.1–1.3 for specific directions.)

Note: If a child's performance on *all* objectives was scored with a 2, the goal is scored 2. If a child's performance on the objectives was scored with *any* combination of a 0, 1, or 2, the goal is scored 1. If a child's performance on *all* objectives was scored with a 0, the goal is scored 0.

Objective 1.1 Demonstrates functional use of books

CRITERION The child performs three of the following prereading tasks:

- Correctly positions books
- Turns all pages from beginning to end
- Pretends to read by vocalizing or verbalizing
- Attempts to structure and tell story

Adult may provide general cues (e.g., "Can you read me a story?"). *Example:* Child looks at book and says, "The dragon went up to the boy. He was really scared. Then the dragon gave him a book, and they were friends."

DIRECTIONS

Materials Any age-appropriate book that is interesting to the child.

Procedure *Observation:* Observe child's ability to perform three of the prereading tasks listed in the criterion. Adult may provide general cues (e.g., "Can you read me a story?"). *Example:* During story time, child looks at book, turns page, and says, "The bear is eating honey. The bee will sting him."

Direct Test: Present book and ask child to read it. Observe child's ability to perform three of the prereading tasks listed in the criterion. *Exam-*

ple: Child takes book, opens it to the first page, and says, "I know this story. The little boy loses his dog."

Objective 1.2   Tells about pictures in book

CRITERION   Child tells about pictures in book and makes comments that provide clues that child knows what the story is about. Adult may provide general cues (e.g., "What is this story about?", "Here's a horsie in the barn").

DIRECTIONS

Materials   Any age-appropriate book that is interesting to the child.

Procedure   *Observation:* Observe child's ability to tell about pictures in book and make comments that provide clues that the child knows what the story is about. Adult may provide general cues (e.g., "What is this story about?"). *Example:* "A girl riding her bike to school. She's happy."
Direct Test: Present picture book and ask child to tell story. Observe child's ability to tell about pictures in a book and make comments that provide clues that child knows what the story is about. Adult may provide general cues (e.g., "What is this story about?"). *Example:* "Here's a train; the train is bringing toys to children."

Objective 1.3   Participates actively in storytelling

CRITERION   During story time, when adult reads story, child participates actively by performing four of the following prereading tasks:

- Making comments
- Pointing to pictures
- Turning pages
- Filling in missing words
- Telling the end of a familiar story

Example: While reading a story about animals, adult shows child a picture and reads, "Then, all of a sudden, baby rabbit saw the red...." Child continues appropriately, according to the picture, "fox!"

DIRECTIONS

Materials   Any age-appropriate book that is interesting to the child.

Procedure   *Observation:* Observe child's ability to participate actively when adult reads a story by performing four of the prereading tasks listed in the

Cog I

criterion. *Example:* During story time, child points to the picture and says, "The duck is swimming" and continues appropriately by turning the page.

Direct Test: Read a story. Observe child's ability to participate actively by performing four of the prereading tasks listed in the criterion. *Example:* While reading a story about Winnie the Pooh, adult shows child a picture and reads, "Then Pooh put his paw inside the honey jar..." Child continues appropriately, according to the picture, "and couldn't get it out!"

GOAL 2   Demonstrates prereading auditory skills

CRITERION   Child demonstrates ability to perform the following prereading tasks:

- Blends a series of sounds together to form a word
- Rhymes words with a model

DIRECTIONS   (See Objectives 2.1 and 2.2 for specific directions.)

Note: If a child's performance on *all* objectives was scored with a 2, the goal is scored 2. If a child's performance on the objectives was scored with *any* combination of a 0, 1, or 2, the goal is scored 1. If a child's performance on *all* objectives was scored with a 0, the goal is scored 0.

Objective 2.1   Blends sounds

CRITERION   When a series of three sounds is presented, child puts them together to form a word. *Example:* Adult says "c-a-t"; child says "cat."

DIRECTIONS

Materials   No materials are necessary.

Procedure   *Observation:* It may be necessary to direct test this item.
Direct Test: Present a series of three sounds. Ask child to tell what word the sounds make. *Example:* Adult says: "m-a-n"; child says "man."

Objective 2.2   Rhymes words

CRITERION   On request, child produces a word or nonsense word that rhymes with a model word. *Example:* Adult says "mat"; child says "hat."

DIRECTIONS

Materials   No materials are necessary.

Procedure   *Observation:* It may be necessary to direct test this item.
Direct Test: Present a word. Ask child to produce a word that rhymes with a model word. *Example:* Adult says: "kid"; child says "lid."

GOAL 3   Sounds out words

CRITERION   Child reads by sounding out three words consisting of three phonetic units. *Example:* Child sounds out printed words "bat," "sit," and "man."

DIRECTIONS

Materials   Any age-appropriate printed words consisting of three phonetic units.

Procedure   *Observation:* Observe child's ability to read by sounding out at least three words consisting of three phonetic units.
Direct Test: Present printed word consisting of three phonetic units and ask child to read. Observe child's ability to read at least three words consisting of three phonetic units.

Objective 3.1   Produces phonetic sounds for letters

CRITERION   On request, child produces phonetic sound for at least three letters. *Example:* Adult shows child letter "B"; child says /b/. Adult shows child letter "S"; child says /s/.

DIRECTIONS

Materials   Printed letters.

Procedure   *Observation:* Observe child's ability to produce phonetic sound for at least three letters.
Direct Test: Present printed letter and ask child to produce its sound. Observe child's ability to produce phonetic sound for at least three letters.

GOAL 4   Reads words by sight

CRITERION   Spontaneously or on request, child reads at least two common words by sight. One of the words may be the child's first name.

Cog I

DIRECTIONS

Materials   Printed words.

Procedure   *Observation:* Observe child's ability to read at least two common words by sight. One of the words may be the child's first name.

Direct Test: Present printed word and ask child to read it. Observe child's ability to read at least two common words by sight. One of the words may be child's first name.

Objective 4.1   Identifies letters

CRITERION   Spontaneously or on request, child names at least five letters of the alphabet. *Example:* Adult shows child printed letters and asks, "Can you name any of these letters?" Child names letters.

DIRECTIONS

Materials   Printed letters.

Procedure   *Observation:* Observe child's ability to name at least five letters of the alphabet. *Example:* As child plays with alphabet blocks, child correctly names letters.

Direct Test: Present set of printed letters and ask child to name letters. Observe child's ability to name at least five letters.

Note: Typically, letters learned first are A, B, C, O, S, X, and letters of name. These letters should be presented first.

SOCIAL-COMMUNICATION DOMAIN

Items in the Social-Communication Domain are based on the theoretical view that communication consists of three overlapping and interrelated developmental areas: 1) content (meaning expressed through language), 2) form (syntax and grammar of language), and 3) use (function of communication in social context).

The Social-Communication Domain was designed to assess the child's language and communication skills as they are used in classroom and home activities, conversations, and social interactions. Items in this domain evaluate social-communication interactions, such as the child's use of words and of conversational rules and grammatical structures. Items in this domain measure the acquisition of the following skills:

• Social-communicative interactions
• Production of words, phrases, and sentences

Two forms, the Social-Communication Recording Form and the Social-Communication Summary Form (both forms are contained in Appendix D), are used for the purpose of collecting, recording, and analyzing the child's social-communication behavior. These forms, or similar forms, are recommended for use in scoring the Social-Communication Domain. Information on collecting data in the Social-Communication Domain is provided at the end of this domain.

The user is reminded that items in the Social-Communication Domain are cross-referenced with items in the Cognitive and Social Domains. For example, a child's ability to name and identify colors (skills included in the Cognitive Domain) is dependent on the child's understanding of verbal instructions or questions like, "Show me which one is green" or "What color is this?" A child may know the colors but not be able to say the appropriate word. If a child is unable to perform a given task, the interventionist should ask, "Is there another behavior absent from the child's repertoire that prevents the child from demonstrating this behavior?"

Strand A   Social-Communicative Interactions

   G1   Uses words, phrases, or sentences to inform, direct, ask questions, and express anticipation, imagination, affect, and emotions
      1.1   Uses words, phrases, or sentences to express anticipated outcomes
      1.2   Uses words, phrases, or sentences to describe pretend objects, events, or people
      1.3   Uses words, phrases, or sentences to label own or others' affect/emotions
      1.4   Uses words, phrases, or sentences to describe past events
      1.5   Uses words, phrases, or sentences to make commands to and requests of others

SC

173

1.6   Uses words, phrases, or sentences to obtain information
1.7   Uses words, phrases, or sentences to inform
G2   Uses conversational rules
2.1   Alternates between speaker/listener role
2.2   Responds to topic changes initiated by others
2.3   Asks questions for clarification
2.4   Responds to contingent questions
2.5   Initiates context-relevant topics
2.6   Responds to others' topic initiations
G3   Establishes and varies social-communicative roles
3.1   Varies voice to impart meaning
3.2   Uses socially appropriate physical orientation

Strand B   **Production of Words, Phrases, and Sentences**
G1   Uses verbs
1.1   Uses auxiliary verbs
1.2   Uses copula verb "to be"
1.3   Uses third person singular verb forms
1.4   Uses irregular past tense verbs
1.5   Uses regular past tense verbs
1.6   Uses present progressive "ing"
G2   Uses noun inflections
2.1   Uses possessive "s"
2.2   Uses irregular plural nouns
2.3   Uses regular plural nouns
G3   Asks questions
3.1   Asks yes/no questions
3.2   Asks questions with inverted auxiliary
3.3   Asks when questions
3.4   Asks why, who, and how questions
3.5   Asks what and where questions
3.6   Asks questions using rising inflection
G4   Uses pronouns
4.1   Uses subject pronouns
4.2   Uses object pronouns
4.3   Uses possessive pronouns
4.4   Uses indefinite pronouns
4.5   Uses demonstrative pronouns
G5   Uses descriptive words
5.1   Uses adjectives
5.2   Uses adjectives to make comparisons
5.3   Uses adverbs
5.4   Uses prepositions
5.5   Uses conjunctions
5.6   Uses articles

Strand A Social-Communicative Interactions

GOAL 1 Uses words, phrases, or sentences to inform, direct, ask questions, and express anticipation, imagination, affect, and emotions

CRITERION Child uses words, phrases, or sentences to do the following:

- Express anticipated outcomes
- Describe pretend objects, events, or people
- Label own or others' affect/emotions
- Describe past events
- Make commands to and requests of others
- Obtain information
- Inform

DIRECTIONS (See Objectives 1.1–1.7 for specific directions.)

Notes: If a child's performance on *all* objectives was scored with a 2, the goal is scored 2. If a child's performance on the objectives was scored with *any* combination of a 0, 1, or 2, the goal is scored 1. If a child's performance on *all* objectives was scored with a 0, the goal is scored 0.

Errors in syntax are acceptable.

Take language sample to collect data on this item. (Refer to pages 203–205.)

Objective 1.1 Uses words, phrases, or sentences to express anticipated outcomes

CRITERION Child uses words, phrases, or sentences to relay information about future events. *Examples:* Child says, "Look out" to warn peer about falling when peer climbs. Child predicts the ending of a familiar story. Child says, "Santa will come on my roof at Christmas."

DIRECTIONS

Materials Objects interesting to the child.

SC A

175

Procedure   *Observation:* Observe child's ability to use words, phrases, or sentences to relay information about future events. *Example:* Child says, "I am going to McDonald's after school."

Direct Test: Arrange events, make statements, and ask questions that encourage child to express anticipated outcomes. Observe child's ability to use words, phrases, or sentences to relay information about future events. *Examples:* While reading story, adult pauses and says, "Uh-oh, I wonder what happens next"; child says, "I think the giant will wake up." Adult asks, "What will you do this weekend?"; child says, "My daddy is going to take me fishing."

Notes: Errors in syntax are acceptable.

This item is cross-referenced with Cognitive Domain, Strand B, Goal 7, and Strand F, Objective 2.2.

Take language sample to collect data on this item. (Refer to pages 203–205.)

Objective 1.2   Uses words, phrases, or sentences to describe pretend objects, events, or people

---

CRITERION   Child uses words, phrases, or sentences to tell about imaginary objects, events, or people. *Examples:* Child says, "I am Superman." Child says, "Let's build a campfire. You go get some wood," and acts out a camping scenario.

DIRECTIONS

Materials   No materials are required.

Procedure   *Observation:* Observe child's ability to use words, phrases, or sentences to tell about imaginary objects, people, or events. *Example:* While playing with peer, child says, "You pretend you're He-man, and you have to help me."

Direct Test: Encourage child to describe pretend objects, events, or people by setting up activities that involve pretending. Observe child's ability to use words, phrases, or sentences to tell about imaginary objects, people, or events. *Examples:* Adult says, "Let's play going to the beach"; child says, "I'll get the towels and suntan lotion" and gathers imaginary objects. Adult says, "Let's pretend this is the hospital. I'll be a doctor. Who do you want to be?"; child says, "I'll be the daddy with the sick baby."

Notes: Errors in syntax are acceptable.

This item is cross-referenced with Cognitive Domain, Strand G, Goal 1.

Take language sample to collect data on this item. (Refer to pages 203–205.)

SC A

Objective 1.3   Uses words, phrases, or sentences to label own or others' affect/emotions

CRITERION   Child uses words, phrases, or sentences to label own or others' affect/emotions. *Examples:* Child withdraws from an activity and says, "I don't like to play that." Child watches an adult laugh and says, "You're happy."

DIRECTIONS

Materials   Objects interesting to the child.

Procedure   *Observation:* Observe child's ability to use words, phrases, or sentences to label own or others' affect/emotions. *Example:* Child says, "The witch is bad," referring to a storybook character.
Direct Test: Arrange events or make statements and ask questions that encourage child to express affect/emotions. Observe child's ability to use words, phrases, or sentences to label own or others' affect/emotions. *Example:* During puppet show, adult says, "The boy can't find his puppy. I wonder how he feels?" Child says, "I think he's sad" or "He's sad."

Notes: Errors in syntax are acceptable.

This item is cross-referenced with Social Domain, Strand C, Goal 1.

Take language sample to collect data on this item. (Refer to pages 203–205.)

Objective 1.4   Uses words, phrases, or sentences to describe past events

CRITERION   Child uses words, phrases, or sentences to describe actions and events that occurred in the immediate and distant past. *Examples:* Child says, "The bad guy chased him, and he fell down" when telling about a movie previously viewed. Child says, "I made a hat" when telling parent about an earlier art activity.

DIRECTIONS

Materials   No materials are required.

Procedure   *Observation:* Observe child's ability to use words, phrases, or sentences to describe past events. *Example:* After snack, child tells peer, "I helped pass out snack today."

SCA

Direct Test: Encourage child to describe past events by asking questions that elicit information about past events. Observe child's ability to use words, phrases, or sentences to describe past events. *Example:* Adult asks child what was done in school. Child says, "I painted a picture of a boat."

Notes: Errors in syntax are acceptable.

This item is cross-referenced with Social-Communication Domain, Strand B, Objectives 1.4 and 1.5; Cognitive Domain, Strand B, Goal 7; and Cognitive Domain, Strand E, Goal 1.

Take language sample to collect data on this item. (Refer to pages 203–205.)

Objective 1.5   Uses words, phrases, or sentences to make commands to and requests of others

CRITERION   Child uses words, phrases, or sentences to make commands to and requests of others. *Examples:* Child says, "Give me the red one." When playing on a swing set, child says, "Push me."

DIRECTIONS

Materials   No materials are required.

Procedure   *Observation:* Observe child's ability to use words, phrases, or sentences to make commands to and requests of others. *Example:* When playing with blocks, child says, "Give me a round one."
Direct Test: Direct test is not appropriate for this item.

Notes: Errors in syntax are acceptable.

This item is cross-referenced with Social Domain, Strand A, Goal 2.

Take language sample to collect data on this item. (Refer to pages 203–205.)

Objective 1.6   Uses words, phrases, or sentences to obtain information

CRITERION   Child uses words, phrases, or sentences, using rising intonation, to obtain information. *Examples:* Child can't locate coat and asks, "My coat?" (with rising intonation). Child watches peer eating and says, "That your cookie?" Child asks classroom teachers, "When Mommy come back?"

DIRECTIONS

Materials   Objects interesting to the child.

Procedure   *Observation:* Observe child's ability to ask questions or use statements with rising intonation to obtain information. *Example:* Child points to tools on floor and asks, "What you doing?" or "You gonna fix it?"
Direct Test: Present objects or arrange events that encourage child to obtain information. Observe child's ability to ask questions or make sentences using rising intonation to obtain information. *Example:* Adult presents unfamiliar objects to child. Child says, "What that?" or "What do you do with it?" or "That yours?"

Notes: Errors in syntax are acceptable.

This item is cross-referenced with Social-Communication Domain, Strand B, Goal 3 and Objectives 3.1 through 3.6.

Take language sample to collect data on this item. (Refer to pages 203–205.)

Objective 1.7   Uses words, phrases, or sentences to inform

CRITERION   Child uses words, phrases, or sentences to describe objects, actions, and events and to relay plans, intentions, and experiences to others. *Examples:* Child calls to parent, "I'm going outside." Child approaches a peer and says, "I have red shoes." Child points to truck and says, "That's my daddy's truck."

DIRECTIONS

Materials   Objects interesting to the child.

Procedure   *Observation:* Observe child's ability to use words, phrases, or sentences to provide information. *Example:* Child points to mother and says, "That's my mommy."
Direct Test: Make statements or ask questions that encourage child to describe objects, actions, and events and to relay plans, intentions, and experiences. Observe child's ability to use words, phrases, or sentences to provide information. *Examples:* Child is drawing, and adult says, "Oh, that's a nice picture"; child says, "It's my house." Adult asks, "What color do you want?" and child says, "Red."

Notes: Errors in syntax are acceptable.

Take language sample to collect data on this item. (Refer to pages 203–205.)

SC A

GOAL 2   Uses conversational rules

CRITERION   Child uses conversational rules to initiate and maintain communicative exchanges for two or more consecutive exchanges. An exchange includes a response from both the child and another person. Conversational rules include the following:

- Alternating between speaker/listener role
- Responding to topic changes
- Asking questions for clarification
- Responding to contingent questions
- Initiating context-relevant topics
- Responding to others' topic initiations

DIRECTIONS   (See Objectives 2.1–2.6 for specific directions.)

Notes: If a child's performance on *all* objectives was scored with a 2, the goal is scored 2. If a child's performance on the objectives was scored with *any* combination of a 0, 1, or 2, the goal is scored 1. If a child's performance on *all* objectives was scored with a 0, the goal is scored 0.

Take language sample to collect data on this item. (Refer to pages 203–205.)

Objective 2.1   Alternates between speaker/listener role

CRITERION   Child uses appropriate responses in conversation to alternate between speaker/listener role. *Examples:* Child pauses after making a comment or asking a question and looks toward communicative partner. Child asks, "Where's my book?" Mother says, "Here." Child asks, "Where?"

DIRECTIONS

Materials   Objects interesting to the child.

Procedure   *Observation:* Observe child's ability to use appropriate responses in conversation to alternate between speaker/listener role. *Example:* Child asks, "Is that your dog?" and pauses for response.
Direct Test: Direct test is not appropriate for this item; however, communicative interaction may be encouraged by grouping children together with consideration of individual child interests, peer preference, and developmental levels of functioning. Communicative interaction may also be encouraged by engaging in play with child and allowing child opportunities to engage in communicative exchanges.

Note: Take language sample to collect data on this item. (Refer to pages 203–205.)

SC A

Objective 2.2   Responds to topic changes initiated by others

CRITERION   Child responds to conversational topic changes initiated by others with a comment, answer, or question related to the new topic. *Example:* The child says, "I want to play outside some more," and adult says, "We need to go inside now to fix a special snack." Child responds, "What is it?"

DIRECTIONS

Materials   Objects interesting to the child.

Procedure   *Observation:* Observe child's ability to respond to conversational topic changes initiated by others with a comment, answer, or question related to new topic. *Example:* Child says, "The baby is sleeping," and adult says, "It's time to put the baby doll away and get ready to go outside." Child responds, "I can swing outside."
Direct Test: When engaged in conversation with child, change the topic of conversation. Observe child's ability to respond to topic changes. *Examples:* Child says, "I like to play with cars," and adult says, "Look, it's raining"; child responds, "I need my rainboots." During classroom circle activity, child says "I like the farm animals," and adult says, "It's time for snack"; child responds, "Juice and cracker."

Note: Take language sample to collect data on this item. (Refer to pages 203–205.)

Objective 2.3   Asks questions for clarification

CRITERION   Child indicates a need for clarification (i.e., repetition, elaboration, or confirmation) by commenting or questioning during communicative exchanges. *Examples:* Child says, "What?" when child does not understand what another person said. Child asks, "That one?" when unsure about which object was indicated by another.

DIRECTIONS

Materials   Objects interesting to the child.

Procedure   *Observation:* Observe child's ability to indicate a need for clarification (i.e., repetition, elaboration, or confirmation) by commenting or questioning during communicative exchanges. *Example:* Child points and asks, "Him?" when unsure which person was referred to by another. *Direct Test:* Direct test is not appropriate for this item; however, use of strategies to mend communication gaps may be encouraged by arranging ambiguous events and asking questions or by giving the

SC A

child ambiguous directions. *Example:* Adult points to a shelf of dolls and asks, "Can you give me the doll?" Child asks, "Which one?"

Note: Take language sample to collect data on this item. (Refer to pages 203–205.)

Objective 2.4   Responds to contingent questions

CRITERION   Child supplies relevant information following another person's request for clarification, repetition, elaboration, or confirmation of child's previous statement. *Examples:* Child says, "She threw it"; adult asks, "Who threw it?" and child answers, "Rachel. Rachel threw it." Child says, "These shoes"; adult asks, "Are those your shoes?" and child nods affirmatively and says, "Yep." Adult asks, "Why do you have your coat on?" and child says, "It's cold."

DIRECTIONS

Materials   Objects interesting to the child.

Procedure   *Observation:* Observe child's ability to respond to contingent questions. *Example:* Child says, "I want that," and adult asks, "What do you want?" Child responds, "I want the bear puzzle."
Direct Test: When child makes statement, ask related questions about statement. Observe child's ability to respond to contingent questions. *Example:* Child says, "I'm going shopping with my mom after school." Adults says, "What are you going to buy?" Child says, "Cereal."

Note: Take language sample to collect data on this item. (Refer to pages 203–205.)

Objective 2.5   Initiates context-relevant topics

CRITERION   Child initiates topics relevant to the situation or communicative partner. *Examples:* Child sees peer with crayons and says, "I want the red one." Child sees adult wearing sunglasses and says, "You have glasses."

DIRECTIONS

Materials   Objects interesting to the child.

Procedure   *Observation:* Observe child's ability to initiate topics relevant to the situation or communicative partner. *Example:* Child approaches adult cleaning up after snack and asks, "Can I help clean the table?"
Direct Test: Direct test is not appropriate for this item.

Note: Take language sample to collect data on this item. (Refer to pages 203–205.)

Objective 2.6   Responds to others' topic initiations

CRITERION   Child responds to another's conversation with a related topic, including an acknowledgment of another's statement, an answer to a question, a request for clarification, or a related comment. *Examples:* Adult says, "It's time to get your coats and hats and line up at the door," and the child says, "Okay." An adult comments, "You have new shoes on today," and the child says, "My mommy got them at the store." Adult asks, "What did you do?" and child answers, "Fall down."

DIRECTIONS

Materials   Objects interesting to the child.

Procedure   *Observation:* Observe child's ability to respond to another's topic initiations. *Example:* Peer says, "I have a cat at home," and child responds, "What's his name?"
Direct Test: Initiate conversation with child by making a statement or asking a question that is relevant to child or situation. Observe child's ability to respond to your initiation with a related topic, including an acknowledgment, answer to a question, request for clarification, or related comment. *Example:* Adult approaches child and says, "Your mom brought you to school today." Child says, "Mommy doesn't work today."

Notes: This item is cross-referenced with Cognitive Domain, Strand A, Objectives 1.1, 1.2, and 2.2; Goal 3; and Objective 3.2.

Take language sample to collect data on this item. (Refer to pages 203–205.)

GOAL 3   Establishes and varies social-communicative roles

CRITERION   Child changes form, length, and grammatical complexity of phrases and sentences according to the listener's needs and social role. *Examples:* Child says, "I want some gum" to a parent but uses polite form, "Can I have some gum please?" with less familiar adults. Child uses shorter and less complex sentences to ask a younger child, "Want a cookie?"

SC A

DIRECTIONS

Materials   No materials are required.

Procedure   *Observation:* Observe child's ability to change form, length, voice, and grammatical complexity of phrases and sentences according to the lis-

tener's needs and social role. *Example:* Child says, "Gimme that cookie" to a peer but asks teacher, "Can I have a cookie, please?"
Direct Test: Direct the child to provide or acquire information to and from various people. Observe child's ability to change form, length, voice, and grammatical complexity of phrases and sentences according to the listener's needs and social roles. *Example:* Adult directs child to ask teacher if child has permission to go outside. Adult then directs child to ask younger peer if peer would like to go outside.

Note: Take language sample to collect data on this item. (Refer to pages 203–205.)

Objective 3.1   Varies voice to impart meaning

CRITERION   Child uses voice pitch (high, low) and intensity (loud, soft) appropriate to the situation, listener, and communicative meaning. *Examples:* Child shouts when playing but whispers after noticing father is sleeping. Child uses higher pitch and less intensity when speaking to infants. Child raises pitch at the end of sentences that are questions.

DIRECTIONS

Materials   No materials are required.

Procedure   *Observation:* Observe child's ability to use voice pitch (high, low) and intensity (loud, soft) appropriate to the situation, listener, and communicative meaning. *Example:* Child shouts to peer across the playground and speaks to peer in normal speaking voice when peer is near.
Direct Test: Direct test is not appropriate for this item; however, use of varied voice to impart meaning may be encouraged by setting up pretend situations and having children act out various roles. *Example:* Adult says, "Let's pretend you're the dad and you're mad" or "You're the baby and you're sick."

Note: Take language sample to collect data on this item. (Refer to pages 203–205.)

Objective 3.2   Uses socially appropriate physical orientation

---

CRITERION   Child looks toward speaker's face and establishes appropriate physical proximity and body posture in relation to others during communicative exchange. *Examples:* When child's name is called, child turns and looks to locate the speaker. Child looks at and leans toward a friend who wants to tell a secret.

DIRECTIONS

Materials   No materials are required.

Procedure   *Observation:* Observe child's ability to look toward speaker's face and establish appropriate physical proximity and body posture in relation to others during communicative exchange.
Direct Test: Initiate a communicative exchange with child. Observe child's ability to use socially appropriate physical orientation during exchange.

Notes: This item is cross-referenced with Cognitive Domain, Strand A, Objectives 2.2 and 3.3.

Take language sample to collect data on this item. (Refer to pages 203–205.)

SC A

Strand B Production of Words, Phrases, and Sentences

GOAL 1 Uses verbs

CRITERION Child uses the following verb forms:

- Auxiliary
- Copula verb "to be"
- Third person singular
- Irregular past tense
- Regular past tense
- Present progressive "ing"

DIRECTIONS (See Objectives 1.1–1.6 for specific directions.)

Notes: If a child's performance on *all* objectives was scored with a 2, the goal is scored 2. If a child's performance on the objectives was scored with *any* combination of a 0, 1, or 2, the goal is scored 1. If a child's performance on *all* objectives was scored with a 0, the goal is scored 0.

Take language sample to collect data on this item. (Refer to pages 203–205.)

Objective 1.1 Uses auxiliary verbs

CRITERION Child uses an appropriate form of the following auxiliary (helping) verbs in combination with other verbs:

- To be (e.g., "He is running," "She's jumping," "They were throwing rocks")
- To want (e.g., "I want to go")
- Will (e.g., "You will fall," "He won't tell her," "She would go")
- Can (e.g., "I could eat that," "We can go," "I can't swim")
- To do (e.g., "I do want that," "They don't go to school," "He doesn't like milk")
- Shall (e.g., "She should take a nap")
- May (e.g., "He might not like it")
- Better (e.g., "They had better not do it")
- To have (e.g., "Do I have to do it?")

The number of forms the child uses is less important than the child's ability to use a form appropriate to the grammatical and semantic context of the sentence.

DIRECTIONS

Materials   Objects interesting to the child.

Procedure   *Observation:* Observe child's ability to use appropriate forms of the listed auxiliary verbs. *Example:* Child says, "She is going" or "You should eat your supper."

Direct Test: Direct test is not appropriate for this item; however, use of auxiliary verbs may be encouraged by engaging in play with child and allowing child opportunities to describe objects, people, and events or by arranging events, asking child questions, or making comments about events. *Examples:* Adult pushes car along floor; child says, "It can go fast." Adult puts doll in bed and asks, "What is the baby doing?"; child says, "She is sleeping." Adult gets coat and says, "What should we do?"; child says, "I want to play." Adult observes child and says, "What are you doing?"; child says, "I'm cutting this."

Note: Take language sample to collect data on this item. (Refer to pages 203–205.)

Objective 1.2   Uses copula verb "to be"

CRITERION   Child uses an appropriate form of the verb "to be" to link a subject noun to a predicate. *Examples:* Child says, "I'm happy," "They are sick," "He wasn't at home," "or "She's funny."

DIRECTIONS

Materials   Objects interesting to the child.

Procedure   *Observation:* Observe child's ability to use an appropriate form of the verb "to be." *Examples:* "He is sad," "They are big," or "I am sick."

Direct Test: Direct test is not appropriate for this item; however, use of the verb "to be" may be encouraged by engaging in play with child and allowing child opportunities to describe objects, people, and events or by arranging events, asking child questions, or making comments about events. *Examples:* When playing with blocks, adult selects a large block and says, "This one is big." Adult hands a small block to child; child says, "This one is little." Adult looks around and asks, "Where are the blocks?"; child says, "They're on the shelf." Adult asks, "How do you feel today?"; child says, "I am tired."

Note: Take language sample to collect data on this item. (Refer to pages 203–205.)

SC B

Objective 1.3   Uses third person singular verb forms

CRITERION   Child uses appropriate regular and irregular third person singular verb forms. *Examples of regular third person:* Child says, "She plays it," "It jumps," or "The dog barks." *Examples of irregular third person:* Child says, "She has a bike," or "He does not." *Examples of third person singular irregular verbs:* has, was, does, is, come, went, ran, drank, ate, and wrote.

DIRECTIONS

Materials   Objects interesting to the child.

Procedure   *Observation:* Observe child's ability to use regular and irregular third person singular verb forms. *Examples:* Child says, "He runs fast."
Direct Test: Direct test is not appropriate for this item; however, use of third person singular verb forms may be encouraged by talking with child about people and asking questions or by allowing child opportunities to comment on and describe people. *Examples:* When reading a story, adult pauses and asks, "What does the dog do?"; child says, "The dog barks." When acting out superheroes, adult asks, "What does Superman do?"; child says, "He flies." Adult says, "My dad works on a farm"; child says, "My daddy drives a big truck."

Note: Take language sample to collect data on this item. (Refer to pages 203–205.)

Objective 1.4   Uses irregular past tense verbs

CRITERION   Child uses appropriate irregular forms of past tense verbs (e.g., came, ran, fell, broke, sat, went, told, heard, did, ate, woke, made, drank, wrote). *Example:* Child says, "Mommy went to work" or "I ran fast."

DIRECTIONS

Materials   Objects interesting to the child.

Procedure   *Observation:* Observe child's ability to use irregular forms of past tense verbs. *Example:* Child says, "I had it first."
Direct Test: Direct test is not appropriate for this item; however, use of past tense verbs may be encouraged by talking with child about past events and allowing child opportunities to comment on and describe past events. *Examples:* Adult says, "I had fun on my vacation. I went to see my mother"; child says, "I went to my grandma's, and she made some cookies." Teacher asks, "What did you do before you came to school today?"; child says, "I woke up, and I ate breakfast."

SCB

Notes: This item is cross-referenced with Social-Communication Domain, Strand A, Objective 1.4, and Cognitive Domain, Strand B, Goal 7, and Strand E, Goal 1.

Take language sample to collect data on this item. (Refer to pages 203–205.)

Objective 1.5   Uses regular past tense verbs

CRITERION   Child uses appropriate regular past tense verbs (i.e., verb plus -ed ending). *Example:* Child says, "We walked home" or "I washed my hands."

DIRECTIONS

Materials   Objects interesting to the child.

Procedure   *Observation:* Observe child's ability to use regular past tense verbs. *Example:* Child says, "I jumped over the rope."
Direct Test: Direct test is not appropriate for this item; however, use of regular past tense verbs may be encouraged by talking about past events with child and allowing child opportunities to comment and describe past events. *Example:* Adult asks, "What did you do outside today?" Child says, "I played on the swings."

Notes: This item is cross-referenced with Social-Communication Domain, Objective 1.4; and Cognitive Domain, Strand B, Goal 7, and Strand E, Goal 1.

Take language sample to collect data on this item. (Refer to pages 203–205.)

Objective 1.6   Uses present progressive "ing"

CRITERION   Child uses appropriate present progressive verb forms (i.e., verb plus -ing ending). *Example:* Child says, "I'm going outside" or "Daddy's washing dishes."

DIRECTIONS

Materials   Objects interesting to the child.

Procedure   *Observation:* Observe child's ability to use present progressive verb forms. *Example:* Child says, "He is running fast."
Direct Test: Direct test is not appropriate for this item; however, use of present progressive verb forms may be encouraged by engaging in play with child and allowing child opportunities to describe objects, people, and events or by arranging events and asking child questions

SC B

about them. *Example:* Adult pretends to feed doll and asks, "What is the baby doing?" Child responds, "She's eating."

Note: Take language sample to collect data on this item. (Refer to pages 203–205.)

GOAL 2   Uses noun inflections

CRITERION   Child uses the following noun inflections:

- Possessive "s" (e.g., Susan's)
- Irregular plural (e.g., mice)
- Regular plural (e.g., toys)

DIRECTIONS   (See Objectives 2.1–2.3 for specific directions.)

Notes: If a child's performance on *all* objectives was scored with a 2, the goal is scored 2. If a child's performance on the objectives was scored with *any* combination of a 0, 1, or 2, the goal is scored 1. If a child's performance on *all* objectives was scored with a 0, the goal is scored 0.

Take language sample to collect data on this item. (Refer to pages 203–205.)

Objective 2.1   Uses possessive "s"

CRITERION   Child uses nouns with an apostrophe "s" to express possession. *Example:* "Mom's hat fell off" or "Ann's shoes are lost."

DIRECTIONS

Materials   Objects that belong to familiar people.

Procedure   *Observation:* Observe child's ability to use nouns with "'s" to express possession. *Example:* Child says, "That is Sammy's truck."
Direct Test: Use possessive terms within context of activities. Pause to allow the child opportunities to indicate possession. Ask occasional questions about the ownership of objects. Observe child's ability to use nouns with "'s" to express possession. *Examples:* Teacher passes out art projects, gives child a peer's drawing, and says, "Here is your picture"; child says, "This is Jenny's picture, not mine." Teacher asks, "Whose coat is this?"; child says, "It's Mary's."

Note: Take language sample to collect data on this item. (Refer to pages 203–205.)

Objective 2.2   Uses irregular plural nouns

CRITERION   Child uses irregular plural noun forms. *Example:* Child says, "Those mice are in the cage" or "My teeth are brushed." *Example of irregular plural nouns:* mice, leaves, geese, feet, teeth.

DIRECTIONS

Materials   Groups of two or more like objects or pictures of two or more like objects.

Procedure   *Observation:* Observe child's ability to use irregular plural noun forms. *Example:* Child says, "I hear those men talking."
Direct Test: Within context of activity, present two or more like objects or pictures and ask child to name them. Observe child's ability to use irregular plural noun forms to name objects or pictures. *Example:* Adult presents three toy mice and asks child, "What are these?" Child says "Mice."

Note: Take language sample to collect data on this item. (Refer to pages 203–205.)

Objective 2.3   Uses regular plural nouns

CRITERION   Child uses regular plural noun forms (i.e., noun plus "s" or "es" ending). *Examples:* Child says, "I see the dogs" or "I have two glasses."

DIRECTIONS

Materials   Groups of two or more like objects or pictures of two or more like objects.

Procedure   *Observation:* Observe child's ability to use regular plural noun forms (i.e., noun plus "s" or "es"). *Example:* Child says, "I want to play with the cars."
Direct Test: Within context of activity, present two or more like objects or pictures and ask child to name them. Observe child's ability to use regular plural noun forms to name objects or pictures. *Examples:* Adult presents blocks and asks child, "What do you want?"; child says, "Blocks, please." Adult says, "I want to light these candles. What do I need?"; child responds, "Matches."

Note: Take language sample to collect data on this item. (Refer to pages 203–205.)

SC B

GOAL 3   Asks questions

CRITERION   Child uses the following forms to ask questions:

- Yes/no questions
- Questions with inverted auxiliary
- When questions
- Why, who, and how questions
- What and where questions
- Rising inflection

DIRECTIONS   (See Objectives 3.1–3.6 for specific directions.)

Notes: If a child's performance on *all* objectives was scored with a 2, the goal is scored 2. If a child's performance on the objectives was scored with *any* combination of a 0, 1, or 2, the goal is scored 1. If a child's performance on *all* objectives was scored with a 0, the goal is scored 0.

Take language sample to collect data on this item. (Refer to pages 203–205.)

Objective 3.1   Asks yes/no questions

CRITERION   Child asks questions that require a yes or no response from the listener. *Example:* Child asks, "Am I bigger?" or "Can't I go?"

DIRECTIONS

Materials   Objects interesting to the child.

Procedure   *Observation:* Observe child's ability to ask questions that require a yes or no response from the listener. *Example:* Child asks, "Can Blackie come, too?"
Direct Test: Direct test is not appropriate for this item; however, use of yes/no questions may be encouraged by engaging in play with child and presenting unfamiliar objects, arranging events, and allowing child opportunities to ask questions. *Examples:* Adult is helping child build puzzle; child picks up puzzle piece, points to place on puzzle, and asks, "Does this one go here?" Adult says, "I have cookies," and child asks, "Can I have one?"

Notes: This item is cross-referenced with Social-Communication Domain, Strand A, Objective 1.6.

Take language sample to collect data on this item. (Refer to pages 203–205.)

SC B

Objective 3.2   Asks questions with inverted auxiliary

CRITERION   Child asks questions by reversing the order of the subject and the auxiliary (helping) verb (i.e., verb precedes the noun). *Example:* Child asks, "Why can't I go?" or "Is he hiding?"

DIRECTIONS

Materials   Objects interesting to the child.

Procedure   *Observation:* Observe child's ability to ask questions by reversing the order of the subject and the auxiliary (helping) verb. *Example:* Child asks, "Is she crying?" or "Can I have one?"
Direct Test: Direct test is not appropriate for this item; however, use of questions may be encouraged by engaging in play with child and presenting unfamiliar objects, arranging events, and allowing child opportunities to ask questions. *Examples:* While playing with miniature animals, adult asks child to find animal that hops; child retrieves frog and asks, "Can he hop?" Adult says, "I am going to the store"; child says, "Can I go, too?"

Notes: This item is cross-referenced with Social-Communication Domain, Strand A, Objective 1.6.

Take language sample to collect data on this item. (Refer to pages 203–205.)

Objective 3.3   Asks when questions

CRITERION   Child asks questions beginning with the word *when. Example:* Child asks, "When can we go?" or "When will we eat?"

DIRECTIONS

Materials   Objects interesting to the child.

Procedure   *Observation:* Observe child's ability to ask questions beginning with the word *when. Example:* Child asks, "When will you be finished?"
Direct Test: Direct test is not appropriate for this item; however, use of questions may be encouraged by engaging in play with child and presenting unfamiliar objects, arranging events, and allowing child opportunities to ask questions. *Examples:* Adult plays organized game with a group of children; child asks, "When can I have a turn?" Adult says, "We're going to McDonald's"; child asks, "When can we go?"

SC B

Notes: This item is cross-referenced with Social-Communication Domain, Strand A, Objective 1.6, and Cognitive Domain, Strand B, Goal 7.

Take language sample to collect data on this item. (Refer to pages 203–205.)

Objective 3.4   Asks why, who, and how questions

CRITERION   Child asks questions beginning with the words *why, who,* and *how. Example:* Child asks, "Why did he do that?", "Who is it?", or "How do you do that?"

DIRECTIONS

Materials   Objects interesting to the child.

Procedure   *Observation:* Observe child's ability to ask questions beginning with the words *why, who,* and *how. Example:* Child asks, "Why is she crying?", "Who made that?", or "How did you do that?"
Direct Test: Direct test is not appropriate for this item; however, use of *why, who,* and *how* questions may be encouraged by engaging in play with child and presenting unfamiliar objects, arranging events, and allowing child opportunities to ask questions. *Examples:* Child and adult are playing with dolls, and adult says, "We have to take this baby to the doctor"; child asks, "Why?" Adult hands telephone to child and says, "It's for you"; child asks, "Who is it?" Adult shows child a magic trick; child asks, "How did you do that?"

Notes: This item is cross-referenced with Social-Communication Domain, Strand A, Objective 1.6.

Take language sample to collect data on this item. (Refer to pages 203–205.)

Objective 3.5   Asks what and where questions

CRITERION   Child asks questions beginning with the words *what* and *where. Example:* Child asks, "Where is she going?", "Where Mommy going?", or "What's that?"

DIRECTIONS

Materials   Objects interesting to the child.

Procedure   *Observation:* Observe child's ability to ask questions beginning with the words *what* and *where. Example:* Child asks, "What are you doing?" or "Where is my book?"

Direct Test: Direct test is not appropriate for this item; however, use of *what* and *where* questions may be encouraged by engaging in play with child and presenting unfamiliar objects, arranging events, and allowing child opportunities to ask questions. *Examples:* Adult presents unfamiliar object; child asks, "What is that?" Adult hides object; child asks, "Where is my doll?" Adult says, "Ann is hiding. Can you find her?"; child asks, "Ann, where are you?"

Notes: This item is cross-referenced with Social-Communication Domain, Strand A, Objective 1.6.

Take language sample to collect data on this item. (Refer to pages 203–205.)

Objective 3.6   Asks questions using rising inflection

CRITERION   Child asks questions by using a raised pitch at the end of utterances so that the utterances sound like questions. *Example:* Child asks, "See that airplane?" or "Mommy go too?"

DIRECTIONS

Materials   Objects interesting to the child.

Procedure   *Observation:* Observe child's ability to ask questions by using rising inflection at end of utterances. *Example:* Child asks, "You help me?" *Direct Test:* Direct test is not appropriate for this item; however, questions may be encouraged by engaging in play with child and presenting unfamiliar objects, arranging events, and allowing child opportunities to ask questions. *Example:* Adult and child are playing a game. Child asks, "My turn?"

Notes: This item is cross-referenced with Social-Communication Domain, Strand A, Objective 1.6.

Take language sample to collect data on this item. (Refer to pages 203–205.)

GOAL 4   Uses pronouns

CRITERION   Child uses appropriate pronouns to serve the following functions:

- As subjects in phrases or sentences
- As objects in phrases or sentences
- To show possession
- To represent unspecified people and objects
- To identify or point out objects

DIRECTIONS   (See Objectives 4.1–4.5 for specific directions.)

SC B

Notes: If a child's performance on *all* objectives was scored with a 2, the goal is scored 2. If a child's performance on the objectives was scored with *any* combination of a 0, 1, or 2, the goal is scored 1. If a child's performance on *all* objectives was scored with a 0, the goal is scored 0.

Take language sample to collect data on this item. (Refer to pages 203–205.)

Objective 4.1   Uses subject pronouns

CRITERION   Child uses subject pronouns appropriately as the subject in phrases or sentences. Subject pronouns include I, you, he, she, it, we, and they. *Example:* Child asks, "He went home," "I did it," or "You have ice cream?" The number of different subject pronouns the child uses is less important than the child's ability to use a subject pronoun appropriate to the grammatical and semantic context of the sentence.

DIRECTIONS

Materials   Objects interesting to the child.

Procedure   *Observation:* Observe child's ability to use subject pronouns appropriately in phrases or sentences. *Example:* Child says, "He is big."
Direct Test: Use subject pronouns when referring to others within the context of activities, pausing to allow the child opportunities to refer to others. Ask questions if necessary. Observe child's ability to use subject pronouns to refer to others. *Examples:* Adult and child are playing with toy people, cars, and trucks. Adult describes activity by saying, "He is going to drive the car. Now he is driving to the store"; child says, "He is driving fast." Adult says, "She is jumping off the boat. Oh look! Now, what is she doing?"; child says, "She is swimming."

Note: Take language sample to collect data on this item. (Refer to pages 203–205.)

Objective 4.2   Uses object pronouns

CRITERION   Child uses object pronouns appropriately as the object (i.e., receives an object or relation) in phrases or sentences. Object pronouns include me, you, her, him, it, us, and them. *Example:* Child says, "John hurt me," "I want you to go," or "I gave it to her." The number of different object pronouns used by the child is less important than the child's ability to use an object pronoun appropriate to the grammatical and semantic context of the sentence.

DIRECTIONS

Materials   People and objects interesting to the child.

Procedure   *Observation:* Observe child's ability to use object pronouns appropriately in phrases or sentences. *Example:* Child says, "Give it to me."
Direct Test: Use object pronouns when referring to others within the context of activities, pausing to allow the child opportunities to refer to others. Ask questions if necessary. *Examples:* Adult passes out materials for art project and says, "I'll give him some paint and water. I'll give her some water"; child says, "Give her some paint, too." Adult says, "I gave one cracker to her and one to me. Who should I give this one to?"; child says, "Give it to me."

Note: Take language sample to collect data on this item. (Refer to pages 203–205.)

Objective 4.3   Uses possessive pronouns

CRITERION   Child uses possessive pronouns appropriately to express possession in phrases or sentences. Possessive pronouns include my/mine, your/yours, his, her/hers, its, our/ours, and their/theirs. *Examples:* Child says, "Those are her shoes" or "I like his toy better." The number of different possessive pronouns used by the child is less important than the child's ability to use a possessive pronoun appropriate to the grammatical and semantic context of the sentence.

DIRECTIONS

Materials   Objects that belong to people.

Procedure   *Observation:* Observe child's ability to use possessive pronouns appropriately to express possession in phrases and sentences. *Example:* Child says, "That's his truck."
Direct Test: Use possessive pronouns within context of activities, pausing to allow child opportunities to indicate possession. Ask questions about the ownership of objects. Observe the child's ability to use possessive pronouns appropriately. *Example:* Adult holds up coat and asks, "Whose is this?" Child says, "It's mine."

Note: Take language sample to collect data on this item. (Refer to pages 203–205.)

Objective 4.4   Uses indefinite pronouns

CRITERION   Child uses indefinite pronouns appropriately to refer to an unspecified person or object. Indefinite pronouns include the following:

any	anything	all	everything
some	something	lots	every
none	nothing	many	more

SC B

Examples: Child says, "Can't I have any?", "Do you want some?", "No one wants more," or "There's nothing to do." The number of different indefinite pronouns used by the child is less important than the child's ability to use an indefinite pronoun appropriate to the grammatical and semantic context of the sentence.

DIRECTIONS

Materials   Objects interesting to the child.

Procedure   *Observation:* Observe child's ability to use indefinite pronouns appropriately to refer to an unspecified person or object. *Example:* "I don't have anything."
Direct Test: Direct test is not appropriate for this item; however, use of indefinite pronouns may be encouraged by engaging in play with child and allowing child opportunities to describe objects, people, and events or by arranging events and asking child about them. *Example:* Adult and child are playing with blocks. Adult says, "I need a yellow block." Child says, "I have some here."

Note: Take language sample to collect data on this item. (Refer to pages 203–205.)

Objective 4.5   Uses demonstrative pronouns

CRITERION   Child uses demonstrative pronouns (e.g., this, that, these, those) appropriately to single out or identify objects. *Example:* Child says, "I want those," "That's not my coat," "Can I have this cookie?" or "These are mine." The number of different demonstrative pronouns used by the child is less important than the child's ability to use a demonstrative pronoun appropriate to the grammatical and semantic context of the sentence.

DIRECTIONS

Materials   Objects interesting to the child.

Procedure   *Observation:* Observe child's ability to use demonstrative pronouns appropriately. *Example:* Child says, "Give me that one."
Direct Test: Direct test is not appropriate for this item; however, use of demonstrative pronouns may be encouraged by engaging in play with child and allowing child opportunities to describe objects, people, and events or by arranging events and asking child about them. *Examples:* Child says, "I want a puzzle"; adult says, "Which one do you want?" and child points and says, "That one." Adult puts objects out of reach and asks child to indicate which one she wants.

Note: Take language sample to collect data on this item. (Refer to pages 203–205.)

SCB

GOAL 5   Uses descriptive words

CRITERION   Child uses descriptive, relational, and functional words as

- Adjectives
- Adverbs
- Prepositions
- Conjunctions
- Articles

DIRECTIONS   (See Objectives 5.1–5.6 for specific directions.)

Notes: If a child's performance on *all* objectives was scored with a 2, the goal is scored 2. If a child's performance on the objectives was scored with *any* combination of a 0, 1, or 2, the goal is scored 1. If a child's performance on *all* objectives was scored with a 0, the goal is scored 0.

Take language sample to collect data on this item. (Refer to pages 203–205.)

Objective 5.1   Uses adjectives

CRITERION   Child uses adjectives to modify nouns and pronouns. *Example:* Child says, "My hands are cold" or "I want the red pepper."

DIRECTIONS

Materials   Objects that have obvious physical characteristics.

Procedure   *Observation:* Observe child's ability to use adjectives to modify nouns and pronouns. *Example:* Child says, "Throw the big ball."
Direct Test: Within the context of activities, talk about the attributes of objects. Pause to allow child the opportunity to describe attributes of objects. Ask questions if necessary. Observe child's ability to use adjectives to modify nouns and pronouns. *Example:* Adult comments on child's painting, "You painted a big cat." Child says, "I made a little one, too."

Notes: This item is cross-referenced with Cognitive Domain, Strand B, Goals 1–6.

Take language sample to collect data on this item. (Refer to pages 203–205.)

SC B

Objective 5.2   Uses adjectives to make comparisons

CRITERION   Child uses adjectives to compare degrees of quality or quantity. *Example:* Child says, "My truck is best," "The red one is better," "She's the strongest one," or "I have the most ice cream."

DIRECTIONS

Materials   Objects interesting to the child.

Procedure   *Observation:* Observe child's ability to use adjectives to compare degrees of quality or quantity. *Example:* Child says, "I have more than you." *Direct Test:* Within the context of activities, use adjectives to compare objects. Pause to allow child the opportunity to make comparisons. Ask questions if necessary. Observe child's ability to use adjectives to compare degrees of quality or quantity. *Example:* Adult compares shapes child is using to make a collage by saying, "This circle is smaller than this one. And this circle is bigger." Child says, "Here is the biggest one."

Note: Take language sample to collect data on this item. (Refer to pages 203–205.)

Objective 5.3   Uses adverbs

CRITERION   Child uses adverbs to modify verbs. *Example:* Child says, "That tastes bad," "Let's go fast," or "He's talking loudly."

DIRECTIONS

Materials   Objects interesting to the child.

Procedure   *Observation:* Observe child's ability to use adverbs to modify words, phrases, and sentences. *Example:* Child says, "You're walking too slow." *Direct Test:* Within the context of activities, use adverbs to describe events. Pause to allow child the opportunity to describe events. Ask questions if necessary. Observe child's ability to use adverbs to describe events. *Examples:* When child is pushing cars around race track, adult comments, "Look at those cars going around the track"; child says, "They are going fast." During gross motor activity, adult designates child as leader to tell peers what to do when music begins (e.g., clap fast, walk slow, sing loud, jump high).

Note: Take language sample to collect data on this item. (Refer to pages 203–205.)

SCB

Objective 5.4 Uses prepositions

CRITERION Child uses prepositions or prepositional phrases appropriately. Prepositions include the following:

in	for	of	in front of	on
with	down	like	in back of	under
to	off	at	through	out
up	over	by	near	

The number of different prepositions used by the child is less important than the child's ability to use prepositions and prepositional phrases appropriate to the grammatical and semantic context of the sentence. *Example:* Child says, "Put it in the box," "It's on the table," or "She's sitting beside him."

DIRECTIONS

Materials Objects interesting to the child.

Procedure *Observation:* Observe child's ability to use prepositions and prepositional phrases appropriately. *Example:* Child says, "The doll is on the chair." *Direct Test:* Within the context of activities, use prepositions and prepositional phrases to describe location or direction of objects. Pause to allow child the opportunity to describe the location of objects. Ask questions if necessary. Observe child's ability to use prepositions and prepositional phrases to describe the location and direction of objects. *Example:* Adult says, "The baseball bat is on the chair, but I don't see the ball." Child says, "It's under the table."

Notes: This item is cross-referenced with Cognitive Domain, Strand B, Goal 6.

Take language sample to collect data on this item. (Refer to pages 203–205.)

Objective 5.5 Uses conjunctions

CRITERION Child uses conjunctions to connect words, phrases, and sentences. Conjunctions include the following:

and	or	so	only
but	because	if	except

Example: Child says, "I want juice and a cookie," "We want to play, but we don't want to go to bed," "We could draw or color," or "I like you because you're nice."

SC B

DIRECTIONS

Materials   Objects interesting to the child.

Procedure   *Observation:* Observe child's ability to use conjunctions to connect words, phrases, and sentences. *Example:* Child says, "I have a cat and a dog" or "Do you want ice cream or cake?"
Direct Test: Ask child questions that require child to list items. Observe child's ability to use conjunctions to connect words, phrases, and sentences. *Example:* Adult asks child to name all the things child likes to eat; child says, "I like spaghetti, and I like ice cream and pizza."

Note: Take language sample to collect data on this item. (Refer to pages 203–205.)

Objective 5.6   Uses articles

CRITERION   Child uses articles (i.e., the, a, an) to precede nouns. *Example:* "I want an ice cream cone" or "I can't find the ball."

DIRECTIONS

Materials   Objects interesting to the child.

Procedure   *Observation:* Observe child's ability to use articles to precede nouns. *Example:* Child says, "I want to play with the dump truck" or "May I have a cookie?"
Direct Test: Direct test is not appropriate for this item; however, use of articles may be encouraged by engaging in play with child and allowing child opportunities to describe objects and people or by asking child questions about objects and people. *Example:* When selecting objects for water play, adult says, "I want the bucket. What do you want?" Child says, "I want the sailboat."

Note: Take language sample to collect data on this item. (Refer to pages 203–205.)

DIRECTIONS FOR USING
THE SOCIAL-COMMUNICATION RECORDING FORM

Collecting and Recording Communicative Behavior

The purpose of collecting and recording a sample of a child's communicative behavior is to determine how the child typically communicates, both verbally and nonverbally. Language sampling and observation techniques allow the assessment of a child's comprehension and production of words and sentences, communicative functions and intentions, and interactions with the social environment (Lund & Dunchan, 1993; Retherford, 1987). Following are several procedures outlined for collecting samples of communicative behavior. Select the procedures that ensure the communicative behavior recorded during the observations is typical or representative of the way the child usually communicates.

1. *Become familiar with the child.* Get to know the child before you record a sample of communicative behavior. Children usually do not communicate at the same frequency or in the same way with strangers as they do with familiar people. It is not always possible to establish rapport with a child in an hour or even in a day or two. Allow several days, if necessary, before recording a communication sample, and allow time for the child to warm up at the beginning of an observation session before you begin to record the child's communicative behavior. The extra time invested will yield more accurate and useful information for programming.

2. *Collect several communicative samples.* Collect three or four short samples (e.g., 10–20 minutes) of the child's communicative behavior over several days in several settings, rather than one long sample in a single setting. The frequency of communicative responses may differ greatly for children at different times and under different conditions. Even several recording sessions may not yield an adequate sample of behavior for those children who use language infrequently. Make an effort to collect at least 50 separate communicative utterances (e.g., 50 single words or word combinations) for a single child. If two of the total number of samples recorded are collected in similar settings (e.g., two free play activities with the same materials and same children present), the sample should appear similar in frequency of words and phrases used and in the forms used by the child. If the two samples are not similar, collect a third sample in the same setting to determine which of the samples is more representative of the way the child usually communicates in that setting. Samples collected in different settings may be different in frequency of words and phrases used and in forms used, and may accurately reflect the child's typical performance in each respective setting (Barrie-Blackley, Musselwhite, & Rogister, 1978). For example, most children communicate differently with adults than with peers; hence, a child might use shorter, less complex language with a younger sibling in one setting than with a parent in another setting, yet both samples of behavior are accurate and representative. The task is to determine how the child communicates in a variety of settings typical for the child.

3. *Select routine settings and materials.* Settings used for sampling communicative behavior should be routine for the child (e.g., a free-play activity in the classroom, a parent–child or sibling–child dyad versus a structured activity with one adult and one child in a therapy room). Materials and activities should be centered around play with age-appropriate toys or around usually occurring activities (e.g., eating, dressing). Adult-directed classroom activities will probably not yield an accurate picture of how well the child usually communicates. Some materials that may encourage social-

communicative interactions include dish sets, dress-up clothes, water and sand, and toy buildings with people and vehicles.

4. *Techniques for interacting with children.* While taking the sample, you may interact with the child or you may observe the child's interactions with another adult or peer. In addition to verbatim recording at the time of the interaction, audiotaping and especially videotaping are useful for the collection and analysis of the child's communicative behavior. Children who use rudimentary gestures may be videotaped so that the context of their communicative behaviors can be observed, the meanings of the gestures inferred, and the patterns of interactions between the child and the environment discerned. Verbatim recording can be employed for children who use a formalized gestural system such as Signed English or those who use a communication board. Each word the child signs or points to should be written down just as if the child used the word verbally.

Allow the child to direct the activity and interactions. You may find it helpful at the beginning of the sampling to engage in play alongside the child while you describe your actions, the actions of your toys, and occasionally the actions of the child in a monologue fashion. Frequent, prolonged pauses will allow the child opportunities to request objects or actions, participate in your activity, or talk about the activity. Do not ask questions that require only a yes/no or single-word response, a manual gesture, or a head shake (e.g., Adult asks, "Is the man riding the motorcycle?" and the child nods head affirmatively; or adult asks, "What is the man riding on?" and the child says, "Motorcycle"). Listen to what the child has to say, and base your responses on the content of the child's verbal and gestural behavior.

USING THE SOCIAL-COMMUNICATION RECORDING AND SCORING FORMS

Social-Communication Recording Form

Use the Recording Form to record verbatim the child's understandable words and word combinations and the context in which they occurred. The child's name and a brief description of the activities in which the language sample was collected should be indicated at the top of the Social-Communication Recording Form (see Figure 7.1) The amount of time each language sample took should also be recorded. It may also be helpful to indicate on the form when the activity changed. For example, if 11 utterances were recorded during snack time (15-minute activity) and then utterances 12–22 were recorded during circle time (10-minute activity), an asterisk could be placed at numbers 12 and 23 to indicate a change in activity. This information may be useful when interpreting the results.

When using the recording form, record verbatim in longhand all child communications. For spoken responses, begin a new line each time the child begins a new utterance. A new utterance occurs when the child addresses a new person, when the child pauses for at least 2 seconds, or when the child uses intonation that signals the end of an utterance. If you cannot understand part of a word the child says, use the letter "u" in place of the unintelligible word. If an entire phrase or sentence is unintelligible, write a "u" in parentheses (u) on a separate line.

Information recorded in the column under the heading Context includes brief descriptions of objects and events that occur immediately before, during, or immediately after the child's communication. Information recorded should permit accurate interpretation of the child's words and sentences, but it should not be so detailed that it interferes with the accurate recording of the child's communication.

Under the remaining headings are columns that provide space to note the way the child's communication was used in relation to others. The headings include Initiation, to indicate that the child initiated an appropriate topic; Response to Comment, to indicate that the child responded to another's comment with a related comment; Response to Question, to indicate that the child responded to a question with a related answer; Imitation, to indicate that the child repeated others' words; and Unrelated, to indicate that the child's response appeared to be unrelated to the activity or conversational context.

If time permits after you record each utterance, and if the function of the utterance is clear, place a check mark in the appropriate columns to the right of the recorded utterance, indicating the function the child's utterance served. If the frequency of the child's utterances makes it difficult to check and record the type and the actual utterance, it is more important to concentrate on recording the actual utterance word for word. Many times a lull in the conversation later in the session will allow you to return to categorize the child's utterances. If you are not sure about the function and/or meaning of a child's utterance, leave the column blank.

Social-Communication Summary Form

After recording a child's language on the recording form, the language sample may be analyzed so that the AEPS Test items can be scored based on the sample. The Social-Communication Summary Form was designed for that purpose (see Figure 7.2).

The summary form is completed by reviewing each utterance for its categorization. For example, if the child's first utterance was, "I'm going outside," tally marks (卌) would be placed next to item 4.1: Uses subject pronouns (for the word "I" in "I'm); next to 1.2: Uses copula verb "to be" (for the "am" part of "I'm"); next to 1.6: Uses present progressive "ing" (for the verb "going"); and next to 5.3: Uses adverbs (for the word "outside"). The number of tally marks per objective does not translate directly to a score (i.e., 0, 1, or 2). The number of tally marks should be compared with the specific item criterion listed on the item page. As the complexity of the child's language increases, it may become difficult to categorize some words. For example, the word "outside" can be a noun, adjective, adverb, or preposition depending on its use. Resources such as a dictionary or basic English grammar text can be of help in categorizing language. If there is a speech and language specialist on the child's team, this portion of the AEPS should be analyzed in conjunction with him or her.

After an adequate number of utterances (at least 50 separate utterances or signals/gestures) have been categorized on the Social-Communication Summary Form, the information can be used to score Strand B of the Social-Communication Domain. The AEPS Test Manual should be consulted, and individual item criteria should be compared with data from the Summary Form when determining an item's score.

REFERENCES

Barrie-Blackley, S., Musselwhite, C., & Rogister, S. (1978). *Clinical oral language sampling.* Danville, IL: Interstate Printers and Publishers.

Lund, N.J., & Dunchan, J.F. (1993). *Assessing children's language in naturalistic contexts* (3rd ed.). Englewood Cliffs, NJ: Prentice Hall.

Retherford, S.K. (1987). *Guide to analysis of language transcripts.* Eau Claire, WI: Thinking Publications.

SOCIAL DOMAIN

Items in the Social Domain are designed to assess children's interactions with peers, responses to the environment, and knowledge of self and others. Items in this domain measure the acquisition of the following skills:

- Interaction with others
- Interaction with environment
- Knowledge of self and others

The development of social skills is closely related to and interdependent on the development of cognitive, social-communication, and adaptive skills; therefore, data from all these domains should be considered by the user when reviewing the Social Domain assessment outcomes. The influence of cultural values on children's social behavior should also be considered during administration of the Social Domain.

Strand A   Interaction with Others
- G1   Has play partners
  - 1.1   Responds to peers in distress or need
  - 1.2   Establishes and maintains proximity to peers
  - 1.3   Initiates greetings to familiar peers
  - 1.4   Responds to affective initiations from peers
- G2   Initiates cooperative activity
  - 2.1   Joins others in cooperative activity
  - 2.2   Maintains cooperative participation with others
  - 2.3   Shares or exchanges objects
- G3   Resolves conflicts by selecting effective strategy
  - 3.1   Negotiates to resolve conflicts
  - 3.2   Uses simple strategies to resolve conflicts
  - 3.3   Claims and defends possessions

Strand B   Interaction with Environment
- G1   Meets physical needs in socially appropriate ways
  - 1.1   Meets physical needs when uncomfortable, sick, hurt, or tired
  - 1.2   Meets observable physical needs
  - 1.3   Meets physical needs of hunger and thirst
- G2   Follows context-specific rules outside home and classroom
  - 2.1   Seeks adult permission
  - 2.2   Follows established rules at home and in classroom

Strand C   Knowledge of Self and Others
- G1   Communicates personal likes and dislikes
  - 1.1   Initiates preferred activities
  - 1.2   Selects activities and/or objects

G2   Relates identifying information about self and others
   2.1   States address
   2.2   States telephone number
   2.3   Knows birthday
   2.4   Names siblings and gives full name of self
   2.5   Knows gender of self and others
   2.6   Knows name and age
G3   Accurately identifies affect/emotions in others and self consistent with demonstrated behaviors
   3.1   Accurately identifies affect/emotions of others
   3.2   Accurately identifies own affect/emotions

Strand A   Interaction with Others

GOAL 1   Has play partners

CRITERION   Child establishes and maintains proximity with peers and cooperatively plays with partners during child-directed free choice activity
(e.g., free play, outdoor play, bus ride). *Example:* During free time,
child walks over to peer swinging on tire swing and says, "I'll push
you," and peer and child take turns pushing each other on the swing.

DIRECTIONS

Materials   No materials are required.

Procedure   *Observation:* During free time, observe child's ability to establish and
maintain proximity to play partners and cooperatively play with partners. *Example:* During free time, child walks over to peer in library corner and says, "I'll help make a Lite Brite picture." Peer and child work
together to create a picture.
Direct Test: Direct test is not appropriate for this item; however, social
behavior may be facilitated by grouping children considering individual child interests, peer preference, and developmental levels of functioning. Toys and materials that encourage interaction should be made
available to the child.

Note: Child's behavior may change as child becomes familiar with the environment.

Objective 1.1   Responds to peers in distress or need

CRITERION   Child responds appropriately to peers in distress or need. *Examples:*
Child pats or hugs peer who is crying. Child helps peer move box of
toys that is too heavy to move alone.

DIRECTIONS

Materials   No materials are required.

Procedure   *Observation:* Observe child's ability to respond appropriately to peers in
distress or need. *Example:* Child helps peer clean up spilled juice.
Direct Test: Direct test is not appropriate for this item.

Objective 1.2   Establishes and maintains proximity to peers

CRITERION   Establishes and maintains proximity to peers during unstructured, child-directed activity.

DIRECTIONS

Materials   No materials are required.

Procedure   *Observation:* During free time, observe child's ability to establish and maintain proximity to peer. Child should be close enough to permit interaction with peer. *Examples:* Child moves toward peer playing with blocks and cars and plays with the cars and a ramp next to peer. Child moves toward peer playing in playhouse and plays with toys next to peer (child initiates contact with peer through a play activity and maintains proximity to allow continued interaction).
Direct Test: Direct test is not appropriate for this item; however, social behavior may be facilitated by grouping children considering individual child interests, peer preference, and developmental levels of functioning. Toys and materials that encourage interaction should be available.

Objective 1.3   Initiates greetings to familiar peers

CRITERION   Child greets familiar peers by vocalizing, verbalizing, hugging, patting, touching, or smiling.

DIRECTIONS

Materials   No materials are required.

Procedure   *Observation:* Observe child's ability to initiate a greeting to a familiar peer. *Example:* Child says "Hi" to a peer when peer arrives at school.
Direct Test: Direct test is not appropriate for this item; however, social behavior may be facilitated by grouping children considering individual child interests, peer preference, and developmental levels of functioning. Toys and materials that encourage interaction should be available.

Soc A

Objective 1.4 Responds to affective initiations from peers

CRITERION Child responds with socially appropriate affect to peer's affective initiation. *Examples:* Child smiles in response to peer's smile. Child says "Hi" in response to peer's greeting. Child frowns and turns away in response to peer's anger.

DIRECTIONS

Materials No materials are required.

Procedure *Observation:* When child is with peers, observe child's ability to respond with socially appropriate affect to peers' affective initiations. *Example:* Child hugs peer in response to peer snuggling close to the child.
Direct Test: Direct test is not appropriate for this item; however, social behavior may be facilitated by grouping children considering individual child interests, peer preference, and developmental levels of functioning. Toys and materials that encourage interaction should be available.

GOAL 2 Initiates cooperative activity

CRITERION Child uses verbal or nonverbal strategies to initiate cooperative activity and encourage peer(s) to participate. *Examples:* Child says, "Come on, let's build a house" to group of peers. Child assigns jobs, roles, or identities and encourages peers to carry them out. Child says, "You play with this truck," while handing truck to peer as child pushes another truck.

DIRECTIONS

Materials Toys that encourage interaction.

Procedure *Observation:* Observe child's ability to use verbal or nonverbal strategies to initiate cooperative activity and encourage peers to participate. *Example:* Child says, "It's time to clean up" to group of peers, assigns jobs to be done, and encourages peers to carry them out.
Direct Test: Direct test is not appropriate for this item; however, social behavior may be facilitated by grouping children considering individual child interests, peer preference, and developmental levels of functioning. Toys and materials that encourage interaction should be available.

Note: This item is cross-referenced with Social-Communication Domain, Strand A, Objective 1.5.

Objective 2.1   Joins others in cooperative activity

CRITERION   Child uses socially appropriate verbal or nonverbal strategies to join peers engaged in cooperative activities. *Examples:* Child approaches group of peers building a sand castle, sits next to them for a while, then begins to help peer who is digging a tunnel to the castle. Child approaches peers playing house and says, "Hey, I could be the baby!" and peer says, "Okay."

DIRECTIONS

Materials   Toys that encourage interaction.

Procedure   *Observation:* Observe child's ability to use verbal or nonverbal strategies to join peers engaged in cooperative play. *Example:* Child approaches peers playing doctor and says, "Hey, could I be the doctor?" and peers say, "Well, okay."
Direct Test: Direct test is not appropriate for this item; however, social behavior may be facilitated by grouping children considering individual child interests, peer preference, and developmental levels of functioning. Toys and materials that encourage interaction should be available.

Note: This item is cross-referenced with Cognitive Domain, Strand A, Goal 2.

Objective 2.2   Maintains cooperative participation with others

---

CRITERION   Child maintains job, role, or identity that supplements another child's job, role, or identity during a cooperative activity. *Example:* Child holds two blocks together while peer puts a third block on top to build a house.

DIRECTIONS

Materials   Toys that encourage interaction.

Procedure   *Observation:* Observe child's ability to maintain job or role or identity that supplements another child's job, role, or identity during a cooperative activity. *Example:* Child holds truck axle while peer puts a wheel on the axle.
Direct Test: Direct test is not appropriate for this item; however, social behavior may be facilitated by grouping children considering individual child interests, peer preference, and developmental levels of functioning. Toys and materials that encourage interaction should be available.

Note: This item is cross-referenced with Cognitive Domain, Strand A, Goal 2.

Objective 2.3   Shares or exchanges objects

CRITERION   During group activities, child shares or exchanges objects with peer(s) engaged in the same activity. *Example:* Child shares glue bottle with peer when both are gluing leaves and flowers onto paper.

DIRECTIONS

Materials   Toys that encourage interaction.

Procedure   *Observation:* During group activities, observe child's ability to share or exchange objects with peers engaged in the same activity. *Example:* Child shares watercolor box with peer when both are painting pictures.

Direct Test: Present objects during group activities and observe child's ability to share or exchange objects with peers engaged in the same activity.

GOAL 3   Resolves conflicts by selecting effective strategy

CRITERION   Child selects appropriate strategies for particular situations to resolve conflicts. Strategies include the following:

- Negotiating
- Using simple strategies
- Claiming and defending possessions

DIRECTIONS   (See Objectives 3.1–3.3 for specific directions.)

Note: If a child's performance on *all* objectives was scored with a 2, the goal is scored 2. If a child's performance on the objectives was scored with *any* combination of a 0, 1, or 2, the goal is scored 1. If a child's performance on *all* objectives was scored with a 0, the goal is scored 0.

Objective 3.1   Negotiates to resolve conflicts

CRITERION   Child initiates a solution to bring about agreement when in conflict with a peer or adult. *Example:* Child says to a peer, "I'll dig here, and you dig there" when both want to dig in same corner of sandbox.

DIRECTIONS

Materials   No materials are required.

Procedure   *Observation:* When child is in conflict with another person, observe child's ability to initiate a solution to bring about agreement. *Example:* Child says to another child, "I'll play with the hammer, and you play with the saw," when both want to play with saw.
Direct Test: Direct test is not appropriate for this item.

Objective 3.2   Uses simple strategies to resolve conflicts

CRITERION   Child uses variety of simple strategies (i.e., makes demand, walks/runs away, reports to adult) to resolve conflicts with another person. *Example:* When peer hits child, child turns to adult and says, "Susan hit me," or child moves away from peer.

DIRECTIONS

Materials   No materials are required.

Procedure   *Observation:* Observe child's ability to use variety of simple strategies to resolve conflicts with another person. *Example:* When peer grabs toy from child, child says, "Give that to me."
Direct Test: Direct test is not appropriate for this item.

Objective 3.3   Claims and defends possessions

CRITERION   Child uses verbal or nonverbal strategies to claim and defend possessions. *Example:* Child says, "That toy is mine," and takes toy from peer.

DIRECTIONS

Materials   Objects interesting to the child.

Procedure   *Observation:* Observe child's ability to use verbal or nonverbal strategies to claim and defend possessions. *Example:* Child grabs back a toy from peer who has taken it.
Direct Test: Direct test is not appropriate for this item.

Soc A

Strand B   Interaction with Environment

GOAL 1   Meets physical needs in socially appropriate ways

CRITERION   Child uses socially appropriate strategies to meet physical needs such
as the following:

- Physical needs when uncomfortable, sick, hurt, or tired
- Observable physical needs
- Physical needs of hunger and thirst

DIRECTIONS   (See Objectives 1.1–1.3 for specific directions.)

Note: If a child's performance on *all* objectives was scored with a 2, the goal is scored 2.
If a child's performance on the objectives was scored with *any* combination of a
0, 1, or 2, the goal is scored 1. If a child's performance on *all* objectives was
scored with a 0, the goal is scored 0.

Objective 1.1   Meets physical needs when uncomfortable, sick, hurt, or tired

CRITERION   Child uses socially appropriate ways to meet physical needs when
uncomfortable, sick, hurt, or tired. *Examples:* Child requests adult help
when injured or sick. Child takes nap when tired. Child puts on coat
when cold.

DIRECTIONS

Materials   No materials are required.

Procedure   *Observation:* Observe child's ability to use socially appropriate ways
to meet physical needs when uncomfortable, sick, hurt, or tired.
Examples: Child lies down when not feeling well. Child takes off
sweater when hot.
Direct Test: Direct test is not appropriate for this item.

Objective 1.2　　Meets observable physical needs

CRITERION　　Child uses socially appropriate ways to meet observable physical needs. *Examples:* Child washes hands when hands are dirty. Child removes wet or soiled clothing.

DIRECTIONS

Materials　　No materials are required.

Procedure　　*Observation:* Observe child's ability to use socially appropriate ways to meet observable physical needs. *Example:* Child removes wet socks and shoes.
Direct Test: Direct test is not appropriate for this item.

Objective 1.3　　Meets physical needs of hunger and thirst

CRITERION　　Child uses socially appropriate ways to express or meet physical needs of hunger and thirst. *Examples:* Child requests food or drink. Child gets drink of milk when thirsty.

DIRECTIONS

Materials　　No materials are required.

Procedure　　*Observation:* Observe child's ability to meet physical needs of hunger and thirst. *Example:* Child says, "I'm hungry," when hungry.
Direct Test: Direct test is not appropriate for this item.

GOAL 2　　Follows context-specific rules outside home and classroom

CRITERION　　Child follows context-specific rules outside home and classroom (e.g., store, park, doctor's office, restaurant, bus). *Example:* Child follows rule not to touch things when in grocery store.

DIRECTIONS

Materials　　No materials are required.

Procedure   *Observation:* Observe child's ability to follow context-specific rules outside home and classroom. *Example:* Child follows rule to remain in seat during bus ride.
Direct Test: Present rules contextually specific to the activity/environment and observe child's ability to follow them. *Example:* During a walk, child holds a peer's hand in response to adult's directions.

Note: This item may have to be scored by parent report because not all classrooms take field trips.

Objective 2.1   Seeks adult permission

CRITERION   Child asks adult permission as required to engage in established routines at home, at school, and in the community. *Examples:* Child asks permission to leave the group and go to the bathroom. Child asks caregiver for permission to go to neighbor's house.

DIRECTIONS

Materials   No materials are required.

Procedure   *Observation:* Observe child's ability to ask adult permission as required to engage in established routines at home, at school, and in the community. *Example:* Child asks permission to go outside after finishing group activity.
Direct Test: Direct test is not appropriate for this item.

Objective 2.2   Follows established rules at home and in classroom

---

CRITERION   Child follows established rules at home and in the classroom. Adult may provide group directions/cues (e.g., "It's story time" or "Time to line up"). *Examples:* Child washes hands before snack or waits turn to speak.

DIRECTIONS

Materials   No materials are required.

Procedure   *Observation:* Observe child's ability to follow established rules at home and in the classroom. *Example:* During large group activity, child raises hand to be recognized.
Direct Test: Direct test is not appropriate for this item.

Soc B

Strand C   Knowledge of Self and Others

GOAL 1   Communicates personal likes and dislikes

CRITERION   Child communicates personal likes and dislikes about people, objects, and activities. *Examples:* Child says, "Ummm, I love chocolate cake" while eating cake. Child says, "I don't like to play at Gretchen's house."

DIRECTIONS

Materials   No materials are required.

Procedure   *Observation:* Observe child's ability to communicate personal likes and dislikes about people, objects, and activities. *Example:* Child says, "I don't want to play outside today."
Direct Test: Direct test is not appropriate for this item.

Note: This item is cross-referenced with Social-Communication Domain, Strand A, Objective 1.3.

Objective 1.1   Initiates preferred activities

CRITERION   Child initiates preferred purposeful activities during free time. General cues may be provided by adult (e.g., "Find something to do"). *Examples:* Child goes to shelf and selects book to look at during free time. Child finishes work and gets paper and markers for coloring.

DIRECTIONS

Materials   Objects interesting to the child.

Procedure   *Observation:* During free time, observe child's ability to initiate preferred activity. *Example:* Child chooses to play with blocks with a peer.
Direct Test: Direct test is not appropriate for this item.

Objective 1.2   Selects activities and/or objects

CRITERION   Child selects an activity or object from a choice of at least two in the daily routine. *Examples:* Child selects crackers from a plate of crackers and cheese. Child selects puzzle from a table with books, puzzles, and tea set.

DIRECTIONS

Materials   Objects interesting to the child.

Procedure   *Observation:* Observe child's ability to select an activity or object when given a choice of at least two within the daily routine. *Example:* Child chooses to paint from a choice of three activities.
Direct Test: Present at least two choices of an activity or object and observe child's ability to select an activity or object. *Example:* Child selects an apple from a basket of apples, bananas, and oranges.

GOAL 2   Relates identifying information about self and others

CRITERION   Child correctly communicates the following information about self and others:

- Address (number, street, and town)
- Telephone number
- Birthday (month and day)
- Names of siblings and full name of self
- Gender (self and others)
- First name and age

DIRECTIONS   (See Objectives 2.1–2.6 for specific directions.)

Note: If a child's performance on *all* objectives was scored with a 2, the goal is scored 2. If a child's performance on the objectives was scored with *any* combination of a 0, 1, or 2, the goal is scored 1. If a child's performance on *all* objectives was scored with a 0, the goal is scored 0.

Objective 2.1   States address

CRITERION   Child correctly states own address (including number, street, and town).

DIRECTIONS

Materials   No materials are required.

Procedure   *Observation:* Observe child's ability to correctly state own address.
Direct Test: Ask child to tell you address. Observe child's ability to state own address.

Note: This item is cross-referenced with Cognitive Domain, Strand E, Goal 2.

Objective 2.2   States telephone number

CRITERION   Child correctly states own telephone number.

DIRECTIONS

Materials   No materials are required.

Procedure   *Observation:* Observe child's ability to correctly state own telephone number.
Direct Test: Ask child to tell you telephone number. Observe child's ability to correctly state own telephone number.

Objective 2.3   Knows birthday

CRITERION   Child correctly states month and day of own birthday.

DIRECTIONS

Materials   No materials are required.

Procedure   *Observation:* Observe child's ability to correctly state own birthday, including month and day.
Direct Test: Ask child to tell you birthday. Observe child's ability to correctly state month and day of own birthday.

Note: This item is cross-referenced with Cognitive Domain, Strand E, Objective 2.1.

Objective 2.4   Names siblings and gives full name of self

CRITERION   Child correctly states first names of siblings and first and last names of self.

DIRECTIONS

Materials   No materials are required.

Procedure   *Observation:* Observe child's ability to correctly state first names of siblings and first and last names of self.

Direct Test: Ask child to tell you names of siblings and own name. Observe child's ability to correctly state first names of siblings and first and last names of self.

Note: This item is cross-referenced with Cognitive Domain, Strand E, Objective 2.1.

Objective 2.5   Knows gender of self and others

CRITERION   Child correctly identifies self and others as a girl or a boy.

DIRECTIONS

Materials   No materials are required.

Procedure   *Observation:* Observe child's ability to correctly identify self and others as a girl or a boy.
Direct Test: Ask child to identify self and others as girl or boy. Observe child's ability to correctly identify self and others as a girl or a boy.

Objective 2.6   Knows name and age

CRITERION   Child correctly states own first name and age in years.

DIRECTIONS

Materials   No materials are required.

Procedure   *Observation:* Observe child's ability to correctly state own first name and age in years.
Direct Test: Ask child to tell you name and age. Observe child's ability to correctly state own first name and age in years

Note: This item is cross-referenced with Cognitive Domain, Strand E, Objective 2.1.

GOAL 3   Accurately identifies affect/emotions in others and self consistent with demonstrated behaviors

CRITERION   Child accurately identifies affect/emotions (e.g., happy, sad, angry, mad, lonely) displayed by self and others.

DIRECTIONS   (See Objectives 3.1–3.2 for specific directions.)

Soc C

Note: If a child's performance on *all* objectives was scored with a 2, the goal is scored 2. If a child's performance on the objectives was scored with *any* combination of a 0, 1, or 2, the goal is scored 1. If a child's performance on *all* objectives was scored with a 0, the goal is scored 0.

Objective 3.1   Accurately identifies affect/emotions of others

CRITERION   Child identifies affect/emotions of others that are consistent with behaviors being displayed. *Example:* Child signs, "He's hurt," in response to a peer's crying after falling on the playground.

DIRECTIONS

Materials   No materials are required.

Procedure   *Observation:* Observe child's ability to identify affect/emotions of others that are consistent with demonstrated behaviors. *Example*: Child says, "She likes it," in response to a peer smiling at getting a favorite cookie during snack time.
Direct Test: Present a picture or situation of person showing some identifiable emotions and ask child how the person feels. Observe child's ability to accurately identify affect/emotions.

Objective 3.2   Accurately identifies own affect/emotions

CRITERION   Child identifies own affect/emotions that are consistent with displayed behaviors. *Example:* Child frowns and says, "Yuk, I don't like it," after sampling distasteful food.

DIRECTIONS

Materials   No materials are required.

Procedure   *Observation:* Observe child's ability to identify own affect/emotions that are consistent with demonstrated behaviors. *Example*: Child cries after losing a doll and says, "I'm sad."
Direct Test: Ask child to identify own affect/emotions and observe child's ability to be consistent with own behaviors. *Example:* Child throws toy and stomps away from play area. Teacher asks, "How do you feel?" Child says, "I'm mad."

Family Participation in the Assessment, Evaluation, and Programming System

Family Participation Process

The differences among families and their strengths and needs require considerable flexibility in approach in order to be successful in assisting them to achieve their selected outcomes. A seven-step procedure for encouraging family participation in assessment, IEP/IFSP development, intervention, and subsequent evaluation of child progress is described in this chapter. This process should be viewed as a set of suggested guidelines rather than an immutable sequence.

A schematic of the seven steps and their sequence and relationships is shown in Figure 8.1. Each of the seven steps is described below.

1. The first step in this process is an *introductory meeting*. During this meeting, the program philosophy and goals are explained to the family, and the network of services and available program resources is briefly reviewed. In addition, the family describes their concerns and interests, determines the areas of assessment they think are important and the roles they want to play, and decides on the format for assessment procedures. (This step is described in further detail later in this chapter.)
2. *Programmatic assessments* are initiated in the second step. The family completes the AEPS Family Interest Survey and AEPS Family Report independently, or, if the family prefers, these tools may be completed by the family and interventionist working together. At the same time, the professional team can administer the AEPS Test or it can be completed with the child by an individual team member who shares the results with the other team members.
3. The third step in the process is the *outcome and intervention planning meeting*. When the test administrations are complete, the information should be summarized; therefore, the purpose of this meeting is to accumulate information for writing the IEP/IFSP. Priorities are established, outcomes are defined, and intervention

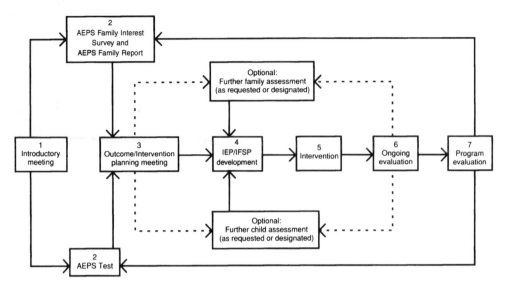

Figure 8.1.   The AEPS process for family participation in assessment, intervention, and evaluation.

and evaluation plans are designed to achieve the outcomes. (This step is discussed in detail later in this chapter.)

4.   The *IEP/IFSP document* is written and signed. Additional assessment information is included, and outcomes are chosen.

5.   *Intervention* begins on the prioritized IEP/IFSP outcomes and in the setting specified in the IEP/IFSP. Progress is monitored as specified in the IEP/IFSP.

6.   *Ongoing evaluations* are conducted as specified in the IEP/IFSP. The AEPS Child Progress Record can be used to help families monitor their child's progress. Outcome statements and intervention activities are revised as needed based on progress or evaluation information.

7.   Annual *program evaluation* is completed.

Except for the introductory meeting and the outcome and planning meeting, procedures for implementing these seven steps are described in Chapters 2, 3, 4, and 5 of this volume. Procedures for conducting the interviews are presented below.

INTRODUCTORY MEETING

The first phase in involving families is an introductory meeting during which intake procedures and program preliminaries are explained to parents and other family members. The setting for this meeting should be comfortable and convenient for the family. The program representative should be familiar with the referral source, knowledgeable about the program, and skilled in interviewing and communicating information verbally.

There are two main purposes for the introductory meeting: 1) to provide information and clarification about the program and 2) to establish the format for the programmatic assessments. The meeting is an opportunity for the family to become familiar with the program. In addition, confidentiality is discussed and the necessary program forms are completed.

The program information needs will vary with each family depending on their source of referral and their previous experiences. For some, a brief interview will be sufficient, whereas others may request detailed information. The program philosophy and goals should be explained to the family, as well as the network of services and program resources. The family may be ready to consider various program services and resources or they may need more time and assessment information. Supportive print materials can be helpful if requested. Caution must be taken to avoid providing more information than the family can manage.

When establishing the format for future meetings and assessments, the family should describe their concerns, determine the areas of assessment they believe are important, and decide on the format for assessment procedures. Providing families with choices about the type or level of involvement in the assessment process helps to establish their role as decision makers and partners in the program. Some families will choose to complete the Family Interest Survey and Family Report independently, whereas others will prefer to provide the information through a meeting. Some families will want to participate in the child's assessment; others will want to watch and offer comments. Some families may choose to have the professional team complete the assessment. All options are acceptable, and the best way to find out which format the family prefers is to ask.

OUTCOME AND INTERVENTION PLANNING MEETING

The outcome and intervention planning meeting is scheduled to occur on completion of the child's programmatic assessment (i.e., AEPS Test) and the family's identification of strengths and interests (i.e., AEPS Family Interest Survey). By this time, the assessment information has been summarized and possible priorities for intervention have been identified by the family and professionals. The purpose of the outcome and intervention planning meeting is to prepare for the IEP/IFSP meeting by 1) identifying priorities for developing outcomes, 2) designing intervention activities, and 3) determining an acceptable evaluation plan for each outcome.

The meeting should be attended by a program staff member(s) familiar with the child and family and with whom parents or caregivers are comfortable. It is helpful if the professional person primarily responsible for assisting the family in the development of the IEP/IFSP (e.g., service coordinator) attends this meeting.

The procedure for the outcome and intervention planning meeting may vary for each family; however, there are some basic elements that should be included in the process. These include an explanation of the planning process and the tasks to be accomplished; a summary of available assessment information; and an opportunity to update, change, add, or delete assessment information. Family priorities should be identified, and outcome statements should be developed with associated intervention activities and evaluation plans. The service coordinator should be selected if this has not already been done. At the end, a summary of the meeting is helpful to remind all participants of their future roles, to clarify any concerns, and to confirm the time and place for the next meeting, if appropriate.

1. **How would you like to see this outcome achieved? Can you think of some ways you would like to make this happen?**

   Purpose: These exploratory questions encourage the family to identify the "ideal" plan for developing this outcome. They encourage the family and the other team participants to think of several strategies and to explore a range of alternatives before identifying specific activities.

2. **Who could participate?**

   Purpose: This exploratory question identifies possible participants and agencies.

   A. *Are these people or agencies willing and able to participate?*
   B. *Will the participation of these individuals or agencies result in the family gaining the information or skills that will improve their ability to enhance their child's development?*

   Purpose: These confirmatory questions are designed to ensure that the individuals identified are truly potential participants and that their services will be able to produce the outcome as it is stated. This will help the team use their time effectively by encouraging them to choose the best resources before developing the intervention activities.

3. **How would we (you) go about doing this? Where should we start? How shall we proceed?**

   Purpose: Brainstorming intervention activities helps to ensure that the activities fit within the structure and values of the family. Exploring a variety of options offers opportunities for all participants to have input and make suggestions. Decisions about the preferred activities should be made collaboratively with the final decision made by the family.

   A. *Do the activities proceed in a logical or sequential progression?*
   B. *Will the activities selected achieve the outcome?*
   C. *Are the activities compatible with the family values?*
   D. *Will participation by any family member adversely affect any other family member? If so, is the ratio of cost to benefit acceptable to the family? If not, are there any other alternatives?*

   Purpose: These confirmatory questions assist the team in planning an effective and efficient intervention plan. These questions provide a check and balance system for developing not only an innovative and individualized plan, but one that includes instructional design components with established efficacy. These questions again remind all team members to consider the family first. Be sure the family accepts and agrees with the plan. Be sure that the plan does not isolate any family member from the rest of the family or neglect other family members.

4. **What resources are needed to complete these activities?**

   Purpose: The identification of resources is similar to the identification of key participants.

   A. *Are the resources available?*
   B. *Can they be acquired?*
   C. *By whom?*
   D. *At whose expense?*

   Purpose: Careful plans often have to be abandoned for lack of resources. To save time and frustration, it is helpful to ensure that the resources necessary to complete the activities are readily available or can be acquired.

5. **How will we (you) know when the outcome is achieved? What are effective evaluation activities? What evaluation activities are the most functional for the desired outcome and the family?**

   Purpose: Developing criteria may be a new and challenging task for many families. Developing criteria that are written in "family friendly" language may be a new and challenging task for many professionals. This is an area where the IFSP differs substantially from the IEP. Families do not have to reach a certain percentage of performance in a specified number of days. The statement should reflect what the family identifies as mastery. The evaluation activities should also reflect the needs and interests of the family and the other participants in the intervention plan.

   A. *Are the timelines acceptable to participants?*
   B. *Who will assume responsibility for monitoring progress?*
   C. *When and how often will progress be monitored?*

   Purpose: This final set of confirmatory questions focuses on the details of the intervention and evaluation plan to ensure that it will be carried out in a timely manner.

Figure 8.2.   Questions for the outcome and intervention planning meeting. Exploratory questions are printed in **bold**, and confirmatory questions are printed in *italic*.

IEP/IFSP Planning Guide

Child's name: Taylor   Birthdate: 1/5/92   Family Name: McClure

Date of IEP/IFSP: 6/6/95   Time: 4:30 PM   Location: McClure's home

Family Members/Professionals/Agency Representatives your family wishes to attend meeting:
Mary (grandmother), Ray (classroom interventionist), Kate (physical therapist), Linda (service coordinator)

Strengths

Child Strengths:
(Include recent progress or changes, favorite activities, special qualities)

Starting to use 2-word sentences

Likes her new glasses

Loves circle time and washing babies

Family Strengths:
(Include available resources, special qualities, abilities, supports)

Insurance is okay

Good child care

Family Priorities

Child Goals:
(Taken from AEPS Family Report)

1. Playing more with friends
2. Referral to physical therapist

3. Using longer sentences

4.

5.

Family Interests
(Taken from AEPS Family Interest Survey)

1. Want to know more about services
2. Want information on vision training
3. Want child care teacher to know how to work with Taylor
4. Want to know more about positioning Taylor for eating and driving in the car
5.

Figure 8.3.   A completed example of an IEP/IFSP Planning Guide.

The planning can begin with a summary of available assessment information. The family should be encouraged to determine the format for presenting the information. They may feel comfortable leading the discussion or they may prefer to hear the summaries of the other participants first. It is critical to let the family identify their own and their child's strengths and interests. Additional information may be gathered from the family at this time, or the request for additional assessments or information may be made. Priorities are established by the family based on their information and the information presented to them. From these priorities, goals, outcome statements, or both are developed. For each goal or outcome statement, an intervention and evaluation plan should be developed.

To assist in the development of intervention and evaluation plans, a series of exploratory (open-ended) and confirmatory (close-ended) questions can be posed. A list of possible questions is contained in Figure 8.2 (on p. 228). The exploratory questions are printed in bold and are followed by the confirmatory questions, which are

---

Family Intervention Planning Worksheet

Child's Name: Taylor   Priority Number: 4

Date: 5/25/95   Assessment Instrument: Family Interest Survey (FIS)

Outcome Statement:

Joe and Alice, Taylor's parents, will be able to position Taylor comfortably at home and while traveling in the car.

Intervention Activities:

During a home visit, Kate, a physical therapy consultant from the local hospital, will demonstrate the most appropriate ways to transfer and position Taylor. This visit will take place on a Saturday morning so that both parents can participate.

Kate will adapt the car seat that Taylor's mother has already purchased to provide the best support for Taylor. Joe has confirmed that the family insurance plan will cover the cost of the adaptations. Kate will also help adapt a chair for Taylor to use during meals.

Parents will use the adapted car seat when traveling and the chair during mealtimes instead of holding Taylor on their laps.

Ray, the classroom interventionist, and Linda, the service coordinator, will provide follow-up information and assistance as requested by parents or as observed to be necessary.

Linda will contact Kate for additional assistance at the family's request.

Evaluation Activities:

The initial visit by the physical therapist should occur within 30 days, with adaptations completed 2 weeks after the visit. Parents and interventionists will rate the success of the activities on a 3-point scale:

1. Outcome completed as desired.
2. Progress made; ongoing monitoring to continue.
3. Outcome unchanged; revise activities.

Review process will be completed within 90 days by Joe, Alice, Kate, Ray, and Linda.

Figure 8.4.   A completed example of a Family Intervention Planning Worksheet.

printed in italic. These questions may be helpful to ensure that the information necessary to achieve the desired outcome is included. The exploratory questions offer opportunities to generate ideas, identify alternatives, and share information. They should be used to initiate discussion about the intervention or evaluation plan. The confirmatory questions are designed to provide clarification and offer a check system to ensure that the selected options will be useful in achieving the outcome in a timely and effective manner.

These questions should be used only as a guide. For some outcome statements, the intervention and evaluation plan may be straightforward and not require the generating of options and alternative strategies. Other outcome statements may need considerable exploration to develop an effective and functional plan for the family. The family should be asked their views first; then, after considering the family's response, the other participants can add information or suggestions.

Some families may find it useful to write down information as the interview proceeds or at its termination. The IEP/IFSP Planning Guide and the Family Intervention Planning Worksheet may be useful forms for this purpose. Completed examples of these forms are shown in Figures 8.3 (on p. 229) and 8.4, respectively.

It may be decided at the outcome and intervention planning meeting or the IEP/IFSP meeting that additional information will be useful. At that time, referrals may be initiated for specific family or child assessments, such as a parent–child interaction scale or an articulation evaluation.

AEPS
Family Interest Survey

The AEPS Family Interest Survey has 30 items and an open-ended question to identify family interests. Priority interests can also be designated. In addition, the Family Interest Survey permits families to indicate the service delivery method they prefer.

DEVELOPMENT OF
THE FAMILY INTEREST SURVEY

Item development for the Family Interest Survey was based on a comprehensive review of the family assessment and intervention literature. An analysis was conducted of the more relevant and frequently used surveys developed for families of children with disabilities (e.g., *Family Needs Survey* [Bailey & Simeonsson, 1988]; the *Family Information Preference Inventory* [Turnbull & Turnbull, 1986]; *Parent Needs Survey* [Seligman & Darling, 1989]; *Prioritizing Family Needs Scale* [Finn & Vadasy, 1988]). Based on the reviewed work, a preliminary survey was developed. The draft was reviewed by 12 early interventionists, 8 parents of young children with disabilities, and 20 parents of typically developing children. Comments and feedback from this group of reviewers were used to delete, add, and clarify items.

The revised Family Interest Survey was used by 30 interventionists and 30 families. Feedback from these users suggested that families and interventionists found that the Family Interest Survey generated useful information. In addition, families reported finding it nonintrusive and helpful in focusing on their needs and interests.

The reading level for items on the Family Interest Survey was analyzed using the Fry method (Collins-Cheek & Collins, 1984). Sentence length was found to be at the sixth-grade reading level while syllable length was at the ninth-grade level. A decision was made to include words such as *positioning* and *development* rather than replace them with more simplified descriptors that might not represent concepts as accurately.

CHAPTER 9

Content

The 30 items on the Family Interest Survey are divided into the categories of child, family, and community interests. The content of the Family Interest Survey is designed to assist parents or caregivers and interventionists in identifying the following types of interests: 1) child focused (e.g., adaptive equipment for assisting the child in eating); 2) family focused (e.g., having access to family recreational programs); and 3) community focused (e.g., finding child care or respite for the family). Each of the three categories includes items that identify needs for having access to information, formal and informal support, participation in activities, and utilizing resources.

Items on the Family Interest Survey are designed to reflect family interest in information, activities, resources, or services rather than on problems associated with parenting a child with special needs (e.g., "I am interested in learning to talk and play with my child", "I am interested in gaining support for my child's brothers and sisters"). To avoid a problem focus or orientation, items on the Family Interest Survey have been worded in a positive manner. Families are asked to indicate their interests rather than identify their problems, needs, or impairments. The intent is to keep interventionists focused on activities seen as productive and positive by parents and caregivers. Items formed as positive statements help promote a partnership role for the family. Wording focused on "needs" and "wants" tends to place the family in the role of the recipient of services provided by interventionists rather than as partners working jointly to solve problems.

Format

The Family Interest Survey is designed as a booklet that includes a cover page for confidentiality and for identifying information (e.g., child and family name). Directions for using the survey and examples are included prior to the survey.

The Child's Interests section contains 11 items, the Family's Interests section contains 9 items, and the Community Interests section contains 10 items. An open-ended question is included at the end to encourage families to identify any child, family, or community interest not addressed in the previous items. For example, the family may be interested in obtaining information about residential treatment programs.

Following each item are two sets of three boxes that allow families to indicate if the item is a "priority interest," an "interest but not a current priority," or "not an interest at this time." The first set of boxes can be used for an initial determination of interests, and the second set of boxes can be used later as a review for updating IFSP outcomes. A sample page from the Family Interest Survey is shown in Figure 9.1. The complete survey is contained in Appendix D.

ADMINISTRATION

The AEPS Family Interest Survey can be used at any time with families; however, it is useful to have families complete the survey at the conclusion of the introductory meeting or before the outcome and intervention planning meeting is conducted. For families that would like assistance, the Family Interest Survey can be completed during the outcome and intervention planning meeting.

If possible, the survey should be completed by all primary caregivers. Caregivers can complete forms independently or together depending on the families' preference. Directions for completing the survey should be carefully explained to families. Families

For each date used, check one box in each row.

Date: _____   Date: _____

Child's Interests
I am interested in...

	Priority interest	Interest but not a current priority	Not an interest at this time	Priority interest	Interest but not a current priority	Not an interest at this time
Knowing more about my child's current strengths and needs						
Learning about services and programs for my child						
Knowing more about my child's condition/disability						
Making plans for future services and programs						
Knowing how my child grows and learns (such as social, motor, self-care)						
Learning ways to care for and help my child (such as positioning, diet, health)						
Learning about laws that affect my child, my rights, and how to advocate for my child						
Teaching my child						
Managing my child's behavior						
Learning to talk and play with my child						
Talking with teachers and professionals about my child's program						

Family's Interests
I am interested in...

	Priority interest	Interest but not a current priority	Not an interest at this time	Priority interest	Interest but not a current priority	Not an interest at this time
Explaining my child's special needs to siblings, grandparents, and friends						
Gaining support for my child's brothers and sisters						
Involving family and friends in my child's care or free time						
Counseling for my family						
Learning to solve family problems ourselves						

Figure 9.1.   Sample page from the AEPS Family Interest Survey.

can leave items blank if they prefer to complete them during the outcome and intervention planning meeting. It may be helpful to suggest that the survey be completed in pencil, so changes can be made easily.

REFERENCES

Bailey, D., & Simeonsson, R. (1988). Assessing family stress and needs. In D. Bailey & R. Simeonsson (Eds.), *Family assessment in early intervention* (pp. 95–118). Columbus, OH: Charles E. Merrill.

Collins-Cheek, M., & Collins, E. (1984). *Reading instruction through content teaching.* Columbus, OH: Charles E. Merrill.

Finn, D., & Vadasy, P. (1988). *Prioritizing Family Needs Scale.* Birmingham: University of Alabama.

Seligman, M., & Darling, R. (Eds.). (1989). Applying a systems approach to the identification of family strengths and needs: The individualized family service plan and beyond. In M. Seligman & R. Darling (Eds.), *Ordinary families, special children: A systems approach to childhood disability* (pp. 245–260). New York: Guilford.

Turnbull, A., & Turnbull, H.R. (Eds.). (1986). Family participation in developing the IEP. In A. Turnbull & H.R. Turnbull III (Eds.), *Families, professionals, and exceptionality: A special partnership* (pp. 269–303). Columbus, OH: Charles E. Merrill.

AEPS Family Report

The AEPS Family Report is a concrete and relevant assessment/evaluation activity for parents and caregivers. It allows families to gain insight into their child's abilities and to further develop their observational skills. Participating in the assessment/evaluation process by using the AEPS Family Report can also help to demystify the assessment/evaluation process and clarify for the family the roles of the professionals.

FEATURES OF THE AEPS FAMILY REPORT

The AEPS Family Report has several important features. First, the AEPS Family Report corresponds directly to the AEPS Test, which is used by professionals. The AEPS Family Report items are simple paraphrases of the goals and selected objectives on the AEPS Test. This feature permits a direct comparison between the caregivers' and professionals' assessments of the child.

Second, the AEPS Family Report measures skills that are functional for young children; that is, only skills that may enhance the child's ability to cope with and adapt to the demands of the social and physical environment are included. This focus on functional skills ensures that all of the items have the potential of being appropriate intervention targets. This feature of the AEPS Family Report makes the assessment outcome of direct relevance and use to the development of the child's IEP/IFSP. The assessment information can be used to assist in developing the child's IEP/IFSP and to formulate subsequent programming to be delivered by an intervention program.

A third feature of the AEPS Family Report that makes it valuable both as an initial assessment tool and in monitoring the child's subsequent progress is the comprehensive nature of the instrument. The major developmental areas of fine motor, gross motor, adaptive, cognitive, social-communication, and social behavior are included in the instrument.

Fourth, although caregivers may complete the AEPS Family Report from their knowledge of and experience with the child, they are encouraged to verify their knowledge through observation of the child in familiar environments. This feature of the AEPS Family Report provides information about what responses the child uses in a functional manner and when and how they are used.

TARGET POPULATION

The AEPS Family Report was developed for use by parents and other caregivers of young children who are at risk for or who have disabilities and who function developmentally between 3 and 6 years of age. This instrument is particularly appropriate for caregivers of young children enrolled in home- or center-based intervention programs in which the goal is to collect child information to formulate appropriate intervention targets.

The AEPS Family Report is *not* recommended for caregivers of children whose developmental level is less than 3 years but whose chronological age exceeds 6 years. The content of the instrument is appropriate for caregivers of young children but is of questionable relevance for caregivers of school-age children.

CONTENT AND ORGANIZATION

Similar to the AEPS Test, the AEPS Family Report is divided into the following six domains:

Fine Motor Domain—focuses on manipulating objects and prewriting skills.
Gross Motor Domain—focuses on balance and mobility in standing and walking and on play skills.
Adaptive Domain—focuses on feeding, hygiene, and dressing.
Cognitive Domain—focuses on participation in group activities, understanding of concepts, categorizing, sequencing, recalling events, problem solving, play, premath, and prereading skills.
Social-Communication Domain—focuses on social-communicative interactions and the production of words, phrases, and sentences.
Social Domain—focuses on interactions with others and the environment and knowledge of self and others.

Each item is numbered consecutively by domain. The Fine Motor Domain has 5 items, the Gross Motor Domain has 6 items, the Adaptive Domain has 8 items, the Cognitive Domain has 31 items, the Social-Communication Domain has 40 items, and the Social Domain has 8 items. Several items have associated subitems denoted by letters.

Items have been written in clear, simple language to assist parents in reading and understanding the content. The report is designed to accommodate the results of four separate administrations. Space is provided at the top of each page to enter the date from each administration. Boxes are located below the column headings for entering scores. A sample page from the AEPS Family Report is shown in Figure 10.1. A complete copy of the AEPS Family Report is contained in Appendix D.

ADMINISTRATION

The AEPS Family Report is an observation-based assessment/evaluation instrument. Parents or caregivers are encouraged to complete the AEPS Family Report without assistance from professionals. Before scoring an item, caregivers should observe their

Gross Motor Domain

1. Does your child walk up and down stairs, putting one foot on each stair, without holding on to a handrail or wall? (A1)

2. Does your child jump forward with feet together? (B1)

3. Does your child run without help around large toys, furniture, and people without bumping into them? (B2)

4. Does your child bounce, catch, kick, and throw different-size balls? (B3)

   (*Note:* If you scored Question 4 with an "S" or an "N," please indicate if your child is able to do a–d by placing a check mark beside the item.)

   ____ a. Does your child bounce a large ball at least twice in a row? (B3.1)

   ____ b. Does your child catch a ball thrown from 6 to 10 feet, using both hands? (B3.2)

   ____ c. Does your child kick a ball placed in front of him or her, without falling? (B3.3)

   ____ d. Does your child throw a ball forward with one hand, using an overhand throw? (B3.4)

5. Does your child skip at least 15 feet? (B4)

6. Does your child ride and steer a two-wheel bicycle without training wheels at least 20 feet? (B5)

Y = Yes; S = Sometimes; N = Not Yet.

Figure 10.1. Portion of a sample page from the Gross Motor Domain of the AEPS Family Report.

child attempting or doing the target behavior. However, there may be items that caregivers can score based on their knowledge of what their child can and cannot do (e.g., parents likely know if their child can walk up and down stairs). Items that are not observed may require that the parents or caregivers create a situation to directly elicit the target behavior.

Caregivers should observe or test a behavior several times before scoring an item to ensure that the child demonstrates the skill consistently and independently. If parents have questions about the intent of an item or are unable to interpret a behavior exhibited by their child, they should seek assistance from a professional. If necessary, the AEPS Family Report can be administered using an interview format. For example, if a parent has limited reading skills, the interventionist may read each item and the response categories to the parent and record his or her response.

Before using the Family Report, it is important that interventionists tell caregivers that they should not expect their child to be able to successfully perform all items. This point should be emphasized for caregivers of young children with severe disabilities.

No specific sequence for administration of the AEPS Family Report is required; however, caregivers should be strongly encouraged to score all 98 items plus the subitems at the first administration. If the AEPS Family Report is used to monitor child progress over time, subsequent administrations can be focused on intervention targets only.

SCORING ITEMS

Caregivers are instructed to score each of the 98 items by selecting one of the three response choices that most accurately reflects their child's current level of functioning: "Yes," "Sometimes," and "Not Yet." When the child performs the skill or behavior consistently and independently across settings, materials, and people, a "Y" is entered in the appropriate box. "Y" is also used when the child previously performed the skill but now uses a more advanced skill (e.g., if the item asks if the child can copy shapes but he or she can draw them independently).

When the child's performance of a specific skill or behavior may be questionable, such as an emerging skill, an "S" is entered in the appropriate box. For example, the child may demonstrate a skill only with certain materials (e.g., drinks from a special cup) or in specific situations (e.g., uses words with caregivers but not with others). The "S" response should also be used if the child needs several verbal or physical prompts to produce the behavior. When a child clearly does not demonstrate a skill, an "N" is entered in the appropriate box. At the end of each domain, space is provided to write the priority goal(s) for the domain.

Some items on the AEPS Family Report contain a series of subitems that ask caregivers to provide additional or clarifying information. A subitem requesting additional information may, for example, ask the caregivers to list which colors their child knows after scoring the item, "Does your child know eight colors?" with a "Yes," "Sometimes," or "Not Yet." Other subitems allow parents or caregivers to identify the portions of a skill their child is able to do. For example, item 3 in the Adaptive Domain asks, "Does your child put a proper amount of food in his or her mouth, drink a proper amount of liquid from a cup, stay at the table for the entire meal, use a napkin to wipe face and hands, and help with clearing the table?" If the caregiver has observed the child only to place the proper amount of food in his or her mouth, he or she would score the item as "S." He or she would then only place a check next to the one behavior that the child was able to do.

All items on the AEPS Family Report correspond with goals and objectives found on the AEPS Test and can be matched by referring to the key at the end of each item. For example, if an item from the Cognitive Domain of the AEPS Family Report is followed by (C1), an interventionist would know that the item corresponds with Strand C within the Cognitive Domain, Goal 1. Another example would be an AEPS Family Report item in the Fine Motor Domain followed by (A3.1). This code tells the interventionist that the item corresponds with Objective 3.1 in Strand A. An example of a portion of a completed AEPS Family Report is shown in Figure 10.2.

AEPS   Gross Motor Domain

Gross Motor Domain

1. Does your child walk up and down stairs, putting one foot on each stair, without holding on to a handrail or wall? (A1)

| Y | Y | | |

2. Does your child jump forward with feet together? (B1)

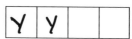

| Y | Y | | |

3. Does your child run without help around large toys, furniture, and people without bumping into them? (B2)

| Y | Y | | |

4. Does your child bounce, catch, kick, and throw different-size balls? (B3)

| S | S | | |

   (*Note*: If you scored Question 4 with an "S" or an "N," please indicate if your child is able to do a—d by placing a check mark beside the item.)

   1-96 ✔ a. Does your child bounce a large ball at least
   1-96   twice in a row? (B3.1)

   ✔ b. Does your child catch a ball thrown from 6 to
   6-96   10 feet, using both hands? (B3.2)

   ✔ c. Does your child kick a ball placed in front of him or her, without falling? (B3.3)

   ____ d. Does your child throw a ball forward with one hand, using an overhand throw? (B3.4)

5. Does your child skip at least 15 feet? (B4)

| N | N | | |

6. Does your child ride and steer a two-wheel bicycle without training wheels at least 20 feet? (B5)

| N | S | | |

Y = Yes; S = Sometimes; N = Not Yet.

Figure 10.2.   Portion of a completed page from the Gross Motor Domain of the AEPS Family Report.

OUTCOMES SUMMARY

If desired, interventionists may convert AEPS Family Report scores by assigning a 2 to the "Y" responses, a 1 to the "S" responses, and a 0 to the "N" responses. The Domain Raw Score can be obtained for each domain by adding all of the numbered items scored as a 2 or 1. Lettered subitems do not have accompanying scoring boxes. Subitems should not be added in when summarizing the Domain Raw Scores.

A Domain Percent Score for each domain is obtained by dividing the Domain Raw Score by the Total Domain Possible Score. Figure 10.3 shows an example of an AEPS Family Report Summary Form for two administrations 6 months apart.

Family Report Summary Form

Child's Name: Jimmy Jones

First Administration				**Second Administration**			
Date 1/96	Parent Mom			Date 6/96	Parent Mom		
Domain	Domain Raw Score	Total Domain Score Possible	Domain Percent Score	Domain	Domain Raw Score	Total Domain Score Possible	Domain Percent Score
Fine Motor	7	10	70	Fine Motor	8	10	80
Gross Motor	10	12	83	Gross Motor	10	12	83
Adaptive	12	16	75	Adaptive	13	16	81
Cognitive	40	62	65	Cognitive	45	62	73
Social-Communication	42	80	53	Social-Communication	51	80	64
Social	8	16	50	Social	9	16	56
TOTAL	119	196	61	TOTAL	136	196	69

Figure 10.3.   Example of an AEPS Family Report Summary Form.

The converted scores from the Family Report, as well as the additional information provided by many of the items' subitems, assist the interventionist (team) in scoring the AEPS Data Recording Form. If discrepancies are found between team member observations, the parents and the professionals should attempt to observe the targeted behavior again and work to understand and resolve the discrepancy. For example, caregivers and professionals may find behaviors the child uses at home but not at school or the reverse.

The AEPS Family Report allows families the opportunity to observe their child in various natural settings, to provide critical information for IEP/IFSP development, and to participate fully in the decision-making process regarding the assessment, intervention, and evaluation of their child's growth and development.

Psychometric Properties and Utility of the AEPS Test

APPENDIX

A

The forerunner to the AEPS Test for Three to Six Years was the AEPS Test for Birth to Three Years, which was, in turn, inspired by the Adaptive Performance Instrument (API) (Consortium on Adaptive Performance Evaluation [CAPE], 1978). Work was begun on the API in the early 1970s by a group of investigators identified as the Consortium on Adaptive Performance Evaluation (CAPE). Although many individuals were associated with CAPE and participated in the early development and testing of the API, Dale Gentry, Owen White, Lisbeth Vincent, Evelyn Brown, Jeff Seibert, Verna Hart, Kathleen McCartan, and Diane Bricker provided the sustaining leadership for this project from the mid-1970s to the early 1980s.

Formal field test data were collected on the API from 1977 to 1981. These data are contained in a final report submitted to the U.S. Office of Special Education Programs that provided support for examining the reliability and validity of the API. Readers interested in these findings are referred to Bricker (1981). Formal psychometric investigations of the AEPS Test for Birth to Three Years was begun in 1981, whereas work was initiated on the AEPS Test for Three to Six Years in 1985.

PSYCHOMETRIC PROPERTIES

A study of selected psychometric properties of the AEPS Test for Three to Six Years was completed in 1986 (Slentz, 1986). Fifty-three children who ranged in age from 34 to 76 months participated in the study. Half of the children were at risk for or had disabilities, whereas the remaining children were developing without difficulty. Interobserver data were collected on all 53 subjects. Pearson product–moment correlations for individual domains ranged from $r = .60$ for the Social Domain to $r = .94$ for the Fine Motor Domain. The total test correlation was $r = .94$. All correlations were significant at the $p < .0001$ level. Test–retest reliability data were collected on 18 children. Pearson product–moment correlations were .86 ($p < .0001$) for the Fine Motor Domain, .07 for the Gross Motor Domain, .13 for the Adaptive Domain, .91 ($p < .0001$) for the Cognitive Domain, .77 ($p < .0001$) for the Social-Communication Domain, .50 ($p < .05$) for the Social Domain, and .91 ($p < .0001$) for the total test.

Slentz (1986) reported congruent validity data on 18 children. These children's AEPS Test performances were compared with their performances on the McCarthy Scales of Children's Abilities (McCarthy, 1972) and the Uniform Performance Assessment System (Haring, White, Edgar, Affleck, & Hayden, 1981). For the McCarthy Scales, Pearson product–moment correlations were .35 and .06 between the Motor Scale and the AEPS Fine Motor Domain and Gross Motor Domain, respectively. Agreement was .66 ($p < .001$) between the McCarthy General Cognitive Index and the AEPS Cognitive Domain and .72 ($p < .0001$) between the McCarthy Verbal Scale and the AEPS Social-Communication Domain. Correlations between the Uniform Performance Assessment System and the AEPS were significant for the Fine Motor Domain ($r = .52$, $p < .01$), Cognitive Domain ($r = .77$, $p < .0001$), Social-Communication Domain ($r = .87$, $p < .0001$), and Social Domain ($r = .75$, $p < .0001$). Correlations were low and nonsignificant for the Gross Motor ($r = .39$) and Adaptive ($r = .30$) Domains.

The mean rank order of AEPS Test total scores was calculated for 3-year-olds in comparison with 4-year-olds and for 4-year-olds in comparison with 5-year-olds. A Mann–Whitney U test found that 4-year-olds scored significantly higher than 3-year-olds ($p < .0009$). The difference in total test scores between the 4- and 5-year-old groups was not significant.

AEPS Test protocols from 53 children were used to examine the relationship of domains and total test scores. All correlations were significant and ranged from .37 ($p < .01$) for the Adaptive Domain to .97 ($p < .0001$) for the Cognitive Domain. Relationships between strands and domains were generally moderate to strong.

A second study focused on examining selected psychometric properties of the AEPS Test for Three to Six Years was completed in 1993 by Hsia. Eighty-two children who ranged in age from 3 to 6 years participated in this study. Fifty-one of these children were classified as having no disabilities, 11 were classified as at risk, and 20 were classified as having disabilities (i.e., had been determined eligible to receive early intervention services). An AEPS Test was completed on each child by a trained examiner. The test was scored primarily through observation of the children as they participated in planned and free play activities while attending a center-based program.

Interobserver reliability was examined by correlating the children's domain scores and total test scores from the AEPS Test protocols of two independent coders. Data from all 82 children were included in this analysis, although not all children had the opportunity to participate in all gross motor and adaptive activities necessary for scoring a complete protocol. Pearson product–moment coefficients were used to correlate the AEPS Test domain and total test scores. A high degree of consistency ($r = .99$) was found for the total group (children with and without disabilities combined, $N = 82$) and for the two subgroups (children with or who are at risk for disabilities, $r = .97$; children without disabilities, $r = .93$). At the domain level, the total group correlations were .75 for the Fine Motor Domain, .82 for the Adaptive Domain, .83 for the Gross Motor and Social Domains, .95 for the Cognitive Domain, .96 for the Social-Communication Domain, and .97 for the total domain scores. All correlations were significant at the $p < .01$ level. Correlations tended to be lower for the subgroups, but all were still significant except for the Social Domain for the subgroup with disabilities.

TEST SENSITIVITY

The AEPS Test was designed to be sensitive to variations in the performance of children of different ages and with different levels of disability; therefore, children who are older and are more able should score higher on the test than younger or less able children. The AEPS Test sensitivity was also examined by Hsia (1993).

Sensitivity to Age

In analyzing the test's accuracy at distinguishing children of different ages, only children *without disabilities* were included. For this analysis children were assigned to one of three age groups (3-, 4-, and 5-year-old groups) based on their date of birth.

A one-way analysis of variance was used to examine subjects' scores in each of the six domains and for the total test score. A multiple comparison procedure, the Scheffé test, was performed when a significant F was obtained. With the exception of the Adaptive Domain, a significant F ratio was obtained for the other five domains and for the total test scores. The 5-year-olds scored significantly higher than the 3- and 4-year-olds, but the 3- and 4-year-olds were not significantly different from each other.

Sensitivity to Level of Disability

Because a number of children with disabilities were not involved in activities that assessed their gross motor and adaptive abilities, total scores for the children with disabilities for this analysis were obtained by summing the other four domain scores (i.e., Fine Motor, Cognitive, Social-Communication, and Social). A one-way analysis of variance was performed using three groups of children: those without disabilities, those at risk or with mild disabilities, and those with moderate/severe disabilities. A statistically significant difference was found for all groups for all domains and for the total test. The Scheffé test indicated that children in the group without disabilities had higher domain and total test scores than the children in both of the other groups.

With the exception of the Fine Motor Domain, significant score differences were found between the three groups. The Fine Motor scores of the group without disabilities were significantly higher than those of the group with moderate/severe disabilities but not those of the group at risk or with mild disabilities. The group at risk or with mild disabilities had significantly higher total test scores than the group with moderate/severe disabilities, but, at the domain level, only Social-Communication Domain scores were significantly different.

SUMMARY

Examining the psychometric properties of a test such as the AEPS is a difficult task from a logistical, technical, and financial perspective. Nevertheless, it is critically important that the validity and reliability of measurement tools be established for the users. Much work remains to be done on the AEPS Test for Three to Six Years; however, the studies to date suggest that this instrument possesses the qualities of a well-designed test.

The developers of the AEPS Test are continuing to study its properties, effectiveness, and usefulness. The conduct of this research is being assisted, in part, by channeling the royalties from the sale of AEPS materials into a fund dedicated to supporting this ongoing work.

REFERENCES

Bricker, D. (1981). *Adaptive assessment for evaluating the progress of severely/profoundly handicapped children functioning between birth and two years.* Final report submitted to the U.S. Department of Education, Office of Special Education Programs, Washington, DC.

The Consortium on Adaptive Performance Evaluation (CAPE). (1978). *Adaptive Performance Instrument (API).* Seattle: Author.

Haring, N., White, O., Edgar, E., Affleck, J., & Hayden, A. (1981). *Uniform performance assessment system.* Columbus, OH: Charles E. Merrill.

Hsia, T. (1993). *Evaluating the psychometric properties of the Assessment, Evaluation, and Programming System for Three to Six Years: AEPS Test.* Unpublished doctoral dissertation, University of Oregon, Eugene.

McCarthy, D. (1972). *McCarthy Scales of Children's Abilities.* New York: Psychological Corporation.

Slentz, K. (1986). *Evaluating the instructional needs of young children with handicaps: Psychometric adequacy of the Evaluation and Programming System—Assessment Level II (EPS–II).* Unpublished doctoral dissertation, University of Oregon, Eugene.

IEP/IFSP
Goals and Objectives

B

FINE MOTOR DOMAIN

Strand A: Manipulation of Objects

G1   The child will manipulate two small objects at the same time (e.g., string small beads; build with blocks, Tinkertoys).

1.1   The child will manipulate two hand-size objects at the same time (e.g., string large beads, put large pop beads together).

G2   The child will cut out shapes with curved lines (e.g., circles, ovals) within ¼ inch of the lines.

2.1   The child will cut out shapes with straight lines (e.g., squares, rectangles, triangles) within ¼ inch of the lines.

2.2   The child will cut paper in two. The edge may be jagged.

G3   The child will tie string-type fastener (e.g., shoelace, ribbon, string).

3.1   The child will fasten buttons.

3.2   The child will thread and zip zippers.

Strand B: Prewriting

G1   The child will copy complex shapes with angular contours (e.g., rectangles, squares, triangles) from a drawn model.

1.1   The child will copy simple shapes with circular contours or lines (e.g., circles, crosses, Ts).

G2   The child will print own first name without a model. Letters must be in correct order, but printing errors are permissible (e.g., a letter printed backward); however, the name should be recognizable.

2.1   The child will print three upper- or lowercase letters without a model. Printing errors are permissible (e.g., a letter printed backward); however, the individual letters should be recognizable. Verbal cues may be provided (e.g., "Can you write some letters?").

2.2   The child will copy own first name from a model. Letters should be in correct order. Printing errors are permissible (e.g., a letter printed backward); however, the name should be recognizable.

2.3   The child will copy three upper- or lowercase letters from a model. Printing errors are permissible (e.g., a letter printed backward); however, the individual letters should be recognizable.

GROSS MOTOR DOMAIN

Strand A: Balance and Mobility in Standing and Walking

G1   The child will walk up and down stairs, alternating feet without holding a handrail or the wall.

1.1   The child will walk up and down stairs without alternating feet. The child may hold a handrail or the wall with one hand for support.

Strand B: Play Skills

G1   The child will jump forward with feet together and land on two feet without falling.

1.1   The child will jump up and down in place and land on two feet without falling. An adult may model the action.

1.2   The child will jump from a low platform (e.g., curb, low step, raised platform) to the supporting surface and land on two feet without falling. An adult may model the action.

1.3 The child will maintain balance during at least two of the following walking positions:

- Walks 6 feet on a 4-inch–wide balance beam
- Walks 10 feet on a line
- Walks 10 feet on tiptoe
- Walks 10 feet backward

An adult may model the action.

1.4 The child will balance on one foot for at least 5 seconds. An adult may model the action.

G2 The child will avoid obstacles while running by controlling starts, stops, and sudden changes in direction.

2.1 The child will run with trunk inclined slightly forward, arms swinging freely, and legs alternately flexing and extending, with a period of no support by either leg.

G3 The child will bounce, catch, kick, and throw a large ball.

3.1 Using the palm of one hand, the child will bounce a large ball at least twice.

3.2 From a distance of 6–10 feet, the child will catch a ball (at least 6 inches in diameter) using the palms of both hands.

3.3 While maintaining balance, the child will kick a large stationary ball with one foot.

3.4 Using an overhand throw, the child will throw a hand-size ball forward with one hand.

G4 The child will skip at least 15 feet using an alternating step–hop pattern.

4.1 The child will hop forward with five or more consecutive hops on one foot.

G5 While sitting on a two-wheel bicycle, the child will pedal forward and steer for at least 20 feet.

5.1 While sitting on a two-wheel bicycle with training wheels with both feet on the pedals, the child will pedal forward and steer for at least 10 feet.

ADAPTIVE DOMAIN

Strand A: Dining

G1 The child will eat and drink a variety of foods using appropriate utensils with little or no spilling.

1.1 The child will eat food of different textures (e.g., soft, liquid, chewy).

1.2 The child will select and eat a variety of foods from different food groups (e.g., dairy, meat, fruit).

1.3 After choosing appropriate utensils (e.g., spoon for soup, fork for meat), the child will eat by spearing with a fork and scooping with a spoon, bringing food to the mouth with minimal spilling.

G2 The child will perform the following activities prior to eating:

- Prepare food for eating
- Use a knife to spread food
- Pour liquids into a variety of containers
- Serve food with utensils

2.1 The child will prepare food for eating by removing inedible parts (e.g., peel an orange, shell a nut, paper wrapping).

2.2   The child will use a knife to spread soft, spreadable foods (e.g., peanut butter, cream cheese, jam) on bread or a cracker. The bread or cracker should be covered with the food and be intact after the child spreads the food. The food does not have to be spread smoothly.

2.3   The child will pour liquid from one container (e.g., pitcher, bottle) into another container (e.g., cup, bowl, glass). The child should not spill the liquid and should stop pouring at an appropriate time to avoid overfilling the receiving container.

2.4   The child will use utensils to transfer food from one container to another.

G3   The child will display social dining skills by performing the following activities:

- Put proper amounts of food in mouth, chew with mouth closed, and swallow before taking another bite
- Take in proper amount of liquid and return the cup to table
- Remain seated during meals or ask to be excused
- Use a napkin to clean face and hands
- Assist in clearing off the table

3.1   While eating, the child will put an appropriate amount of food in mouth (i.e., does not overfill mouth), chew with mouth closed, and swallow before taking another bite.

3.2   While eating, the child will take in an appropriate amount of liquid from a child-size cup without spilling and return the cup to the table at least once before emptying the cup.

3.3   The child will remain seated during meals or until excused.

3.4   After eating, the child will use a napkin to clean food from face and hands. The child may be given assistance to clean thoroughly.

3.5   After eating, the child will remove own dishes and silverware from the table and put them in an appropriate place (e.g., in the sink, on the counter, in the dishwasher).

Strand B: Personal Hygiene

G1   The child will initiate trips to the bathroom, pull down pants, use toilet paper, flush the toilet, pull up pants, wash hands, and remain dry and unsoiled between trips to the bathroom. Reminders are acceptable.

1.1   The child will complete the following toileting routine: pull down pants, use toilet paper after using the toilet, pull up pants, flush toilet, and wash hands.

1.2   The child will initiate a trip to the bathroom and use the toilet for urination or bowel movements, remaining dry and unsoiled between trips to the bathroom. Reminders are acceptable. The child may have assistance with other toileting skills (e.g., pulling pants down and up, washing hands).

1.3   The child will accurately indicate (e.g., tell, sign, gesture) to an adult the need to use a toilet for urination or bowel movement.

G2   The child will perform the following washing and grooming activities:

- Use a tissue to clean nose
- Brush teeth
- Bathe and dry body
- Brush or comb hair
- Wash and dry face

2.1   The child will use a tissue to blow or wipe nose. The child may be given assistance to thoroughly clean nose.

2.2   The child will put toothpaste on a toothbrush, brush teeth, and rinse mouth. Reminders are acceptable (e.g., "What should you do next?").

2.3   The child will perform the following bathing routine: remove clothing, get into a tub or shower, use soap to clean body, rinse off, obtain a towel, dry body, and return the towel to towel rack. Reminders are acceptable, and the child may be given assistance to thoroughly clean and dry body.

2.4   The child will use a brush or a comb to groom hair.

2.5   The child will complete face washing and drying routine by turning on the faucet, washing face with soap, rinsing off face, turning off faucet, drying face with a towel, and returning the towel to a towel rack.

Strand C: Dressing and Undressing

G1   The child will use any functional means to perform all of the following unfastening activities:

- Unfasten buttons/snaps/Velcro fasteners on garments
- Untie string-type fasteners
- Unzip zippers

1.1   The child will unfasten buttons/snaps/Velcro fasteners on garments (e.g., shirt, dress, pants) when dressing, using any functional means that does not damage the clothing or fastener.

1.2   The child will untie string-type fasteners (e.g., shoelace, hood string) when undressing using any functional means that does not damage the clothing or fastener.

1.3   The child will unzip and detach zipper when undressing, using any functional means that does not damage the clothing or zipper.

G2   The child will select appropriate clothing (i.e., shorts in summer, sweater in winter, nightgown at bedtime) and dress self at a designated time (e.g., after breakfast). Reminders are acceptable.

2.1   The child will use any functional means to pull long pants over both feet and up to the waist. Adult may fasten any fasteners.

2.2   The child will use any functional means to put on front-opening garments (e.g., blouse, shirt, coat). An adult may fasten any fasteners.

2.3   The child will use any functional means to put on pullover garments (e.g., T-shirt, dress, sweater).

2.4   The child will use any functional means to put shoes on both feet. An adult may fasten any fasteners.

2.5   The child will use any functional means to pull garments (e.g., underpants, shorts, skirt) over feet and up to waist. Adult may fasten any fasteners.

G3   The child will use any functional means to perform the following activities:

- Tie string-type fasteners
- Fasten buttons, snaps, and Velcro fasteners
- Thread and zip zipper

3.1   The child will use any functional means to tie string-type fasteners (e.g., shoelace) when dressing.

3.2   The child will use any functional means to fasten buttons, snaps, and Velcro fasteners when dressing.

3.3   The child will use any functional means to thread and zip zippers when dressing.

COGNITIVE DOMAIN

Strand A: Participation

G1   The child will initiate and complete age-appropriate activities without adult prompting (e.g., during free play, child gets out puzzle, puts it together, then puts it away).

1.1   The child will respond to the first request to finish activities (e.g., child carries out adult's request to pick up all of the blocks).

1.2   The child will respond to the first request to begin activities (e.g., child sits at table watching peers draw with crayons; in response to an adult's first request, the child begins to draw).

G2   The child will engage in the following behaviors during structured small group activities (i.e., groups of five or fewer children):

- Interact appropriately with materials
- Respond appropriately to directions
- Look at appropriate object, person, or event
- Remain with the group

An adult may provide group directions.

2.1   The child will interact with materials in a functional or demonstrated fashion (e.g., use a hammer to pound pegs into a pegboard) during structured small group activities (i.e., groups of five or fewer children). An adult may provide group directions.

2.2   The child will respond with appropriate verbal or motor actions to group directions provided by an adult (e.g., child follows directions to dip paintbrush in paint and stroke paintbrush across paper) during structured small group activities (i.e., groups of five or fewer children).

2.3   The child will look at object, person, or event that is the focus of activity (e.g., the child looks at a person while that person is talking) during small group activities (i.e., groups of five or fewer children). An adult may provide group directions.

2.4   The child will stay seated or in an indicated area (e.g., at the table for table activities) for the duration of structured small group activities (i.e., groups of five or fewer children). An adult may provide group directions.

G3   The child will engage in the following behaviors during large group activities (i.e., groups of six or more children):

- Interact appropriately with materials
- Respond appropriately to directions
- Look at appropriate object, person, or event
- Remain with the group

An adult may provide group directions.

3.1   The child will interact with materials in a functional or demonstrated fashion (e.g., the child passes a ball to the next child during a group game) during structured large group activities (i.e., groups of six or more children). An adult may provide group directions.

3.2   The child will respond with appropriate verbal or motor actions to group directions provided by an adult (e.g., child selects a musical instrument and follows directions to play instrument while marching) during structured large group activities (i.e., groups of six or more children).

3.3   The child will look at object, person, or event that is the focus of activity (e.g., the child looks at a person who is talking and showing a toy boat) during structured large group activities (i.e., groups of six or more children). An adult may provide group directions.

3.4 The child will stay seated or in an indicated area (e.g., at the table for snack time) for the duration of large group activities (i.e., groups of six or more children).

Strand B: Demonstrates Understanding of Concepts

G1 The child will follow directions; answer questions; or identify objects, people, or events using at least eight different terms that describe color (e.g., the child selects a red crayon and begins coloring in response to an adult's direction to "Color the car red").

1.1 The child will follow directions; answer questions; or identify objects, people, or events using at least six different terms that describe color (e.g., in response to a peer's request to "Give me a yellow one," the child gives the peer a yellow block).

1.2 The child will follow directions; answer questions; or identify objects, people, or events using at least three different terms that describe color (e.g., while painting with green paint, the child says, "I'm painting the house green").

G2 The child will follow directions, answer questions, or identify objects using at least five different terms that describe shape (e.g., the child finds a square and gives it to an adult in response to the adult's request to "Find a square").

2.1 The child will follow directions, answer questions, or identify objects using at least three different terms that describe shape (e.g., while gluing cut-out triangles onto a piece of paper, the child says, "This triangle goes here").

2.2 The child will follow directions; answer questions; or identify objects using at least one term that describes shape (e.g., while looking at pictures in a book, the child says, "The clock looks like a circle").

G3 The child will follow directions, answer questions, or identify objects or people using at least six different terms that describe size (e.g., the child hands the adult a small block in response to adult's request to "Give me a small one").

3.1 The child will follow directions, answer questions, or identify objects or people using at least four different terms that describe size (e.g., while coloring, the child chooses a short crayon and says, "I like this little crayon").

3.2 The child will follow directions, answer questions, or identify objects or people using at least two different terms that describe size (e.g., the child selects a large car from a group of cars and says, "This person wants to ride in the big car").

G4 The child will follow directions; answer questions; or identify objects, people, or events using at least 10 different terms that describe quality (e.g., the child pushes a truck across the floor and says, "This truck can go fast").

4.1 The child will follow directions; answer questions; or identify objects, people, or events using at least six different terms that describe quality (e.g., the child tastes a spoonful of soup and says, "This is hot").

4.2 The child will follow directions; answer questions; or identify objects, people, or events using at least four different terms that describe quality (e.g., after washing hands, the child says, "I got wet").

4.3 The child will follow directions; answer questions; or identify objects, people, or events using at least two different terms that describe quality (e.g., while coloring, the child picks up two blue crayons and says, "These are the same color").

G5 The child will follow directions, answer questions, or identify objects or events using at least eight different terms that describe quantity (e.g., the child gathers empty cups in response to an adult's request to "Bring me the empty cups").

5.1 The child will follow directions, answer questions, or identify objects or events using at least five different terms that describe quantity (e.g., while stringing beads, a peer says, "Can I have some more beads?" and the child hands the peer a few beads).

5.2   The child will follow directions, answer questions, or identify objects or events using at least two different terms that describe quantity (e.g., during snack time, the child sees that other children have crackers and says, "I don't have any crackers!").

G6   The child will follow directions; answer questions; or identify objects, people, or events using at least 12 different terms that describe spatial relations (e.g., the child lines up dolls and, while placing the last one, says, "This baby is last").

6.1   The child will follow directions; answer questions; or identify objects, people, or events using at least nine different terms that describe spatial relations (e.g., while the child is drawing, the child says, "I'm going to make a kitty next to this flower," and does so).

6.2   The child will follow directions; answer questions; or identify objects, people, or events using at least six different terms that describe spatial relations (e.g., when asked, "Who's in back of Sam?" the child correctly names that person).

6.3   The child will follow directions; answer questions; or identify objects, people, or events using at least three different terms that describe spatial relations (e.g., the child sees another child hiding and says, "Chris is hiding behind the door").

G7   The child will follow directions, answer questions, or identify events using at least seven different terms that describe temporal relations (e.g., while building a tower of blocks, the child says, "After I make this big, I'm going to knock it down"; the child then builds the tower and knocks it down).

7.1   The child will follow directions, answer questions, or identify events using at least five different terms that describe temporal relations (e.g., when told to wash up before snack time, the child does so).

7.2   The child will follow directions, answer questions, or identify events using at least three different terms that describe temporal relations (e.g., the child approaches a peer and says, "Today is my birthday").

Strand C: Categorizing

G1   The child will devise a criterion (e.g., category, function, attribute) and sort all objects into groups according to that criterion (e.g., the child separates miniature toys into the following groups: people, animals, and vehicles). An adult may provide a general cue (e.g., "Put all of the ones together that look the same").

1.1   The child will sort all objects into groups according to some categorical criterion (e.g., food, animals, clothing). An adult may provide the categories (e.g., "Put the food on the table and the vehicles in the box").

1.2   The child will sort all objects into groups according to their function (e.g., the child chooses from a group of objects all those appropriate for water play).

1.3   The child will sort all objects into groups according to some physical attribute (e.g., the child puts large vehicles on one shelf and small vehicles on another).

Strand D: Sequencing

G1   In response to functional (i.e., within context) three-step directions that are not routinely given, the child will correctly perform the sequence as directed (e.g., during a gross motor activity, an adult gestures and tells the child to "Run to the bench, pick up the ball, then run to the slide"; the child then follows these directions in the correct sequence). Contextual cues such as gestures may be given.

1.1   In response to functional (i.e., within context) three-step directions that are routinely given, the child will correctly perform the sequence as directed (e.g., after outside time, an adult gestures and tells the child to "Take off your coat, hang it up, then wash your hands"; the child follows the directions in the correct sequence). Contextual cues such as gestures may be given.

G2   The child will place three or more objects in series according to length or size (e.g., the child puts books on a bookshelf in order by height). The child may correct self.

2.1   The child will match two related sets of two or more objects by assigning each object from one set to its matching object from the other set (e.g., the child fits a set of two different-size lids to correct bowls). The child may correct self.

G3   The child will retell sequences of at least three events verbally, through gestures and demonstration, or by arranging pictures into correct sequence (e.g., an adult tells a three-part story and asks the child to retell the story; the child gestures, tells the story verbally, or arranges the story pictures in correct sequence to retell the story).

3.1   The child will respond appropriately to questions about the sequence of stories or events verbally, through gestures and demonstration, or by arranging pictures in the correct sequence (e.g., when telling a story, the child responds appropriately to an adult's question, "Then what happened?").

Strand E: Recalling Events

G1   Without contextual cues, the child will spontaneously and accurately relate (e.g., tell, demonstrate) events that occurred on the same day at least 30 minutes after the occurrence of the event (e.g., at the end of the school day, an adult asks "What did you make in art today?" when art project and materials are not present in the environment; the child responds by accurately telling what was made during the activity).

1.1   With contextual cues, the child will spontaneously and accurately relate (e.g., tell, demonstrate) events that occurred on the same day at least 30 minutes after the occurrence of the events (e.g., during circle time with the toys present, an adult asks, "What did you play with during play time?"; the child responds by telling which toys were used).

1.2   Spontaneously or on request, the child will accurately relate (e.g., tell, demonstrate) events that occurred immediately before (e.g., child washes hands, walks out of the bathroom and tells an adult, "I washed my hands").

G2   Spontaneously or on request, the child will recite two of the following verbal sequences:

- Telephone number
- Alphabet
- Numbers from 1 to 20
- Spelling of name
- Days of the week

2.1   Spontaneously or on request, the child will tell two of the following:

- First name and last name
- Birthday
- Age
- First name(s) of sibling(s)
- First name(s) of parent(s)

Strand F: Problem Solving

G1   Spontaneously or on request the child will indicate (e.g., tell, demonstrate) why particular solutions to problems that occur within context would or would not work (e.g., the child responds with a reason when asked, "Why couldn't we glue these on with water?").

1.1   Spontaneously or on request, the child will indicate (e.g., tell, demonstrate) acceptable solutions to problems (e.g., the child is having difficulty cutting and points to a different pair of scissors when asked, "What can we try?"). Adult may provide general cues.

1.2 Spontaneously or on request, the child will name or select appropriate or functional means to goals when problems and their solutions have been identified (e.g., the child brings a large empty container in response to an adult's request to "Find something for carrying the blocks").

G2 The child will make statements and appropriately answer questions that require the child to

- Give reasons for inferences
- Make predictions about future or hypothetical events
- Determine possible causes for events

2.1 Spontaneously or on request, the child will give plausible reasons for making inferences (e.g., the child says, "She is sad"; an adult asks "How do you know that the girl is sad?" and the child answers, "She is crying").

2.2 Spontaneously or on request, the child will make plausible predictions about future or hypothetical events that take place within context (e.g., an adult who is reading an unfamiliar story pauses and asks the child, "What do you think will happen?"; the child tells a possible event).

2.3 Spontaneously or on request, the child will tell possible causes for observed events (e.g., in response to an adult's question, "Why do you think she is crying?" the child tells a possible cause).

Strand G: Play

G1 The child will engage in the following imaginary play behaviors:

- Take on roles or identities
- Plan and act out recognizable events, themes, or story lines
- Use imaginary and representational props

1.1 The child will assume recognizable roles or identities by announcing the roles or changing voice, manner, or behaviors to portray identities (e.g., the child says, "I'll be the bus driver," sits in the front seat of the pretend bus, and in an adult voice tells the children, "Sit down and be quiet while I'm driving").

1.2 The child will plan and enact recognizable events, themes, or story lines (e.g., the child puts on a hat and takes a purse, pretends to go to the store, comes home, cooks dinner).

1.3 The child will play using imaginary props (e.g., the child gallops around the room pretending to hold reins and says, "Giddyup horsie, go fast").

G2 The child will engage in games with rules by

- Maintaining participation
- Conforming to game rules

2.1 The child will continue to participate in organized games until their completion. An adult may provide group directions.

2.2 The child will follow the rules in organized games (e.g., the child waits for a turn, follows an appropriate sequence of steps in a game, knows the beginning and end of the game). An adult may provide group directions.

Strand H: Premath

G1 Spontaneously or on request, the child will recite numbers from 1 to 20 in correct order.

1.1 Spontaneously or on request, the child will recite numbers from 1 to 10 in correct order.

1.2 Spontaneously or on request, the child will recite numbers from 1 to 5 in correct order.

1.3 Spontaneously or on request, the child will recite numbers from 1 to 3 in correct order.

G2 When presented with a set of 10 objects, the child will correctly count the objects.

2.1 When presented with a set of five objects, the child will correctly count the objects.

2.2 When presented with a set of two objects, the child will correctly count the objects.

2.3 Spontaneously or on request, the child will demonstrate understanding of one-to-one correspondence by assigning one object to each of four or more objects or people (e.g., the child places one fork next to each plate).

G3 Spontaneously or on request, the child will identify printed numerals 1–10 (e.g., the child looks at a number book and correctly identifies the numbers 1–10).

3.1 Spontaneously or on request the child will identify printed numerals 1–8 (e.g., an adult shows the child printed numerals and asks, "What numbers are these?" and the child correctly identifies numbers from 1 to 8).

3.2 Spontaneously or on request, the child will identify printed numerals 1–5 (e.g., when the child is playing with magnetic board numbers, the child selects and correctly identifies numbers from 1 to 5).

3.3 Spontaneously or on request, the child will identify printed numerals 1–3 (e.g., when the child is working on number puzzle, an adult points to a number and asks, "What number is this?"; the child correctly identifies numbers from 1 to 3).

G4 On request, the child will match printed numerals to sets of 1–10 objects (e.g., when the child is playing with cards with the printed numerals 1, 2, 3, 4, 5, 6, 7, 8, 9, and 10, the child will correctly match printed numerals with corresponding sets of objects).

4.1 On request, the child will match printed numerals to sets of 1–8 objects (e.g., when asked to match the printed numeral with a group of 8 objects, the child will correctly select and match the printed numeral 8 with the group of 8 objects).

4.2 On request, the child will match printed numerals to sets of 1–5 objects (e.g., when asked to match the printed numeral with a group of 5 objects, the child will correctly select and match the printed numeral 5 with the group of 5 objects).

4.3 On request, the child will match printed numerals to sets of 1–3 objects (e.g., when asked to match the printed numeral with a group of 3 objects, the child will correctly select and match the printed numeral 3 with the group of 3 objects).

Strand I: Prereading

G1 The child will demonstrate understanding of the purpose, function, and use of books by performing the following prereading tasks:

• Demonstrating functional use of book
• Telling about pictures in book
• Participating actively in storytelling

1.1 The child will perform three of the following prereading tasks:

• Correctly position the book
• Turn each page from beginning to end
• Pretend to read by vocalizing or verbalizing
• Attempt to structure and tell the story

1.2 The child will tell about pictures in books and make comments that provide clues indicating that the child knows what the stories are about. An adult may provide general cues (e.g., "What is this story about?").

1.3 During story time, the child will participate actively when an adult reads stories by performing four of the following prereading tasks:

- Making relevant comments
- Pointing to pictures
- Turning pages
- Filling in missing words
- Telling the ends of familiar stories (e.g., while reading a story about animals, an adult shows the child a picture and reads, "Then, all of a sudden, baby rabbit saw the red..."; child continues appropriately, according to the picture, "fox!").

G2 The child will demonstrate the ability to perform the following prereading tasks:

- Blend a series of sounds together to form a word
- Rhyme words with a model

2.1 When a series of three sounds is presented, the child will put them together to form a word (e.g., an adult says "s-i-t" and the child says "sit").

2.2 On request, the child will produce words or nonsense words that rhyme with a model word (e.g., an adult says "mat" and the child says "hat").

G3 The child will read three words consisting of three phonetic units by sounding them out (e.g., the child sounds out the printed words "bat," "sit," and "man").

3.1 On request, the child will produce the phonetic sounds for at least three letters (e.g., an adult shows the child the letter "B" and the child says /b/).

G4 Spontaneously or on request, the child will read at least two common words by sight. One of the words may be the child's first name.

4.1 Spontaneously or on request, the child will name at least five letters of the alphabet (e.g., an adult shows the child printed letters and asks, "Can you name any of these letters?" and the child names five of the letters).

SOCIAL-COMMUNICATION DOMAIN

Strand A: Social-Communicative Interactions

G1 The child will use words, phrases, or sentences to do the following:

- Express anticipated outcomes
- Describe pretend objects, events, or people
- Label own or others' affect/emotions
- Describe past events
- Make commands to and requests of others
- Obtain information
- Inform

Errors in syntax are acceptable.

1.1 The child will use words, phrases, or sentences to relay information about future events (e.g., the child says, "Tomorrow we are going to the park"). Errors in syntax are acceptable.

1.2 The child will use words, phrases, or sentences to describe pretend objects, events, or people (e.g., the child pretends to be driving a car and says, "My car is really fast"). Errors in syntax are acceptable.

1.3   The child will use words, phrases, or sentences to label own or others' affect/emotions (e.g., the child sees a peer frowning and says, "Terry's mad"). Errors in syntax are acceptable.

1.4   The child will use words, phrases, or sentences to describe actions and events that occurred in the immediate and distant past (e.g., the child says, "I made a hat," when telling a parent about what she made earlier during an art activity). Errors in syntax are acceptable.

1.5   The child will use words, phrases, or sentences to make commands to and requests of others (e.g., when a peer takes the child's toy, the child says, "Give that back!"). Errors in syntax are acceptable.

1.6   The child will use words, phrases, or sentences, using rising intonation, to obtain information (e.g., the child asks a peer, "How old are you?") Errors in syntax are acceptable.

1.7   The child will use words, phrases, or sentences to describe objects, actions, and events and to relay plans, intentions, and experiences to others (e.g., the child calls to a parent, "I'm going outside"). Errors in syntax are acceptable.

G2   The child will use conversational rules to initiate and maintain communicative exchanges for two or more consecutive exchanges. An exchange includes a response from both the child and another person.

2.1   The child will use appropriate responses in conversation to alternate between speaker and listener roles (e.g., the child pauses after making a comment and looks toward communicative partner).

2.2   The child will respond to conversational topic changes initiated by others with comments, answers, or questions related to the new topic (e.g., the child says, "I want to play outside some more," and the adult says, "We need to go inside now to fix a snack"; the child responds, "What are we gonna eat?").

2.3   The child will indicate a need for clarification (i.e., repetition, elaboration, or confirmation) by commenting or questioning during communicative exchanges (e.g., the child asks "What?" when the child does not understand what another person has said).

2.4   The child will supply relevant information following another person's request for clarification, repetition, elaboration, or confirmation of the child's previous statement (e.g., the child says, "She threw it"; an adult asks, "Who?" and the child answers, "Rachel").

2.5   The child will initiate topics relevant to situations or communicative partners (e.g., the child sees a peer with crayons and asks, "Can I have a red one?").

2.6   The child will respond to another's conversation with related topics, including acknowledgment of another's statement, an answer to a question, a request for clarification, or a related comment (e.g., an adult comments, "You have new shoes on today," and the child says, "My mommy got them at the store").

G3   The child will change the form, length, and grammatical complexity of phrases and sentences according to listeners' needs and social roles (e.g., the child uses shorter and less complex sentences to ask a younger child, "Want a cookie?").

3.1   The child will use voice pitch (e.g., high, low) and voice intensity (e.g., loud, soft) that is appropriate to the situation, listener, and communicative meaning (e.g., the child shouts when playing but begins to whisper after noticing that his or her father is sleeping).

3.2   The child will look toward the speaker's face and establish an appropriate physical proximity and body posture in relation to others during communicative exchanges (e.g., when the child's name is called, the child turns and looks to locate the speaker).

Strand B: Production of Words, Phrases, and Sentences

G1   The child will use the following verb constructs:

- Auxiliary verbs
- The copula verb "to be"
- Third person singular verb forms
- Irregular past tense verbs
- Regular past tense verbs
- Present progressive "ing"

1.1   The child will use appropriate forms of the following auxiliary (helping) verbs in combination with other verbs:

- To be (e.g., "He is running")
- To want (e.g., "I wanna go")
- Will (e.g., "She won't tell")
- Can (e.g., "I could eat that")
- To do (e.g., "He doesn't like milk")
- Shall (e.g., "She should take a nap")
- May (e.g., "He might not like that")
- Better (e.g., "They'd better do it")
- To have (e.g., "Do I hafta do it?")

1.2   The child will use appropriate forms of the verb "to be" to link subject nouns to predicates (e.g., the child says, "I'm happy").

1.3   The child will use appropriate regular and irregular third person singular verb forms (e.g., regular: "It jumps"; irregular: "She has a bike").

1.4   The child will use appropriate irregular forms of past tense verbs (e.g., came, ran, fell, broke, sat) (e.g., the child says, "Mommy went to work").

1.5   The child will use appropriate regular past tense verbs (i.e., verb plus -ed ending) (e.g., the child says, "We walked home").

1.6   The child will use appropriate present progressive verb forms (i e., verb plus -ing ending) (e.g., the child says, "I'm going outside").

G2   The child will use the following noun inflections:

- Possessive "s" (e.g., Susan's)
- Irregular plural (e.g., mice)
- Regular plural (e.g., toys)

2.1   The child will use nouns with an apostrophe "s" to express possession (e.g., the child says, "Mom's hat fell off").

2.2   The child will use irregular plural noun forms (e.g., the child says, "Those mice are in the cage").

2.3   The child will use regular plural noun forms (i.e., noun plus -s or -es ending) (e.g., the child says, "I see the dogs").

G3   The child will use the following forms to ask questions:

- Yes/no question
- Questions with inverted auxiliary
- When questions
- Why, who, and how questions

- What and where questions
- Rising inflection

3.1 The child will ask questions that require a yes or no response from the listener (e.g., the child asks, "Can't I go?").

3.2 The child will ask questions by reversing the order of the subject and the auxiliary (helping) verb (e.g., the child asks, "Is he hiding?").

3.3 The child will ask questions beginning with the word *when* (e.g., the child asks, "When will we eat?").

3.4 The child will ask questions beginning with the words *why, who,* and *how* (e.g., the child asks, "Why did he do that?", "Who is it?", or "How you do that?").

3.5 The child will ask questions beginning with the words *what* and *where* (e.g., the child asks, "Where she going?" or "What that?").

3.6 The child will ask questions by using raised pitch at the end of utterances so that the utterances sound like questions (e.g., the child asks, "See that airplane?").

G4 The child will use appropriate pronouns to serve the following functions:

- As subjects in phrases or sentences
- As objects in phrases or sentences
- To show possession
- To represent unspecified people and objects
- To identify or point out objects

4.1 The child will use subject pronouns (e.g., she, he, they) appropriately as subjects in phrases or sentences.

4.2 The child will use object pronouns (e.g., her, him, them) appropriately as objects (i.e., receives an object or relation) in phrases or sentences.

4.3 The child will use possessive pronouns (e.g., hers, his, their) appropriately to express possession in phrases or sentences.

4.4 The child will use indefinite pronouns (e.g., some, lots, more) appropriately to refer to unspecified people or objects.

4.5 The child will use demonstrative pronouns (e.g, this, that, these) appropriately to single out or identify objects.

G5 The child will use descriptive, relational, and functional words as

- Adjectives
- Adverbs
- Prepositions
- Conjunctions
- Articles

5.1 The child will use adjectives to modify nouns and pronouns (e.g., the child says, "My hands are cold").

5.2 The child will use adjectives to compare degrees of quality or quantity (e.g., the child says, "My truck is best" or "I got the most ice cream").

5.3 The child will use adverbs to modify verbs (e.g., the child says, "That tastes bad").

5.4 The child will use prepositions or prepositional phrases appropriately (e.g., the child says, "The person goes in the car").

5.5 The child will use conjunctions to connect words, phrases, and sentences (e.g., the child says, "I want a cup and some juice").

5.6 The child will use articles (i.e., the, a, an) preceding nouns (e.g., the child says, "I can't find the ball").

SOCIAL DOMAIN

Strand A: Interaction with Others

G1 The child will establish and maintain proximity with peers and cooperatively play with partners during child-directed free choice activities (e.g., the child walks over to a peer swinging on a swing and says, "I'll push you"; the child and peer then take turns pushing each other and swinging).

1.1 The child will respond appropriately to peers in distress or need (e.g., the child pats or hugs a peer who is crying).

1.2 The child will establish and maintain proximity with peers during unstructured, child-directed activities (e.g., the child walks over to a peer playing with dolls and begins playing beside the peer).

1.3 The child will greet familiar peers by vocalizing, verbalizing, hugging, patting, touching, or smiling.

1.4 The child will respond with socially appropriate affect to peers' affective initiations (e.g., the child smiles in response to a peer's smile).

G2 The child will use verbal or nonverbal strategies to initiate cooperative activities and encourage peers to participate (e.g., the child says, "Come on, let's build a house," to a group of peers).

2.1 The child will use socially appropriate verbal or nonverbal strategies to join peers engaged in cooperative activities (e.g., the child approaches a group of peers building a sand castle, sits next to them for a while, then begins to help peer who is digging a tunnel).

2.2 The child will maintain jobs, roles, or identities that supplement other children's jobs, roles, or identities during cooperative activities (e.g., the child holds two blocks together while a peer puts a third block on top in building a house).

2.3 During group activities, the child will share or exchange objects with peers engaged in the same activity (e.g., the child shares a glue bottle with a peer when both are engaged in a gluing activity).

G3 The child will select appropriate strategies to resolve conflicts. Strategies include the following:

- Negotiating
- Using simple strategies
- Claiming and defending possessions

3.1 The child will initiate solutions to bring about agreement when in conflict with a peer or an adult (e.g., when both the child and a peer want to play in a corner of the sandbox, the child says, "I'll dig here and you dig there").

3.2 The child will use a variety of simple strategies (e.g., whines, makes demand, walks/runs away, tattles) to resolve conflicts with other people (e.g., when a peer hits the child, the child turns to an adult and says, "Susan hit me").

3.3 The child will use verbal or nonverbal strategies to claim and defend possessions (e.g., the child says, "That coat is mine," and takes the coat from peer).

Strand B: Interaction with Environment

G1 The child will use socially appropriate strategies to meet physical needs such as the following:

- Physical needs when uncomfortable, sick, hurt, or tired
- Observable physical needs
- Physical needs of hunger and thirst

1.1   The child will use socially appropriate ways to meet physical needs when uncomfortable, sick, hurt, or tired (e.g., the child requests an adult to help when injured or sick).

1.2   The child will use socially appropriate ways to meet observable physical needs (e.g., the child removes wet or soiled clothing).

1.3   The child will use socially appropriate ways to express or meet physical needs of hunger and thirst (e.g., the child requests food or drink).

G2   The child will follow context-specific rules outside of the home and classroom (e.g., store, park, doctor's office; the child follows a rule not to touch things when in the grocery store).

2.1   The child will ask adults for permission as required to engage in established routines at home, at school, and in the community (e.g., the child asks a parent for permission to go to a neighbor's house).

2.2   The child will follow established rules at home and within the classroom. Group directions or cues may be provided by an adult (e.g., "It is story time").

Strand C: Knowledge of Self and Others

G1   The child will communicate personal likes and dislikes about people, objects, and activities (e.g., the child says, "Yumm, I love chocolate cake" while eating a piece of cake).

1.1   The child will initiate preferred purposeful activities during free time. General cues may be provided by an adult (e.g., "Find something to do").

1.2   The child will select activities or objects when given a choice of at least two within the daily routine (e.g., the child selects crackers from a plate of crackers and cheese).

G2   The child will correctly communicate the following information about self and others:

- Address (number, street, and town)
- Telephone number
- Birthday (month and day)
- Name(s) of sibling(s) and full name of self
- Gender (self and others)
- First name and age

2.1   The child will correctly state own address, including the number, street, and town.

2.2   The child will correctly state own telephone number.

2.3   The child will correctly state own birthday, including the month and the day.

2.4   The child will correctly state the first name(s) of sibling(s) and own first and last names.

2.5   The child will correctly identify self and others as being either a girl or a boy.

2.6   The child will correctly state own first name and age in years.

G3   The child will accurately identify affect/emotions (e.g., happy, sad, angry, mad, lonely) displayed by self and others.

3.1   The child will identify affect/emotions of others that are consistent with displayed behaviors (e.g., the child signs, HE'S HURT, in response to a peer's crying after falling on the playground).

3.2   The child will identify own affect/emotions that are consistent with displayed behaviors (e.g., when sampling distasteful food, the child frowns and says, "Yuck, I don't like it").

AEPS Assessment
Activity Plans

This appendix contains six AEPS assessment activity plans that may serve as models for the development of additional plans or can be modified to meet the needs of particular groups of children and settings. Each plan contains the following elements: a description of the activity, materials that will be needed, and directions for execution of the activity. The modification of these plans or the development of alternative activity plans is encouraged in order to meet the needs of children with varying developmental levels or who have specific disabilities.

The use of activity plans should have two important outcomes. First, the use of the activity format should help ensure that the assessor will obtain an accurate picture of the child's skills and capabilities. Second, the use of the activity format with groups of children will enhance the efficiency of the assessment process, permitting interventionists and caregivers to begin intervention activities more quickly.

The sample plans contained in this appendix describe activities that are likely to occur in center-based settings. Employing such activities to assess groups of children often results in little disruption to the ongoing program. In addition, the use of such activities to assess children should yield outcomes that accurately reflect their functional repertoires.

Groups of children can be assessed during a period of several days by organizing assessment stations. A different activity can be conducted at each station and small groups of children can rotate from station to station throughout the day. The activities conducted at each station should be designed to ensure that target goals and objectives will occur frequently. It is important to remember that modification in plans and format will be likely if the individual needs of children are to be met appropriately.

ACTIVITY CENTERS/FREE PLAY

Preparation

Establish activity centers in the classroom that are equipped with materials available to the children during unstructured play periods. One center should be equipped with blocks in various shapes, sizes, and colors; simple puzzles; and toys that the children can assemble (e.g., Tinkertoys, Legos, or Lincoln Logs). These materials can be placed on easy-to-reach shelves, in toy chests, or in large containers with lids.

Another center can be supplied with paper and crayons for coloring or art. Place posters or pictures with familiar characters, objects, or shapes on the walls. The children's artwork can also be placed on this wall.

A third center should have a variety of dress-up clothing and a mirror. The shirts and coats can be hung on low hooks; hats, jewelry, and shoes can be placed on shelves or in boxes.

Access to bathroom facilities will also be necessary for cleaning up after messy activities and for daily toileting. Place a low stool under a hard-to-reach sink to promote independence in washing.

Outdoors, the children should have access to tricycles, balls, and a variety of playground equipment.

Domains: Fine Motor (FM), Gross Motor (GM), Adaptive (Adap), Cognitive (Cog), Social-Communication (SC), Social (Soc)

Materials

Art Center	**Dress-Up Center**
Crayons	Coats
Pencils	Hats
Paper	Shoes
	Pants
Manipulative Center	Shirts
Puzzles	Socks
Blocks	
Tinkertoys	**Outdoors**
Legos	Bicycles
Lincoln Logs	Balls
	Playground equipment

Domain and strand		Targeted goals and/or objectives	Description/sequence
Soc A	1.3	Initiates greetings to familiar peers	**Morning Routine** As the children arrive in the classroom, observe each child's ability to greet others.
FM B	G1	Copies complex shapes	**Art Center** In this center, model writing and drawing. Watch the children for demonstration of these skills. Use the posters on the wall as examples of shapes, objects, and letters for the children to copy. Model drawing and writing letters as needed.
	1.1	Copies simple shapes	
	G2	Prints first name	
	2.1	Prints three letters	
	2.2	Copies first name	
	2.3	Copies three letters	
FM A	G1	Manipulates two small objects at same time	**Manipulative Center** In this center, observe each child's ability to handle blocks, to put puzzles together, and to assemble Tinkertoys, Lincoln Logs, or Legos.
	1.1	Manipulates two hand-size objects at same time	

Domain and strand		Targeted goals and/or objectives	Description/sequence
FM A	G3	Ties string-type fastener	**Dress-Up Center**
	3.1	Fastens buttons	In the dress-up center, observe each child's ability to dress and undress.
	3.2	Threads and zips zipper	
Adap C	G1	Unfastens fasteners on garments	
	1.1	Unfastens buttons/snaps/Velcro fasteners on garments	
	1.2	Unties string-type fastener	
	1.3	Unzips zipper	
	2.1	Puts on long pants	
	2.2	Puts on front-opening garment	
	2.3	Puts on pullover garment	
	2.4	Puts on shoes	
	2.5	Puts on underpants, shorts, or skirt	
	G3	Fastens fasteners on garments	
	3.1	Ties string-type fastener	
	3.2	Fastens buttons, snaps, and Velcro fasteners	
	3.3	Threads and zips zipper	
Cog G	G1	Engages in imaginary play	As the children are playing with the dress-up clothing, observe them for demonstration of imaginary play skills (e.g., a child puts on a hat and high heels and pretends to be Mommy going shopping, or a child says "I'm going to ride my motorcycle," holding her hands in front of her and making "motor" noises).
	1.1	Enacts roles or identities	
	1.2	Plans and acts out recognizable event, theme, or story line	
	1.3	Uses imaginary props	
GM A	G1	Alternates feet walking up and down stairs	**Outside**
	1.1	Walks up and down stairs	As children move and play around the building or playground, watch for demonstration of gross motor skills.
GM B	G1	Jumps forward	
	1.1	Jumps in place	
	1.2	Jumps from platform	
	1.3	Maintains balance in walking	
	1.4	Balances on one foot	
	G2	Runs avoiding obstacles	
	2.1	Runs	
	G3	Bounces, catches, kicks, and throws ball	
	3.1	Bounces ball	
	3.2	Catches ball	
	3.3	Kicks ball	
	3.4	Throws ball	
	G4	Skips	
	4.1	Hops	
	G5	Rides and steers two-wheel bicycle	
	5.1	Pedals and steers two-wheel bicycle with training wheels	
Cog G	G2	Engages in games with rules	As the children participate in organized games outside, observe for their participation skills (e.g., several children play "tag" or "follow-the-leader").
	2.1	Maintains participation	
	2.2	Conforms to game rules	

Domain and strand		Targeted goals and/or objectives	Description/sequence
Soc A	1.1	Responds to peers in distress or need	While the children are involved in activities outside, watch for them to look for and respond to peers.
	1.2	Establishes and maintains proximity to peers	
	1.4	Responds to affective initiations from peers	
Adap B	G1	Carries out all toileting functions	**Toileting/Washing**
	1.1	Uses toilet paper, flushes toilet, washes hands after using toilet	During toileting, watch each child for demonstration of personal hygiene and undressing skills.
	1.2	Uses toilet	
	1.3	Indicates need to use toilet	
Adap C	2.5	Puts on underpants, shorts, or skirt	
	G3	Fastens fasteners on garments	
Adap B	G2	Washes and grooms self	**Throughout the day**
	2.2	Brushes teeth	When the children are washing up after a messy activity and before or after snack time, watch for demonstration of grooming skills as appropriate.
	2.4	Brushes or combs hair	
	2.5	Washes and dries face	
Soc C	G1	Communicates personal likes and dislikes	As the children are given choices in activities or objects, watch for the children to make choices appropriately.
	1.1	Initiates preferred activities	
	1.2	Selects activities and/or objects	
Soc A	G3	Resolves conflicts by selecting effective strategy	During activities throughout the day, observe each child's ability to resolve conflicts that arise (e.g., when a peer says that she wants a child's toys, the child says "You can play with this one," handing the peer one of the toys).
	3.1	Negotiates to resolve conflicts	
	3.2	Uses simple strategies to resolve conflicts	
	3.3	Claims and defends possessions	
Adap B	2.1	Uses tissue to clean nose	Observe the children's ability to meet their physical needs appropriately (e.g., a child asks to get a tissue for her nose or tells an adult "I'm hungry").
Soc B	G1	Meets physical needs in socially appropriate ways	
	1.1	Meets physical needs when uncomfortable, sick, hurt, or tired	
	1.2	Meets observable physical needs	
	1.3	Meets physical needs of hunger and thirst	
Soc A	G1	Has play partners	As the children play independently, watch for each child's interaction skills with peers (e.g., a child asks a peer to play with her, or a child hands a peer some toys).
	G2	Initiates cooperative activity	
	2.1	Joins others in cooperative activity	
	2.2	Maintains cooperative participation with others	
	2.3	Shares or exchanges objects	
Soc B	2.1	Seeks adult permission	At the end of the unstructured play periods, observe each child's ability to follow classroom rules such as cleaning up, moving to other activities, preparing for snack time or outdoor activities, toileting, and getting ready to go home at the end of the day.
	2.2	Follows established rules at home and in classroom	
Cog D	G1	Follows directions of three or more related steps that are not routinely given	Also, watch for each child's ability to follow directions during these times.
	1.1	Follows directions of three or more related steps that are routinely given	

Domain and strand		Targeted goals and/or objectives	Description/sequence
Cog A	G1	Initiates and completes age-appropriate activities	Observe each child's ability to participate appropriately in small and large group activities.
	1.1	Responds to request to finish activity	
	1.2	Responds to request to begin activity	
	G2	Watches, listens, and participates during small group activities	
	2.1	Interacts appropriately with materials during small group activities	
	2.2	Responds appropriately to directions during small group activities	
	2.3	Looks at appropriate object, person, or event during small group activities	
	2.4	Remains with group during small group activities	
	G3	Watches, listens, and participates during large group activities	
	3.1	Interacts appropriately with materials during large group activities	
	3.2	Responds appropriately to directions during large group activities	
	3.3	Looks at appropriate object, person, or event during large group activities	
	3.4	Remains with group during large group activities	
SC A	G2	Uses conversational rules	Observe the children for demonstration of communication skills. Unstructured play times and transition times are often good opportunities for taking language samples.
	2.1	Alternates between speaker/listener role	
	2.2	Responds to topic changes initiated by others	
	2.3	Asks questions for clarification	
	2.4	Responds to contingent questions	
	2.5	Initiates context-relevant topics	
	2.6	Responds to others' topic initiations	
SC B	G1	Uses verbs	
	G2	Uses noun inflections	
	G3	Asks questions	
	G4	Uses pronouns	
	G5	Uses descriptive words	
Cog D	G3	Retells event in sequence	At the end of activities or the class session, observe each child's ability to describe a story or classroom events to a naive listener (e.g., a parent).
	3.1	Completes sequence of familiar story or event	

ACTIVITY: POST OFFICE

Preparation

Set up an area to be the post office, with a counter and a mail box. Have shapes of various sizes and colors drawn on construction paper. Larger shapes will be used for cards and smaller shapes will be used for stamps. Tape some of the scissors shut beforehand to give the children an opportunity to solve problems. Limit the number of scissors and pencils available to provide opportunities for peer interaction.

Domains: Fine Motor (FM), Cognitive (Cog), Social-Communication (SC), Social (Soc)

Materials

Scissors
Toy money
Mail carrier's hat
Mail bag
Rubber stamps
Pencils
Markers
Tape
Paper
Mailbox
Envelopes (different sizes)

Domain and strand		Targeted goals and/or objectives	Description/sequence
Cog A	G2	Watches, listens, and participates during small group activities	Introduce the activity by describing the sequence of events for when a person sends a letter (i.e., "First we write a letter and put it in the envelope. Then we write an address and put a stamp on it. Last, we put it in the mailbox"). Ask the children to name the steps. Tell the children that they will follow these steps to send letters to friends or family members.
Cog E	G2	Recalls verbal sequences	
Cog D	G1	Follows directions of three or more related steps that are not routinely given	Observe the children's ability to follow directions.
Cog A	1.2	Responds to request to begin activity	Encourage the children to cut out cards and stamps to use for the activity, identifying various shapes, sizes, and colors (i.e., ask the children what colors of paper they want, which shapes they would like to cut out, what size paper they would like).
FM A	G1	Manipulates two small objects at same time	
	1.1	Manipulates two hand-size objects at same time	
	G2	Cuts out shapes with curved lines	
	2.1	Cuts out shapes with straight lines	
	2.2	Cuts paper in two	
Cog B	G1	Demonstrates understanding of eight different colors	
	G2	Demonstrates understanding of five different shapes	
	G3	Demonstrates understanding of six different size concepts	

Domain and strand		Targeted goals and/or objectives	Description/sequence
Cog F	G1	Evaluates solutions to problems	Observe the children's abilities to problem-solve with taped scissors and limited supplies.
	1.1	Suggests acceptable solutions to problems	
Soc C	2.3	Knows birthday	As the children are cutting, ask them when their birthdays are so that they can decide if they should send birthday cards to people in the class.
Cog E	2.1	Recalls verbal information about self	
Soc C	2.6	Knows name and age	During this discussion, have the children state how old they are.
Soc C	2.4	Names siblings and gives full name of self	Then, ask the children to name people in their families and tell if any of their family members have birthdays coming up.
Cog I	4.1	Identifies letters	Present children with cards with printed letters on them. Have the children select or identify letters to write their names. The children can then write letters and draw pictures for other children or for family members.
Cog B	G3	Demonstrates understanding of six different size concepts	When the children have finished writing or coloring their letters, ask them to select an envelope from a selection of various sizes.
Soc C	2.1	States address	Ask each child for his or her name and address to write on the envelope (also ask the child for his or her telephone number).
	2.2	States telephone number	
	2.4	Names siblings and gives full name of self	
	2.6	Knows name and age	
FM B	G1	Copies complex shapes	Have each child print the name and address of the letter's recipient on the envelope. (The child may need a printed model to copy from.)
	1.1	Copies simple shapes	
	G2	Prints first name	
	2.1	Prints three letters	
	2.2	Copies first name	
	2.3	Copies three letters	
Cog A	G1	Initiates and completes age-appropriate activities	Once the letters are ready, let the children dramatize a post office situation. The children can take turns being customers and postal workers. The customers need to buy stamps and mail letters; the workers need to talk to the customers and sell stamps.
	1.1	Responds to request to finish activity	
Cog G	G1	Engages in imaginary play	
	1.1	Enacts roles or identities	
SC A	G2	Uses conversational rules	
	2.1	Alternates between speaker/listener role	
	2.2	Responds to topic changes initiated by others	
	2.3	Asks questions for clarification	
	2.4	Responds to contingent questions	
	2.5	Initiates context-relevant topics	
	2.6	Responds to others' topic initiations	
Soc A	G2	Initiates cooperative activity	
	2.1	Joins others in cooperative activity	
	2.2	Maintains cooperative participation with others	
	2.3	Shares or exchanges objects	

Domain and strand		Targeted goals and/or objectives	Description/sequence
Cog I	4.1	Identifies letters	The children can identify names and letters on the envelopes, collect the mail, and deliver the mail to the children's boxes or cubbies.
Cog E	1.1	Recalls events that occurred on same day, with contextual cues	When the children have finished mailing and delivering the letters, have the children name the steps they performed to do so.

ACTIVITY: WASHING BABIES

Preparation

Have an area set aside with tables with plastic or towels around it. Have dressed dolls, folded towels, washcloths, soap, shampoo, tubs, sponges, containers, and aprons on the counter or another table nearby.

Domains: Fine Motor (FM), Adaptive (Adap), Cognitive (Cog), Social (Soc)

Materials

Washcloths
Dishpans or tubs
Dolls (waterproof)
Water containers
Aprons or smocks
Towels
Sponges
Soap
Shampoo

Domain and strand		Targeted goals and/or objectives	Description/sequence
Cog A	G2	Watches, listens, and participates during small group activities	Group three to five children around the prepared table and tell the children that they are going to give the "babies" or dolls a bath today.
Cog F	1.1	Suggests acceptable solutions to problems	Ask the children what they will need to give the dolls a bath.
Cog F	G1	Evaluates solutions to problems	Tell the children before they start that they need to find a way to keep their own clothes dry. Suggest some possible solutions (e.g., "What if you tucked a paper napkin in your shirt?" or "What if you didn't stand near the tub?"). Allow the children opportunity to respond.
	1.1	Suggests acceptable solutions to problems	
Cog H	2.1	Counts five objects	After the suggestion of wearing aprons has been made, ask one of the children to count the number of children in the group and ask another child to get that number of aprons from the box and give one to each child.
	2.3	Demonstrates understanding of one-to-one correspondence	
Adap C	G3	Fastens fasteners on garments	Ask each child to put his or her smock on, pick out a doll from the box, and bring it to the table, or give a similar three-step direction.
Cog D	G1	Follows directions of three or more related steps that are not routinely given	
Cog F	1.2	Identifies means to goal	Let the children fill the tubs with water using the containers to carry water from the sink.
Cog B	G4	Demonstrates understanding of 10 different qualitative concepts	Ask the children questions and give directions using a variety of qualitative and quantitative concepts (e.g., Is the water *hot* or *cold*?" or "Give me the *empty* container").
	G5	Demonstrates understanding of eight different quantitative concepts	
Cog D	3.1	Completes sequence of familiar story or event	Tell the children, "First we will undress the dolls, then wash the dolls, then dry them and dress them again." See if the children can verbally repeat this sequence.

Domain and strand		Targeted goals and/or objectives	Description/sequence
FM A	G1	Manipulates two small objects at same time	Allow the children to wash the dolls using the sponges, washcloths, soap, and shampoo.
	1.1	Manipulates two hand-size objects at same time	
Cog B	G3	Demonstrates understanding of six different size concepts	Follow the children's lead and, as opportunity allows, ask questions or give directions that will demonstrate the child's functional use of size concepts (e.g., "Are your fingers bigger or smaller than the doll's?"); spatial relationships (e.g., "Put your doll next to mine" or "Wash between the doll's fingers"); and premath concepts (e.g., "Let's count our dolls' toes").
	G6	Demonstrates understanding of 12 different spatial relations concepts	
Cog H	G2	Counts 10 objects	
	2.1	Counts five objects	
	2.2	Counts two objects	
Cog A	G2	Watches, listens, and participates during small group activities	Throughout the activity, observe the children's abilities to watch, listen, and participate during small group activities.
	2.1	Interacts appropriately with materials during small group activities	
	2.2	Responds appropriately to directions during small group activities	
	2.3	Looks at appropriate object, person, or event during small group activities	
	2.4	Remains with group during small group activities	
Soc A	G2	Initiates cooperative activity	Also, observe the children's social interactions with others and encourage these interactions (e.g., "Maybe you can share the soap with Tommy" or "What can we do? We have only one bottle of shampoo").
	2.1	Joins others in cooperative activity	
	2.2	Maintains cooperative participation with others	
	2.3	Shares or exchanges objects	
	G3	Resolves conflicts by selecting effective strategy	
	3.1	Negotiates to resolve conflicts	
	3.2	Uses simple strategies to resolve conflicts	
	3.3	Claims and defends possessions	
Cog C	G1	Groups objects, people, or events on the basis of specified criteria	After the dolls are washed, dried, and redressed, ask the children to help clean up. Clean up by grouping the items that go together in separate containers: all the wet towels and washcloths in one container, the soaps and shampoos in another, sponges in a third, and tubs on the sink counter.
Cog E	1.2	Recalls events immediately after they occur	The activity could end by discussing the events of the activity and how each child proceeded to wash his or her baby or what he or she did during the activity.

ACTIVITY: PLAY-DOH

Preparation

Place various sizes and shapes of cookie cutters into several containers with very tight lids. In another container, place items that can be used to change the texture of the Play-Doh (toothbrushes, screen, forks, spoons, rollers, and so forth). Have several colors of Play-Doh available for the children's use.

Domains: Fine Motor (FM), Gross Motor (GM), Cognitive (Cog), Social-Communication (SC), Social (Soc)

Materials

Rollers
Forks
Spoons
Cookie cutters
Pieces of screen
Toothbrushes
Play-Doh (various colors)
Containers with lids (at least four)

Domain and strand		Targeted goals and/or objectives	Description/sequence
Soc C	G1	Communicates personal likes and dislikes	Introduce the activity by asking each child to choose a canister of cookie cutters.
	1.2	Selects activities and/or objects	
Cog B	G1	Demonstrates understanding of eight different colors	Allow them to choose Play-Doh and any other objects they would like to work with. One child may be put "in charge" of a specific color or toy. Encourage the children to identify items by color or shape.
	G2	Demonstrates understanding of five different shapes	
Cog A	1.2	Responds to request to begin activity	See if the children are able to use problem-solving skills to open their canisters.
Cog F	G1	Evaluates solutions to problems	
	1.1	Suggests acceptable solutions to problems	
	1.2	Identifies means to goal	
Cog H	G2	Counts 10 objects	Make balls of Play-Doh and model counting them. Observe the children's ability to do so. Ask children who do not imitate this action how many pieces of Play-Doh they have.
	2.1	Counts five objects	
	2.2	Counts two objects	
FM A	G1	Manipulates two small objects at same time	Allow the children to play independently with the Play-Doh. Observe them for demonstration of fine motor skills.
	1.1	Manipulates two hand-size objects at same time	
Soc A	G2	Initiates cooperative activity	Watch for each child to initiate, join, and maintain participation with others (e.g., children ask each other for different cookie cutters or for a piece of Play-Doh in a particular color; a child offers to trade a roller for a toothbrush).
	2.1	Joins others in cooperative activity	
	2.2	Maintains cooperative participation with others	
	2.3	Shares or exchanges objects	

Domain and strand		Targeted goals and/or objectives	Description/sequence
Soc A	G3	Resolves conflicts by selecting effective strategy	Observe the children's ability to resolve their own conflicts.
	3.1	Negotiates to resolve conflicts	
	3.2	Uses simple strategies to resolve conflicts	
	3.3	Claims and defends possessions	
Cog D	G1	Follows directions of three or more related steps that are not routinely given	Give the children instructions to follow involving several steps. Have the children take turns giving each other instructions too (e.g., "Put the cookie cutter on the table, take a fork and push it into your cookie").
Cog B	G1	Demonstrates understanding of eight different colors	While giving instructions, use color, shape, size, qualitative, quantitative, spatial, and temporal concepts.
	G2	Demonstrates understanding of five different shapes	
	G3	Demonstrates understanding of six different size concepts	
	G4	Demonstrates understanding of 10 different qualitative concepts	
	G5	Demonstrates understanding of eight different quantitative concepts	
	G6	Demonstrates understanding of 12 different spatial relations concepts	
	G7	Demonstrates understanding of seven different temporal relations concepts	
Cog A	G2	Watches, listens, and participates during small group activities	Watch for children to demonstrate skills involving small group participation.
	2.1	Interacts appropriately with materials during small group activities	
	2.2	Responds appropriately to directions during small group activities	
	2.3	Looks at appropriate object, person, or event during small group activities	
	2.4	Remains with group during small group activities	
Cog C	1.3	Groups objects on the basis of physical attribute	To end the activity, have the children sort the materials on the basis of physical attribute (e.g., "Put the Play-Doh into the container with a lid of the same color"; demonstrate with pieces of Play-Doh).
SC A	G1	Uses words, phrases, or sentences to inform, direct, ask questions, and express anticipation, imagination, affect, and emotions	Have a container for each of three groups but not for a fourth to elicit communication.
Cog H	G2	Counts 10 objects	As the children are putting the materials away, encourage them to count the cookie cutters.
	2.1	Counts five objects	
	2.2	Counts two objects	

Domain and strand		Targeted goals and/or objectives	Description/sequence
Soc B	2.2	Follows established rules at home and in classroom	Observe each child's ability to follow the typical routine for cleaning up after an activity.
GM B	1.3	Maintains balance in walking	Observe each child's ability to walk as the children put materials away and move to the next activity.

ACTIVITY: OBSTACLE COURSE

Preparation

Using balance beams, jump ropes, stairs, and playground equipment, set up an area to be used as an obstacle course that children can move through follow-the-leader style. Use string or tape to identify boundaries. This activity can be set up outside or in a large open space such as a gym or activity room. Provide a private area for changing clothes.

As with all of the AEPS Assessment Activity Plans, portions of this activity (e.g., changing clothes) may be excluded as necessary to allow for time constraints. Also, if particular objectives have been assessed previously, those items may be omitted. Similarly, if additional assessment items are needed, they may be incorporated into the activity.

Domains: Fine Motor (FM), Gross Motor (GM), Adaptive (Adap), Cognitive (Cog), Social-Communication (SC), Social (Soc)

Materials

Bicycles
Tape
Balance beam
String
Jump rope
Balls
Playground equipment
Stairs
From home:
  T-shirts
  Shorts
  Athletic shoes
  Socks

Domain and strand		Targeted goals and/or objectives	Description/sequence
Cog D	1.1	Follows directions of three or more related steps that are routinely given	For this activity, tell the children that they will be doing an obstacle course and exercises. Give the children directions involving three steps (e.g., "Take off your school shoes and put them on the bench. Then put on your tennies," or "Go to the bathroom, put on your shorts, and line up by the door").
Adap C	G1	Unfastens fasteners on garments	If the children are asked to change their clothes, observe each child's ability to unfasten buttons, snaps, and Velcro fasteners on garments, to untie string fasteners, and to open zippers.
	1.1	Unfastens buttons/snaps/Velcro fasteners on garments	
	1.2	Unties string-type fastener	
	1.3	Unzips zipper	
FM A	G3	Ties string-type fastener	Watch for fine motor skills as the children put on their exercise clothing.
	3.1	Fastens buttons	
	3.2	Threads and zips zipper	

Domain and strand		Targeted goals and/or objectives	Description/sequence
Adap C	2.3	Puts on pullover garment	Also as the children dress, watch for them to demonstrate adaptive skills.
	2.4	Puts on shoes	
	2.5	Puts on underpants, shorts, or skirt	
	G3	Fastens fasteners on garments	
	3.1	Ties string-type fastener	
	3.2	Fastens buttons, snaps, and Velcro fasteners	
	3.3	Threads and zips zipper	
Cog B	G6	Demonstrates understanding of 12 different spatial relations concepts	When the children are dressed, use spatial concepts to tell them to put their clothes away and to get into a line (e.g., "Put your shoes *on* the shelf," "Put your socks *in* your shoes," "Stand *behind* the line," or "Line up *in front of* the swings").
GM B	1.3	Maintains balance in walking	Throughout the preparation period, observe each child's balance and movement while walking.
GM A	G1	Alternates feet walking up and down stairs	Have an adult lead the children through the obstacle course the first time through. Model walking up and down stairs.
	1.1	Walks up and down stairs	
GM B	G1	Jumps forward	Observe the children using the equipment. Encourage them to stand on one foot, jump in place, jump from a platform, and jump over a jump rope placed on the ground.
	1.1	Jumps in place	
	1.2	Jumps from platform	
	1.4	Balances on one foot	
GM B	G2	Runs avoiding obstacles	Observe each child's ability to run through an open portion of the course and around obstacles in another part.
	2.1	Runs	
GM B	G4	Skips	Later, encourage the children to hop and then skip through the course.
	4.1	Hops	
GM B	G5	Rides and steers two-wheel bicycle	Allow the children to ride bicycles through another portion of the course.
	5.1	Pedals and steers two-wheel bicycle with training wheels	
GM B	G3	Bounces, catches, kicks, and throws ball	Encourage the children to stand in a circle in a clear spot. Give each pair of children a ball. Encourage the children to bounce, throw, catch, and kick their balls.
	3.1	Bounces ball	
	3.2	Catches ball	
	3.3	Kicks ball	
	3.4	Throws ball	
SC A	1.5	Uses words, phrases, or sentences to make commands to and requests of others	After the first time through the course, have the children take turns being the leader and giving instructions.
Soc A	G1	Has play partners	Watch for social interactions between children.
	1.1	Responds to peers in distress or need	
	1.2	Establishes and maintains proximity to peers	

Domain and strand		Targeted goals and/or objectives	Description/sequence
Cog A	G3	Watches, listens, and participates during large group activities	Throughout the activity, observe the children for demonstration of large group participation skills.
	3.1	Interacts appropriately with materials during large group activities	
	3.2	Responds appropriately to directions during large group activities	
	3.3	Looks at appropriate object, person, or event during large group activities	
	3.4	Remains with group during large group activities	
			Allow the children to play independently with the obstacle course materials toward the end of the activity. This will provide additional opportunities to observe target behaviors.
Cog D	1.1	Follows directions of three or more related steps that are routinely given	To end the activity, give three-step directions to instruct the children to take off their exercise clothing and to put on their street clothes or to make the transition to the next activity (e.g., "Go to the bathroom, wash your hands, and sit down for snack").
FM A	G3	Ties string-type fastener	If the children are wearing gym clothes, watch for fine motor skills as they change into their street clothing.
	3.1	Fastens buttons	
	3.2	Threads and zips zipper	
Adap C	G1	Unfastens fasteners on garments	Also, watch for self-care skills as the children are changing.
	1.1	Unfastens buttons/snaps/Velcro fasteners on garments	
	1.2	Unties string-type fastener	
	1.3	Unzips zipper	
	G3	Fastens fasteners on garments	
	3.1	Ties string-type fastener	
	3.2	Fastens buttons, snaps, and Velcro fasteners	
	3.3	Threads and zips zipper	
Cog D	1.1	Follows directions of three or more related steps that are routinely given	When the children have finished dressing, use three-step directions to tell them to put their clothes away (e.g., "Put your shoes and shorts in your bag, put your bag in your cubby, and go wash for snack").

ACTIVITY: STORY

Preparation

Choose some books that would be appropriate for beginning readers to sound out and rhyme words. Other books can be about the country, animals, the alphabet, colors, or shapes. In order to isolate objectives (e.g., particular concepts), choose books in which those concepts are frequently used. Place pillows around the area to make comfortable seating available.

Domains: Cognitive (Cog), Social (Soc)

Materials

Books
Pillows

Domain and strand		Targeted goals and/or objectives	Description/sequence
Soc C	1.2	Selects activities and/or objects	Have several books available for the children to choose from.
Cog I	1.1	Demonstrates functional use of books	Allow the children to look at or read the books.
	1.2	Tells about pictures in book	
Cog I	G1	Demonstrates prereading skills	Observe each child's ability to demonstrate book-related skills.
Cog I	G3	Sounds out words	Ask each child to identify letters, produce phonetic sounds for letters, sound out printed words, and read words by sight.
	3.1	Produces phonetic sounds for letters	
	G4	Reads words by sight	
	4.1	Identifies letters	
Cog F	G2	Makes statements and appropriately answers questions that require reasoning about objects, situations, or people	Observe the children's ability to use reasoning skills. If necessary, ask questions to elicit these skills (e.g., "Why is the dog barking?" or "What will the little pigs do if the wolf comes?").
	2.1	Gives reason for inference	
	2.2	Makes prediction about future or hypothetical events	
Cog B	G1	Demonstrates understanding of eight different colors	As the children look at their books, ask them to identify colors, shapes, sizes, quality, quantity concepts, as well as spatial and temporal relations concepts. (e.g., "What *color* is the ball?", "Show me the *biggest* cat," "*How many* ducks do you see?", or "This picture has a moon and stars. Is it *morning* or *night?*").
	G2	Demonstrates understanding of five different shapes	
	G3	Demonstrates understanding of six different size concepts	
	G4	Demonstrates understanding of 10 different qualitative concepts	
	G5	Demonstrates understanding of eight different quantitative concepts	
	G6	Demonstrates understanding of 12 different spatial relations concepts	
	G7	Demonstrates understanding of seven different temporal relations concepts	

Domain and strand		Targeted goals and/or objectives	Description/sequence
Cog D	G3	Retells event in sequence	After the children have finished looking at their books, encourage each of them to tell what their book was about.
	3.1	Completes sequence of familiar story or event	
Cog F	2.3	Gives possible cause for some event	Next, read a book containing rhymes to the children and watch for their ability to participate in storytelling (i.e., Do they attend to the storyteller, anticipate what will happen next in the story, or comment as the story goes on?).
Cog I	1.3	Participates actively in storytelling	
Cog I	2.2	Rhymes words	Also, observe their ability to think of words that rhyme with words in the book (e.g., "'Mat' and 'hat' rhyme with 'cat.' What else rhymes with 'cat'?").
Cog A	G2	Watches, listens, and participates during small group activities	Throughout the activity observe each child's ability to watch, listen, and participate during a small group activity (i.e., Does the child remain with the group? Does she continue looking at books or go get a doll? Does she attend to the storyteller?).
	2.1	Interacts appropriately with materials during small group activities	
	2.2	Responds appropriately to directions during small group activities	
	2.3	Looks at appropriate object, person, or event during small group activities	
	2.4	Remains within group during small group activities	
Soc B	2.2	Follows established rules at home and in classroom	Encourage the children to put their books away when the activity is finished.

Variations

Read

Read a popular children's story to the children and allow them to participate in the storytelling by making comments and asking questions.

Animal Sounds

Read a story that includes various types of animals. Have the children make the noise of a particular animal each time the animal is mentioned. In addition, allow the children to comment on what they know about the different types of animals.

Flannel Board

Use a flannel board and flannel cutouts to tell the children a story. The flannel board can be set up to portray a scene, and the flannel characters can be moved around on the board as events take place in the story.

Acting Out Story

Allow the children to dress up and act out a story that they have read. Choose a story that they are very familiar with, such as *The Three Little Pigs, Goldilocks and the Three Bears,* or *The Little Red Hen.*

Puppets

Have the children use puppets to act out a story. The children can make the puppets ahead of time as an art activity.

Collage Book

Prepare several blank sheets of paper and staple them together to form a book. Collect some old magazines. Select a general theme for the books such as families, animals, transportation, buildings, and so forth. Allow the children to choose pictures and cut them out. Then they can glue the pictures into their books.

Classroom Story

Take pictures of a classroom field trip, party, or other special event. Later in the week, have the children work cooperatively to make a book that tells about the event. The children can paste the pictures into their book, draw additional pictures, glue them into the book, and dictate what they would like to have written.

My Book About Me

Have each child draw pictures of him- or herself on the covers of their books. They can write their names and other personal information below the pictures. Inside the books, the children can draw pictures of friends, pets, family members, hobbies, their homes, or whatever interests them.

Recording a Story

Find picture books portraying a series of events. Have the children tell their stories into an audiotape recorder. When the first child has finished, play the tape back so that the children can listen to part of the story as they follow along in the book.

AEPS Forms

APPENDIX

D

Appendix D contains forms to assist in utilizing the AEPS. These forms include:

AEPS Data Recording Forms
AEPS Family Report
AEPS Family Interest Survey
AEPS Child Progress Record

The AEPS Data Recording Forms, Family Report, Family Interest Survey, and Child Progress Record may be purchased in packets from Paul H. Brookes Publishing Co., P.O. Box 10624, Baltimore, Maryland 21285-0624; 1-800-638-3775.

DATA RECORDING FORMS

for

Assessment, Evaluation, and Programming System (AEPS) for Infants and Children

AEPS Measurement for Three to Six Years

edited by

Diane Bricker, Ph.D., and Kristie Pretti-Frontczak, Ph.D.

Child's name: _____

Child's date of birth: _____

Family name: _____

Name of person

   completing form: _____

Date: _____

Family's address: _____

_____

_____

DIRECTIONS

Before beginning the assessment, read Chapter 6 for a comprehensive description of how to use the AEPS Test. In addition, review the Scoring Key and Qualifying Notes.

To begin, fill in the blanks on the cover sheet of the scoring form, which ask for the child's name, date of birth, family information, and name of the person completing the form. The Data Recording Form is designed to be used across four test administrations; therefore, space is available to enter four test dates and the names of the observer for each test interval. It is recommended that the AEPS Test be administered at 3-month intervals, which permits using one scoring form for an entire year.

The scoring form for each domain lists the strands, which are shaded, and their associated goals and objectives. Beside each item (goal and objective) are five columns. The first column, the IFSP column, can be checked if the item is to become an IEP or IFSP goal. The second and subsequent columns are headed "S" and "Q." The boxes under the "S" column are used to record the item score, whereas the boxes under the "Q" column are used to record any necessary qualifying notes. The "S" and "Q" columns appear four times to accommodate four test periods.

For a specific test period, the box under the "S" column should be used to record the child's score for each item. A score should appear in each box for each test period. The scoring key appears at the top of each domain and indicates that the child's performance can be scored with a 2, 1, or 0. A score of 2 indicates that the child has consistently met the item's criterion, a 1 indicates that the child inconsistently met the criterion, and a 0 means that the child did not meet the criterion stated in the AEPS Test manual. Items that are clearly above the child's performance level and cannot be observed can be scored with a 0 with an accompanying R (reported assessment) noted in the "Q" column. Likewise, items clearly below the child's performance level can be scored with a 2, with an accompanying R noted in the "Q" column.

Each "S" column has an associated "Q" column for indicating qualifying notes. The qualifying notes key appears at the top of each domain. As necessary for individual items, the appropriate qualifying note should be written in the appropriate box located under the "Q" column. Depending on the child's performance, items may or may not have qualifying notes indicated in the "Q" column.

At the bottom of the form, the Total Domain Score Possible is indicated along with space for recording the child's Domain Raw Score and the Domain Percent Score.

At the end of each domain of the Data Recording Form, space is provided for comments for each of the four test periods. Observers might want to indicate particular child or environmental features that might have affected the child's performance (e.g., the child appeared ill or several new children were present in the classroom). At the end of the Social-Communication Data Recording Form, in addition to the above-mentioned space for comments, there is a Social-Communication Recording Form and Summary Form. Refer to pages 203–205 for directions on how to complete these forms.

Fine Motor Domain

S = Scoring Key	Q = Qualifying Notes
2 = Pass consistently	A = Assistance provided
1 = Inconsistent performance	B = Behavior interfered
	R = Reported assessment
0 = Does not pass	M = Modification/adaptation
	D = Direct test

Name: _____

	Test Period:								
	Test Date: /			/		/		/	
	Examiner:								
	IFSP	S	Q	S	Q	S	Q	S	Q
A. Manipulation of objects									
1. Manipulates two small objects at same time									
1.1 Manipulates two hand-size objects at same time									
2. Cuts out shapes with curved lines									
2.1 Cuts out shapes with straight lines									
2.2 Cuts paper in two									
3. Ties string-type fastener									
3.1 Fastens buttons									
3.2 Threads and zips zipper									
B. Prewriting									
1. Copies complex shapes									
1.1 Copies simple shapes									
2. Prints first name									
2.1 Prints three letters									
2.2 Copies first name									
2.3 Copies three letters									

A Total Domain Raw Score can be computed for the domain by adding all of the 2 and 1 scores entered in the S column for a specific test period. To determine the Domain Percent Score, divide the Total Domain Raw Score by the Total Domain Score Possible, then multiply by 100.

RESULTS				
Test Date	_____	_____	_____	_____
Total Domain Raw Score	_____	_____	_____	_____
Total Domain Score Possible	28	28	28	28
Domain Percent Score	_____	_____	_____	_____

_____*AEPS*_____

Fine Motor Domain

EXAMINER: _____ DATE: _____

COMMENTS: _____

_____

_____

_____

EXAMINER: _____ DATE: _____

COMMENTS: _____

_____

_____

_____

EXAMINER: _____ DATE: _____

COMMENTS: _____

_____

_____

_____

EXAMINER: _____ DATE: _____

COMMENTS: _____

_____

_____

_____

Gross Motor Domain

S = Scoring Key	Q = Qualifying Notes
2 = Pass consistently	A = Assistance provided
1 = Inconsistent	B = Behavior interfered
performance	R = Reported assessment
0 = Does not pass	M = Modification/adaptation
	D = Direct test

Name: _____

	Test Period:								
	Test Date: __/__		__/__		__/__		__/__		
	Examiner:								
	IFSP	S	Q	S	Q	S	Q	S	Q
A. Balance and mobility in standing and walking									
1. Alternates feet walking up and down stairs									
1.1 Walks up and down stairs									
B. Play skills									
1. Jumps forward									
1.1 Jumps in place									
1.2 Jumps from platform									
1.3 Maintains balance in walking									
1.4 Balances on one foot									
2. Runs avoiding obstacles									
2.1 Runs									
3. Bounces, catches, kicks, and throws ball									
3.1 Bounces ball									
3.2 Catches ball									
3.3 Kicks ball									
3.4 Throws ball									
4. Skips									
4.1 Hops									
5. Rides and steers two-wheel bicycle									
5.1 Pedals and steers two-wheel bicycle with training wheels									

A Total Domain Raw Score can be computed for the domain by adding all of the 2 and 1 scores entered in the S column for a specific test period. To determine the Domain Percent Score, divide the Total Domain Raw Score by the Total Domain Score Possible, then multiply by 100.

AEPS   Gross Motor Domain

RESULTS				
Test Date				
Total Domain Raw Score				
Total Domain Score Possible	36	36	36	36
Domain Percent Score				

AEPS   Gross Motor Domain

Gross Motor Domain

EXAMINER: _____ DATE: _____

COMMENTS: _____

_____

_____

_____

EXAMINER: _____ DATE: _____

COMMENTS: _____

_____

_____

_____

EXAMINER: _____ DATE: _____

COMMENTS: _____

_____

_____

_____

EXAMINER: _____ DATE: _____

COMMENTS: _____

_____

_____

_____

Adaptive Domain

S = Scoring Key	Q = Qualifying Notes
2 = Pass consistently	A = Assistance provided
1 = Inconsistent	B = Behavior interfered
performance	R = Reported assessment
0 = Does not pass	M = Modification/adaptation
	D = Direct test

Name: _____

	Test Period:								
	Test Date:		/		/		/		/
	Examiner:								
	IFSP	S	Q	S	Q	S	Q	S	Q
A. Dining									
1. Eats and drinks a variety of foods using appropriate utensils with little or no spilling									
1.1 Eats a variety of food textures									
1.2 Selects and eats a variety of food types									
1.3 Eats with fork and spoon									
2. Prepares and serves food									
2.1 Prepares food for eating									
2.2 Uses knife to spread food									
2.3 Pours liquid into a variety of containers									
2.4 Serves food with utensil									
3. Displays social dining skills									
3.1 Puts proper amount of food in mouth, chews with mouth closed, swallows before another bite									
3.2 Takes in proper amount of liquid and returns cup to surface									
3.3 Remains seated during meal or until excused									
3.4 Uses napkin to clean face and hands									
3.5 Assists in clearing table									
B. Personal hygiene									
1. Carries out all toileting functions									
1.1 Uses toilet paper, flushes toilet, washes hands after using toilet									
1.2 Uses toilet									
1.3 Indicates need to use toilet									

AEPS   Adaptive Domain

	Test Period:							
Name: _____	Test Date:	/		/		/		/
	Examiner:							
	IFSP	S	Q	S	Q	S	Q	S	Q

	IFSP	S	Q	S	Q	S	Q	S	Q
2. Washes and grooms self									
2.1 Uses tissue to clean nose									
2.2 Brushes teeth									
2.3 Bathes and dries self									
2.4 Brushes or combs hair									
2.5 Washes and dries face									
C. Dressing and undressing									
1. Unfastens fasteners on garments									
1.1 Unfastens buttons/snaps/Velcro fasteners on garments									
1.2 Unties string-type fastener									
1.3 Unzips zipper									
2. Selects appropriate clothing and dresses self at designated times									
2.1 Puts on long pants									
2.2 Puts on front-opening garment									
2.3 Puts on pullover garment									
2.4 Puts on shoes									
2.5 Puts on underpants, shorts, or skirt									
3. Fastens fasteners on garments									
3.1 Ties string-type fastener									
3.2 Fastens buttons, snaps, and Velcro fasteners									
3.3 Threads and zips zipper									

A Total Domain Raw Score can be computed for the domain by adding all of the 2 and 1 scores entered in the S column for a specific test period. To determine the Domain Percent Score, divide the Total Domain Raw Score by the Total Domain Score Possible, then multiply by 100.

RESULTS

Test Date	_____	_____	_____	_____
Total Domain Raw Score	_____	_____	_____	_____
Total Domain Score Possible	78	78	78	78
Domain Percent Score	_____	_____	_____	_____

AEPS Adaptive Domain

Adaptive Domain

EXAMINER: _____ DATE: _____

COMMENTS: _____

_____

_____

_____

EXAMINER: _____ DATE: _____

COMMENTS: _____

_____

_____

_____

EXAMINER: _____ DATE: _____

COMMENTS: _____

_____

_____

_____

EXAMINER: _____ DATE: _____

COMMENTS: _____

_____

_____

_____

Cognitive Domain

S = Scoring Key	Q = Qualifying Notes
2 = Pass consistently	A = Assistance provided
1 = Inconsistent performance	B = Behavior interfered
	R = Reported assessment
0 = Does not pass	M = Modification/adaptation
	D = Direct test

Name: _____

	IFSP	S	Q	S	Q	S	Q	S	Q
Test Period:									
Test Date:		/		/		/		/	
Examiner:									
A. Participation									
1. Initiates and completes age-appropriate activities									
1.1 Responds to request to finish activity									
1.2 Responds to request to begin activity									
2. Watches, listens, and participates during small group activities									
2.1 Interacts appropriately with materials during small group activities									
2.2 Responds appropriately to directions during small group activities									
2.3 Looks at appropriate object, person, or event during small group activities									
2.4 Remains with group during small group activities									
3. Watches, listens, and participates during large group activities									
3.1 Interacts appropriately with materials during large group activities									
3.2 Responds appropriately to directions during large group activities									
3.3 Looks at appropriate object, person, or event during large group activities									
3.4 Remains with group during large group activities									
B. Demonstrates understanding of concepts									
1. Demonstrates understanding of eight different colors									
1.1 Demonstrates understanding of six different colors									
1.2 Demonstrates understanding of three different colors									

Cognitive Domain

	Test Period:								
Name: _____ Test Date: ___/___ ___/___ ___/___ ___/___ Examiner: _____									
	IFSP	S	Q	S	Q	S	Q	S	Q
2. Demonstrates understanding of five different shapes									
2.1 Demonstrates understanding of three different shapes									
2.2 Demonstrates understanding of one shape									
3. Demonstrates understanding of six different size concepts									
3.1 Demonstrates understanding of four different size concepts									
3.2 Demonstrates understanding of two different size concepts									
4. Demonstrates understanding of 10 different qualitative concepts									
4.1 Demonstrates understanding of six different qualitative concepts									
4.2 Demonstrates understanding of four different qualitative concepts									
4.3 Demonstrates understanding of two different qualitative concepts									
5. Demonstrates understanding of eight different quantitative concepts									
5.1 Demonstrates understanding of five different quantitative concepts									
5.2 Demonstrates understanding of two different quantitative concepts									
6. Demonstrates understanding of 12 different spatial relations concepts									
6.1 Demonstrates understanding of nine different spatial relations concepts									
6.2 Demonstrates understanding of six different spatial relations concepts									
6.3 Demonstrates understanding of three different spatial relations concepts									
7. Demonstrates understanding of seven different temporal relations concepts									
7.1 Demonstrates understanding of five different temporal relations concepts									
7.2 Demonstrates understanding of three different temporal relations concepts									

AEPS   Cognitive Domain

	Test Period:							
Name: _____ Test Date:		/		/		/		/
Examiner:								
	IFSP	S	Q	S	Q	S	Q	S	Q

	IFSP	S	Q	S	Q	S	Q	S	Q
C. Categorizing									
1. Groups objects, people, or events on the basis of specified criteria									
1.1 Groups objects, people, or events on the basis of category									
1.2 Groups objects on the basis of function									
1.3 Groups objects on the basis of physical attribute									
D. Sequencing									
1. Follows directions of three or more related steps that are not routinely given									
1.1 Follows directions of three or more related steps that are routinely given									
2. Places objects in series according to length or size									
2.1 Fits one ordered set of objects to another									
3. Retells event in sequence									
3.1 Completes sequence of familiar story or event									
E. Recalling events									
1. Recalls events that occurred on same day, without contextual cues									
1.1 Recalls events that occurred on same day, with contextual cues									
1.2 Recalls events immediately after they occur									
2. Recalls verbal sequences									
2.1 Recalls verbal information about self									
F. Problem solving									
1. Evaluates solutions to problems									
1.1 Suggests acceptable solutions to problems									
1.2 Identifies means to goal									
2. Makes statements and appropriately answers questions that require reasoning about objects, situations, or people									
2.1 Gives reason for inference									

AEPS   Cognitive Domain

	IFSP	S	Q	S	Q	S	Q	S	Q
2.2 Makes prediction about future or hypothetical events									
2.3 Gives possible cause for some event									
G. Play									
1. Engages in imaginary play									
1.1 Enacts roles or identities									
1.2 Plans and acts out recognizable event, theme, or story line									
1.3 Uses imaginary props									
2. Engages in games with rules									
2.1 Maintains participation									
2.2 Conforms to game rules									
H. Premath									
1. Recites numbers from 1 to 20									
1.1 Recites numbers from 1 to 10									
1.2 Recites numbers from 1 to 5									
1.3 Recites numbers from 1 to 3									
2. Counts 10 objects									
2.1 Counts five objects									
2.2 Counts two objects									
2.3 Demonstrates understanding of one-to-one correspondence									
3. Identifies printed numerals 1–10									
3.1 Identifies printed numerals 1–8									
3.2 Identifies printed numerals 1–5									
3.3 Identifies printed numerals 1–3									
4. Matches printed numerals to sets of 1–10 object(s)									
4.1 Matches printed numerals to sets of 1–8 object(s)									
4.2 Matches printed numerals to sets of 1–5 object(s)									
4.3 Matches printed numerals to sets of 1–3 object(s)									

Test Period: _____
Name: _____
Test Date: ___/___
Examiner: _____

AEPS   Cognitive Domain

		Test Period:								
Name:		Test Date:	/		/		/		/	
		Examiner:								
		IFSP	S	Q	S	Q	S	Q	S	Q

I. Prereading									
1. Demonstrates prereading skills									
1.1 Demonstrates functional use of books									
1.2 Tells about pictures in book									
1.3 Participates actively in story-telling									
2. Demonstrates prereading auditory skills									
2.1 Blends sounds									
2.2 Rhymes words									
3. Sounds out words									
3.1 Produces phonetic sounds for letters									
4. Reads words by sight									
4.1 Identifies letters									

A Total Domain Raw Score can be computed for the domain by adding all of the 2 and 1 scores entered in the S column for a specific test period. To determine the Domain Percent Score, divide the Total Domain Raw Score by the Total Domain Score Possible, then multiply by 100.

RESULTS

Test Date				
Total Domain Raw Score				
Total Domain Score Possible	184	184	184	184
Domain Percent Score				

Cognitive Domain

EXAMINER: _____   DATE: _____

COMMENTS: _____

_____

_____

_____

_____

EXAMINER: _____   DATE: _____

COMMENTS: _____

_____

_____

_____

EXAMINER: _____   DATE: _____

COMMENTS: _____

_____

_____

_____

EXAMINER: _____   DATE: _____

COMMENTS: _____

_____

_____

_____

Social-Communication Domain

S = Scoring Key	Q = Qualifying Notes
2 = Pass consistently	A = Assistance provided
1 = Inconsistent	B = Behavior interfered
performance	R = Reported assessment
0 = Does not pass	M = Modification/adaptation
	D = Direct test

	IFSP	S	Q	S	Q	S	Q	S	Q
Test Period:									
Test Date:		/		/		/		/	
Examiner:									

Name: _____

A. Social-communicative interactions	IFSP	S	Q	S	Q	S	Q	S	Q
1. Uses words, phrases, or sentences to inform, direct, ask questions, and express anticipation, imagination, affect, and emotions									
1.1 Uses words, phrases, or sentences to express anticipated outcomes									
1.2 Uses words, phrases, or sentences to describe pretend objects, events, or people									
1.3 Uses words, phrases, or sentences to label own or others' affect/emotions									
1.4 Uses words, phrases, or sentences to describe past events									
1.5 Uses words, phrases, or sentences to make commands to and requests of others									
1.6 Uses words, phrases, or sentences to obtain information									
1.7 Uses words, phrases, or sentences to inform									
2. Uses conversational rules									
2.1 Alternates between speaker/listener role									
2.2 Responds to topic changes initiated by others									
2.3 Asks questions for clarification									
2.4 Responds to contingent questions									
2.5 Initiates context-relevant topics									
2.6 Responds to others' topic initiations									
3. Establishes and varies social-communicative roles									
3.1 Varies voice to impart meaning									
3.2 Uses socially appropriate physical orientation									

AEPS   Social-Communication Domain

			Test Period:								
Name:			Test Date:	/		/		/		/	
			Examiner:								
		IFSP	S	Q	S	Q	S	Q	S	Q

B. Production of words, phrases, and sentences										
1. Uses verbs										
1.1 Uses auxiliary verbs										
1.2 Uses copula verb "to be"										
1.3 Uses third person singular verb forms										
1.4 Uses irregular past tense verbs										
1.5 Uses regular past tense verbs										
1.6 Uses present progressive "ing"										
2. Uses noun inflections										
2.1 Uses possessive "s"										
2.2 Uses irregular plural nouns										
2.3 Uses regular plural nouns										
3. Asks questions										
3.1 Asks yes/no questions										
3.2 Asks questions with inverted auxiliary										
3.3 Asks when questions										
3.4 Asks why, who, and how questions										
3.5 Asks what and where questions										
3.6 Asks questions using rising inflection										
4. Uses pronouns										
4.1 Uses subject pronouns										
4.2 Uses object pronouns										
4.3 Uses possessive pronouns										
4.4 Uses indefinite pronouns										
4.5 Uses demonstrative pronouns										
5. Uses descriptive words										
5.1 Uses adjectives										
5.2 Uses adjectives to make comparisons										
5.3 Uses adverbs										

AEPS   Social-Communication Domain

	Test Period:							
Name: _____	Test Date:	/		/		/		/
	Examiner:							
	IFSP	S	Q	S	Q	S	Q	S	Q
5.4 Uses prepositions									
5.5 Uses conjunctions									
5.6 Uses articles									

A Total Domain Raw Score can be computed for the domain by adding all of the 2 and 1 scores entered in the S column for a specific test period. To determine the Domain Percent Score, divide the Total Domain Raw Score by the Total Domain Score Possible, then multiply by 100.

RESULTS

Test Date	_____	_____	_____	_____
Total Domain Raw Score	_____	_____	_____	_____
Total Domain Score Possible	98	98	98	98
Domain Percent Score	_____	_____	_____	_____

_____**AEPS**_____

Social-Communication Domain

EXAMINER: _____ DATE: _____

COMMENTS: _____

_____

_____

_____

EXAMINER: _____ DATE: _____

COMMENTS: _____

_____

_____

_____

EXAMINER: _____ DATE: _____

COMMENTS: _____

_____

_____

_____

EXAMINER: _____ DATE: _____

COMMENTS: _____

_____

_____

_____

Social-Communication Recording Form

Child's name: _____ Observer/Activity: _____

Others present: _____

Date: _____ Time (start): _____ Time (stop): _____ Total time: _____

Record child utterances word-for-word u = unintelligible word (u) = unintelligible phrase	Context	Initiation	Response to comment	Response to question	Imitation	Unrelated
1.						
2.						
3.						
4.						
5.						
6.						
7.						
8.						
9.						

AEPS   Social-Communication Domain

Record child utterances word-for-word u = unintelligible word (u) = unintelligible phrase	Context	Initiation	Response to comment	Response to question	Imitation	Unrelated
10.						
11.						
12.						
13.						
14.						
15.						
16.						
17.						
18.						
19.						
20.						

Record child utterances word-for-word u = unintelligible word (u) = unintelligible phrase	Context	Initiation	Response to comment	Response to question	Imitation	Unrelated
21.						
22.						
23.						
24.						
25.						
26.						
27.						
28.						
29.						
30.						
31.						

Record child utterances word-for-word υ = unintelligible word (υ) = unintelligible phrase	Context	Initiation	Response to comment	Response to question	Imitation	Unrelated
32.						
33.						
34.						
35.						
36.						
37.						
38.						
39.						
40.						

Social-Communication Summary Form

Strand B: Production of words and sentences

Review each utterance on the Social-Communication Recording Form one at a time and record the frequency with which specific types of words, word forms, and types of sentences occur by entering tally marks (J卄𝖳) in the appropriate spaces below. *This information should be used to score all items in Strand B of the Social-Communication Domain according to the criterion specified for each individual item.* (See Chapter 7.)

1.1 Uses auxiliary verbs (e.g., will, can, do, shall, have)	
1.2 Uses copula verb "to be" (e.g., I am, they are, she is)	
1.3 Uses third person singular verb forms (e.g., "She plays it," "He does not")	
1.4 Uses irregular past tense verbs (e.g., went, ran, made, ate, drank)	
1.5 Uses regular past tense verbs (e.g., walked, talked, jumped)	
1.6 Uses present progressive "ing" (e.g., going, washing, dancing)	
2.1 Uses possessive "s" (e.g., Mom's, Ann's, Sammy's)	
2.2 Uses irregular plural nouns (e.g., mice, leaves, geese, feet)	
2.3 Uses regular plural nouns (e.g., dogs, cups, blocks, dresses)	
3.1 Asks yes/no questions	
3.2 Asks questions with inverted auxiliary (e.g., "Can I have one?")	
3.3 Asks when questions	
3.4 Asks why, who, and how questions	
3.5 Asks what and where questions	
3.6 Asks questions using rising inflection	
4.1 Uses subject pronouns (e.g., I, he, she, we, you)	
4.2 Uses object pronouns (e.g., me, her, them, us)	
4.3 Uses possessive pronouns (e.g., my, mine, hers, yours)	
4.4 Uses indefinite pronouns (e.g., none, all)	
4.5 Uses demonstrative pronouns (e.g., this, that, these, those)	

5.1 Uses adjectives (e.g., cold, red, big)	
5.2 Uses adjectives to make comparisons (e.g., "The red one is better")	
5.3 Uses adverbs (e.g., "He's over there," "Let's go fast")	
5.4 Uses prepositions (e.g., in, on, for, at, near, through)	
5.5 Uses conjunctions (e.g., and, or, so, only, if)	
5.6 Uses articles (e.g., the, a, an)	

Social Domain

S = Scoring Key	Q = Qualifying Notes
2 = Pass consistently	A = Assistance provided
1 = Inconsistent	B = Behavior interfered
performance	R = Reported assessment
0 = Does not pass	M = Modification/adaptation
	D = Direct test

Name: _____

		Test Period:								
		Test Date:	/		/		/		/	
		Examiner:								
		IFSP	S	Q	S	Q	S	Q	S	Q
A. Interaction with others										
1.	Has play partners									
	1.1 Responds to peers in distress or need									
	1.2 Establishes and maintains proximity to peers									
	1.3 Initiates greetings to familiar peers									
	1.4 Responds to affective initiations from peers									
2.	Initiates cooperative activity									
	2.1 Joins others in cooperative activity									
	2.2 Maintains cooperative participation with others									
	2.3 Shares or exchanges objects									
3.	Resolves conflicts by selecting effective strategy									
	3.1 Negotiates to resolve conflicts									
	3.2 Uses simple strategies to resolve conflicts									
	3.3 Claims and defends possessions									
B. Interaction with environment										
1.	Meets physical needs in socially appropriate ways									
	1.1 Meets physical needs when uncomfortable, sick, hurt, or tired									
	1.2 Meets observable physical needs									
	1.3 Meets physical needs of hunger and thirst									

AEPS   Social Domain

Name: _____

Test Period: _____

Test Date: ___/___ ___/___ ___/___ ___/___

Examiner: _____

	IFSP	S	Q	S	Q	S	Q	S	Q
2. Follows context-specific rules outside home and classroom									
2.1 Seeks adult permission									
2.2 Follows established rules at home and in classroom									
C. Knowledge of self and others									
1. Communicates personal likes and dislikes									
1.1 Initiates preferred activities									
1.2 Selects activities and/or objects									
2. Relates identifying information about self and others									
2.1 States address									
2.2 States telephone number									
2.3 Knows birthday									
2.4 Names siblings and gives full name of self									
2.5 Knows gender of self and others									
2.6 Knows name and age									
3. Accurately identifies affect/emotions in others and self consistent with demonstrated behaviors									
3.1 Accurately identifies affect/ emotions of others									
3.2 Accurately identifies own affect/emotions									

A Total Domain Raw Score can be computed for the domain by adding all of the 2 and 1 scores entered in the S column for a specific test period. To determine the Domain Percent Score, divide the Total Domain Raw Score by the Total Domain Score Possible, then multiply by 100.

RESULTS

Test Date	_____	_____	_____	_____
Total Domain Raw Score	_____	_____	_____	_____
Total Domain Score Possible	66	66	66	66
Domain Percent Score	_____	_____	_____	_____

AEPS   Social Domain

Social Domain

EXAMINER: _____ DATE: _____

COMMENTS: _____

_____

_____

_____

_____

EXAMINER: _____ DATE: _____

COMMENTS: _____

_____

_____

_____

_____

EXAMINER: _____ DATE: _____

COMMENTS: _____

_____

_____

_____

_____

EXAMINER: _____ DATE: _____

COMMENTS: _____

_____

_____

_____

_____

Summary of AEPS Results

For each domain, plot the Domain Percent Score for each test period (1–4) to determine if the child's performance is improving over time.

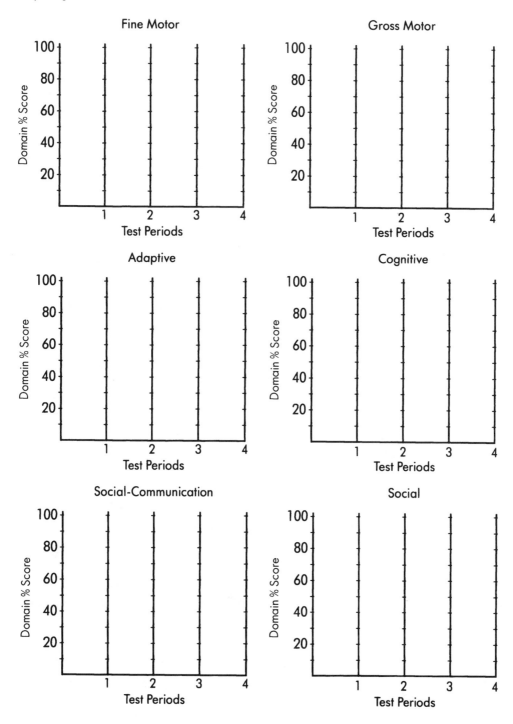

FAMILY REPORT

for

Assessment, Evaluation, and Programming System (AEPS) for Infants and Children
AEPS Measurement for Three to Six Years

edited by

Diane Bricker, Ph.D., and Kristie Pretti-Frontczak, Ph.D.

Child's name: _____

Child's date of birth: _____

Family name: _____

Name of person
   completing form: _____

Date: _____

Family's address: _____

_____

_____

Completion of the 98 items contained on this form will assist you to participate in the assessment and evaluation of your child's skills and abilities. It will also help prepare you to participate in your child's individualized education program (IEP) or individualized family service plan (IFSP) meeting.

DIRECTIONS

Carefully read each of the questions contained on this form. The questions ask if your child can do specific activities such as throwing balls, drawing shapes, and using words. Be sure to ask your child to perform each action before you select an answer. After observing your child do or try to do the action *several* times, enter the letter in the appropriate box.

The AEPS Family Report is designed to accommodate the results from four separate administrations. Space is provided at the top of each page to enter the date of each administration. In the column below the date, boxes are provided to enter a letter to score each item. Enter a "Y" in the box if the item is scored "Yes." Enter an "S" in the box if the item is scored "Sometimes." Enter an "N" in the box if the item is scored "Not Yet." The following are the scoring criteria:

Yes, which is scored with a "Y," is appropriate if your child does the action described in the question (e.g., your child can consistently zip and unzip his or her coat without your assistance). Also enter a "Y" if your child used to do the action but now does a more advanced action or skill. For example, if the question asks if your child can copy shapes and he or she is able to draw them independently, score the item with a "Y."

Sometimes, which is scored with an "S," is appropriate if your child does not always do the action as the question asks, is just starting to do the action, or does a portion of the action and needs your help. For example, if your child can sometimes zip his or her coat but generally needs your help, score the item with an "S."

Not Yet, which is scored with an "N," is appropriate if your child does not or is not able to do the action described in the question. For example, if your child cannot pour juice into a cup, score the item with an "N."

Subitems are indicated by letters (e.g., a, b, c) and are not scored as Y, S, or N. Subitems that your child can do should be indicated with a check mark.

The letters and numbers in parentheses that follow each item refer to the corresponding strand and goal/objective on the AEPS Test, which may be given to your child by the interventionist with whom you are working. Space is provided at the end of each domain to indicate the priority goals for that domain.

Note to interventionists: Please see pages 241–242 for converting Family Report Scores and for using the Family Report Summary Form shown on page 347.

Fine Motor Domain

date

1. Does your child hold a small object in each hand at the same time while building or putting things together? For example, your child builds with blocks, strings small beads/objects together. (A1)

2. Does your child use scissors to cut out shapes such as circles and ovals with curved lines, staying within 1/4 inch of the line? (A2)

3. Does your child tie string-type fasteners such as shoelaces, ribbons, and strings? (A3)

4. If you draw shapes such as squares or rectangles, does your child copy the shapes so that they look like yours? (B1)

5. Without help, does your child print his or her own first name? The letters must be in the correct order but can be upside down or backward. (B2)

Priority Goals: _____

_____

_____

_____

Y = Yes;   S = Sometimes;   N = Not Yet.

323

Gross Motor Domain

1. Does your child walk up and down stairs, putting one foot on each stair, without holding onto a handrail or wall? (A1)

2. Does your child jump forward with feet together? (B1)

3. Does your child run without help around large toys, furniture, and people without bumping into them? (B2)

4. Does your child bounce, catch, kick, and throw different-size balls? (B3)

   (*Note:* If you scored Question 4 with an "S" or an "N," please indicate if your child is able to do a—d by placing a check mark beside the item.)

   ____ a. Does your child bounce a large ball at least twice in a row? (B3.1)

   ____ b. Does your child catch a ball thrown from 6—10 feet, using both hands? (B3.2)

   ____ c. Does your child kick a ball placed in front of him or her, without falling? (B3.3)

   ____ d. Does your child throw a ball forward with one hand, using an overhand throw? (B3.4)

5. Does your child skip at least 15 feet? (B4)

6. Does your child ride and steer a two-wheel bicycle without training wheels at least 20 feet? (B5)

Priority Goals: _____

_____

_____

_____

Y = Yes; S = Sometimes; N = Not Yet.

Adaptive Domain

1. Does your child eat and drink a variety of foods using forks, spoons, and other utensils with little or no spilling? (A1)

   (*Note:* If you scored Question 1 with an "S" or an "N," please indicate if your child is able to do a–c by placing a checkmark beside the item.)

   ____ a. Does your child eat and drink foods of different textures? For example, your child eats soft foods such as bananas, drinks liquids such as milk, and eats hard foods such as raw vegetables. (A1.1)

   ____ b. Does your child choose to eat different kinds of food, such as dairy, meats, and fruit? (A1.2)

   ____ c. Does your child eat with a fork and spoon without much spilling? (A1.3)

2. Does your child help prepare and serve food? For example, your child removes peels and wrappers, uses a knife to spread soft foods, pours liquid, or uses a fork or spoon to serve food from one container to another. (A2)

   (*Note:* If you scored Question 2 with an "S" or an "N," please indicate if your child is able to do a–d by placing a checkmark beside the item.)

   ____ a. Does your child remove peels and wrappers before eating food? For example, your child peels a banana and removes a candy wrapper. (A2.1)

   ____ b. Does your child use a knife to spread soft foods such as cream cheese or peanut butter onto bread or crackers? (A2.2)

   ____ c. Does your child pour liquid from one container into another, such as juice into a cup? (A2.3)

   ____ d. Does your child serve food from one container to another with a fork or spoon? For example, your child spoons applesauce from a jar into a bowl. (A2.4)

Y = Yes; S = Sometimes; N = Not Yet.

3. Does your child put a proper amount of food in mouth, drink a proper amount of liquid from a cup, stay at the table for the entire meal, use a napkin to wipe face and hands, and help with clearing the table? (A3)

   (*Note:* If you scored Question 3 with an "S" or an "N," please indicate if your child is able to do a—e by placing a checkmark beside the item.)

   ____ a. Does your child put a proper amount of food in his or her mouth, chew with mouth closed, and swallow the food before taking another bite? (A3.1)

   ____ b. Does your child drink a proper amount of liquid from a cup and return the cup to the table without spilling? (A3.2)

   ____ c. Does your child stay at the table for the entire meal or until you say the child may leave? (A3.3)

   ____ d. Does your child use a napkin or paper towel to wipe face and hands? (A3.4)

   ____ e. Does your child help clear the table? (A3.5)

4. Does your child use the toilet without help (walk to toilet, adjust clothing, use toilet paper, flush toilet, pull up clothing, wash hands, and stay dry/unsoiled between trips)? (B1)

5. Does your child wash and groom self? For example, your child uses tissue to clean nose, brushes teeth, bathes and dries self, brushes and combs hair, and washes and dries face. (B2)

   (*Note:* If you scored Question 5 with an "S" or an "N," please indicate if your child is able to do a—e by placing a checkmark beside the item.)

   ____ a. Does your child use a tissue to blow or wipe nose? (B2.1)

   ____ b. Does your child brush own teeth (put toothpaste on brush, brush teeth, and rinse mouth)? (B2.2)

AEPS   Adaptive Domain

_____ c.   When bathing, does your child remove cloth-
           ing, get into tub or shower, use soap to clean
           body, get a towel, dry off body, and put the
           towel back on the rack? (B2.3)

_____ d.   Does your child brush and comb own hair?
           (B2.4)

_____ e.   Does your child wash and dry face (turn water
           on and off, use soap, dry with a towel, and put
           towel on the rack or throw paper towel
           away)? (B2.5)

6. Does your child _unfasten_ buttons, snaps, or Velcro fas-
    teners on clothes; untie string-type fasteners such as
    shoelaces or ties on a jacket hood; and unzip zippers
    when _undressing_? (C1)

    (_Note:_ If you scored Question 6 with an "S" or an "N,"
    please indicate if your child is able to do a–c by plac-
    ing a checkmark beside the item.)

    _____ a.   Does your child unfasten buttons, snaps, or
               Velcro fasteners on own clothing? (C1.1)

    _____ b.   Does your child untie string-type fasteners
               such as shoelaces or ties on a jacket hood?
               (C1.2)

    _____ c.   Does your child unzip and separate zippers
               when undressing? (C1.3)

7. Does your child choose, without help, the right clothes
    to wear for the time of day and weather conditions and
    dress self only with a few reminders? For example, your
    child puts on pajamas at bedtime and puts on coat to
    go outside. (C2)

    (_Note:_ If you scored Question 7 with an "S" or an "N,"
    please indicate if your child is able to do a–e by plac-
    ing a checkmark beside the item.)

    _____ a.   Does your child put long pants over both feet
               and pull them up to the waist? (C2.1)

    _____ b.   Does your child put on front-opening clothes
               (e.g., blouse, shirt, coat)? (C2.2)

AEPS   Adaptive Domain

_____ c. Does your child put on pullover clothes (e.g., T-shirts, dress, sweater)? (C2.3)

_____ d. Does your child put shoes on both feet? (C2.4)

_____ e. Does your child pull clothes over feet and up to waist (e.g., underpants, shorts, skirts)? (C2.5)

8. Does your child _fasten_ string-type fasteners such as shoelaces, ties on a jacket hood, and buttons, snaps, and Velcro fasteners on clothes, and thread and zip zippers when dressing? (C3)

    (_Note:_ If you scored Question 8 with an "S" or an "N," please indicate if your child is able to do a–c by placing a checkmark beside the item.)

_____ a. Does your child tie string-type fasteners (shoelaces) when dressing? (C3.1)

_____ b. Does your child fasten buttons, snaps, and Velcro fasteners when dressing? (C3.2)

_____ c. Does your child thread and zip zippers when dressing? (C3.3)

Priority Goals: _____

_____

_____

_____

Cognitive Domain

date

1. Does your child begin playing with toys and finish the activity without being told? For example, your child gets out a puzzle, puts it together, and puts it away. (A1)

2. Does your child watch others, listen, and participate during a small group activity with adult supervision? (A2)

   (*Note:* If you scored Question 2 with an "S" or an "N," please indicate if your child is able to do a–d by placing a checkmark beside the item.)

   ____ a. Does your child use materials in the way they are intended to be used during a small group? For example, your child uses glue to paste pictures. (A2.1)

   ____ b. Does your child follow directions from an adult during a small group activity? (A2.2)

   ____ c. Does your child look at the adult who is talking or the object the adult is talking about during a small group? (A2.3)

   ____ d. Does your child stay with the group during the activity activity? (A2.4)

3. Does your child watch others, listen, and participate during a large group activity with adult supervision? (A3)

   (*Note:* If you scored Question 3 with an "S" or an "N," please indicate if your child is able to do a–d by placing a checkmark beside the item.)

   ____ a. Does your child use materials in the way they are intended to be used during a large group activity? For example, your child passes a ball to the next child during a group game. (A3.1)

   ____ b. Does your child follow directions from an adult during a large group activity? (A3.2)

   ____ c. Does your child look at the adult who is talking or the object the adult is talking about during a large group activity? (A3.3)

   ____ d. Does your child stay with the group during the activity? (A3.4)

Y = Yes; S = Sometimes; N = Not Yet.

4. Does your child use at least eight color words (e.g., red, blue, yellow)? For example, your child says, " I have a green ball" while holding a green ball. (B1)

    Please list the color words your child uses correctly:

    _____   _____

    _____   _____

    _____   _____

    _____   _____

    _____

5. Does your child correctly use at least five shape words (e.g., circle, square, star)? For example, your child hands you a square puzzle piece when you ask for the square puzzle piece. (B2)

    Please list the shape words your child uses correctly:

    _____   _____

    _____   _____

    _____   _____

    _____   _____

    _____

6. Does your child correctly use at least six size words (e.g., little, tall, fat, thick, long)? For example, your child is playing with big blocks and says, "Give me big block." (B3)

    Please list the size words your child uses correctly:

    _____   _____

    _____   _____

    _____   _____

    _____   _____

    _____

7. Does your child correctly use at least 10 quality words (e.g., wet, hot, soft, loud, rough)? For example, your child turns on the water and says, "It's cold." (B4)

   Please list the quality words your child uses correctly:

   _____   _____

   _____   _____

   _____   _____

   _____   _____

   _____   _____

8. Does your child correctly use at least eight quantity words (e.g., few, all, enough, none, some)? For example, your child has a full cup of juice and says, "My cup is full." (B5)

   Please list the quantity words your child uses correctly:

   _____   _____

   _____   _____

   _____   _____

   _____   _____

   _____   _____

9. Does your child correctly use at least 12 words to describe the position of objects or people (e.g., in front of, beside, middle, first, under)? For example, your child says, "My shoes are behind the door." (B6)

   Please list the spatial relations words your child uses correctly:

   _____   _____

   _____   _____

   _____   _____

   _____   _____

   _____   _____

10. Does your child correctly use at least seven time words (e.g., yesterday, early, first, after, later)? For example, you ask your child when he or she is going to the park and your child says, "Later." (B7)

    Please list the time words your child uses correctly:

    _____   _____

    _____   _____

    _____   _____

    _____   _____

    _____

11. Does your child put things into groups on his or her own? For example, when cleaning the bedroom, your child puts all the cars on the shelf, all the airplanes on the bed, and all the boats in the closet. (C1)

12. Does your child carry out three-step directions that you would not typically give? For example, your child follows your directions to go to the bathroom, get a toothbrush, and put it in the bedroom. (D1)

    (_Note:_ If you scored Question 12 with an "S" or an "N," please indicate if your child is able to do a by placing a checkmark beside the item.)

    ____ a. Does your child carry out three-step directions that you _do_ frequently give? For example, your child follows your directions to put the book away, turn off the light, and get into bed. (D1.1)

13. Does your child put three objects in order according to amount, length, size, or color? For example, you give your child three blocks and your child lines them up on a shelf with the smallest first and the biggest last. (D2)

14. Does your child retell an event or story that involves a beginning, middle, and end? For example, you ask your child how he or she made a picture, and your child says, "First we got paper, then we put glue on it, and then we stuck beans on it." (D3)

15. Does your child tell you about something that happened at least 30 minutes earlier on the same day? For example, you ask your child what he or she had for lunch and your child tells you. (E1)

16. Does your child recite at least two of the following: (E2)

    (*Note:* Please place a checkmark beside the ones your child is able to recite.)

    _____ a. Telephone number

    _____ b. Alphabet

    _____ c. Numbers from 1 to 20

    _____ d. Spelling of name

    _____ e. Days of week

17. Does your child tell you at least two of the following: (E2.1)

    (*Note:* Please place a checkmark beside the ones your child is able to recite.)

    _____ a. First and last name

    _____ b. Birthday

    _____ c. Age

    _____ d. First name(s) of sister(s) or brother(s)

    _____ e. First name(s) of parent(s)

18. Does your child tell you why a solution to a problem would or would not work? For example, your child stands on a chair to reach a book on the shelf and says, "This chair is too small. I can't reach." (F1)

19. Does your child make statements and give answers to questions that require him or her to give the following three responses: (F2)

    (*Note*: If you scored Question 19 with an "S" or an "N," please indicate if your child is able to do a–c by placing a checkmark beside the item.)

    _____ a. Give a reason—for example, your child says, "She is sad" and you ask, "How do you know that the girl is sad?" Your child answers, "She is crying." (F2.1)

    _____ b. Make a prediction—for example, when you are reading an unfamiliar story you pause and ask your child, "What do you think will happen?" Your child tells a possible event. (F2.2)

    _____ c. Determine a possible cause—for example, your child tells a possible cause in response to your question, "Why do you think she is crying?" Your child says, "Because she fell down." (F2.3)

20. Does your child engage in the following three imaginary play behaviors: (G1)

    (*Note*: If you scored Question 20 with an "S" or an "N," please indicate if your child is able to do a–c by placing a checkmark beside the item.)

    _____ a. Child pretends to be someone else. For example, your child says, "I'm a bus driver" while driving a pretend bus. (G1.1)

    _____ b. Child plans and acts out a series of three actions when pretending. For example, your child says he or she is going fishing and then pretends to catch some fish and cook them. (G1.2)

    _____ c. Child uses pretend props to play. For example, your child pretends to brush hair without a brush. (G1.3)

21. Does your child engage in games with rules by doing the following two behaviors: (G2)

    (*Note*: If you scored Question 21 with an "S" or an "N," please indicate if your child is able to do a and/or b by placing a checkmark beside the item.)

    ____ a. Child plays games with rules until the game is over, even when he or she is not winning. (G2.1)

    ____ b. Child follows the rules of a game, such as waiting for a turn. (G2.2)

22. Does your child count from 1 to 20? (H1)

    (*Note*: If you scored Question 22 with an "S" or an "N," please indicate how high your child is able to count.)

    My child can count from _____ to _____.
    (H1.1–H1.3)

23. Can your child count a set of 10 objects? For example, your child correctly counts 10 stuffed animals on his or her bed. (H2).

    (*Note*: If you scored Question 23 with an "S" or an "N," please indicate how many sets of objects your child is able to count.)

    My child can count _____ sets of objects.
    (H2.1–H2.2)

24. Can your child identify the printed numerals 1–10? For example, when numerals are seen in books, on cards, or on road signs, your child correctly identifies the numerals. (H3)

    (*Note*: If you scored Question 24 with an "S" or an "N," please circle each numeral your child is able to identify.)

    1   2   3   4   5   6   7   8   9   10
    (H3.1–H3.3)

____**AEPS**_____Cognitive Domain

25. When given cards with the numbers 1–10 printed on them, does your child match them to the correct number of objects? For example, the card with the number 5 is matched to 5 crackers or the card with the number 8 is matched to 8 cars. (H4)

    (*Note:* If you scored Question 25 with an "S" or an "N," please indicate how many sets of objects and printed numerals your child is able to match.)

    My child can match _____ printed numerals to the correct number of objects. (H4.1–H4.3)

26. When your child is reading a book by him- or herself, does your child perform three of the following: (I1.1)

    (*Note:* Please place a checkmark beside the ones your child is able to do.)

    ____ a.   Holds book upright

    ____ b.   Turns all pages from beginning to end

    ____ c.   Pretends to read by vocalizing or verbalizing

    ____ d.   Attempts to structure and tell story

27. Does your child tell you about pictures in a book so that you can tell the child knows what the story is about? (I1.2)

28. When you are reading a story to your child, does your child do four of the following: (I1.3)

    (*Note:* Please place a checkmark beside the ones your child is able to do.)

    ____ a.   Makes comments

    ____ b.   Points to pictures

    ____ c.   Fills in missing words

    ____ d.   Tells the end of a familiar story

    ____ e.   Turns the pages

29. Does your child do both of the following: (12)

    (*Note:* If you scored Question 29 with an "S" or an "N,"
    please indicate if your child is able to do a and/or b by
    placing a checkmark beside the item.)

    ____ a.   When you sound out three letters of a word,
              such as /p/.../a/.../t/, does your child say
              "pat"? (12.1)

    ____ b.   Does your child say a word that rhymes with
              a word you say? For example, you say "pat"
              and your child says "cat." (The word can be a
              nonsense word such as "dat.") (12.2)

30. Does your child sound at least 3 three-letter words? For
    example, your child can look at a word ("mat") and say
    the sound for each letter (/m/.../a/.../t/). (13)

31. Does your child read two common words written on
    paper? (14)

Priority Goals: _____

_____

_____

_____

Social-Communication Domain

1. Does your child talk about the future? For example, your child predicts the ending of a familiar story, or says, "I'm going swimming tonight." (A1.1)

2. Does your child talk about pretend objects, events, or people? For example, your child says, "This is my magic spaceship, and I'm going to drive it to the moon." (A1.2)

3. Does your child tell you what he or she thinks and feels? For example, your child says, "I am happy" while playing with a puppy. (A1.3)

4. Does your child talk about the past? For example, your child says, "I fell down" or "I had soup at school today." (A1.4)

5. Does your child tell other people what to do? For example, your child says, "Give me the red Lego." (A1.5)

6. Does your child ask questions to gain information about what he or she sees, hears, and does? For example, when you are cooking, your child says, "What are you making?" (A1.6)

7. Does your child tell you about what he or she sees, hears, or does? For example, your child says, "I saw a cat today" or "I'm going outside to play." (A1.7)

8. Does your child start, finish, and change conversations? For example, your child finishes a conversation by saying, "I have to go outside now." (A2.1)

9. Does your child change the subject when you do? For example, your child says, "I want to play outside some more," and you say, "We need to go inside now and fix a snack." Your child responds by changing the subject and saying, "What are we going to eat?" (A2.2)

10. Does your child try to keep a conversation going? For example, your child says, "What?" when he or she does not understand what you said. (A2.3)

Y = Yes; S = Sometimes; N = Not Yet.

11. Does your child answer questions about things he or she sees, hears, says, or does? For example, your child says, "I want that," and you ask, "What do you want?" and your child says, "I want the red truck." (A2.4)

12. Does your child talk about things that are relevant to the situation or to the person he or she is talking to? For example, your child sees you cutting carrots and asks for one. (A2.5)

13. Does your child respond to things you talk about? For example, you say, "You look nice," and your child says, "I have on my new sweater." (A2.6)

14. Does your child change the way he or she talks according to the person being spoken to? For example, your child says, "Want cookie?" to a 1-year-old and "Do you want a cookie?" to an adult. (A3)

15. Does your child use verbs such as "She _is_ running" or "You _will_ fall"? (B1.1)

16. Does your child use verbs such as am, is, are, and was? (B1.2)

17. Does your child use the correct verbs when talking about another person? For example, your child says, "She plays, he does not." (B1.3)

18. Does your child use past tense verbs such as came, ran, fell, did, told, went, and sat? (B1.4)

19. Does your child use past tense verbs such as walked, washed, played, and helped? (B1.5)

20. Does your child use "ing" verbs such as washing, going, and eating? (B1.6)

21. Does your child use possessive "s" (a word followed by an apostrophe and "s" to show something belongs to someone)? For example, your child says, "Mom's hat," or "Ann's shoes." (B2.1)

22. Does your child use irregular plural nouns such as men, mice, and children? (B2.2)

AEPS   Social-Communication Domain

date

23. Does your child use regular plural nouns such as dogs, houses, boats, and blocks? (B2.3)

24. Does your child ask questions that you must answer with a yes or no? (B3.1)

25. Does your child ask questions such as, "Can't I go?" or "Is he hiding?" (B3.2)

26. Does your child ask questions that begin with the word "when"? (B3.3)

27. Does your child ask questions that begin with the words "why," "who," and "how"? (B3.4)

28. Does your child ask questions that begin with the words "what" and "where"? (B3.5)

29. Does your child's voice rise in pitch at the end of a question? (B3.6)

30. Does your child use pronouns (e.g., I, she, he, they, we) as the subject in phrases and/or sentences? For example, your child says, "He went home" or "I did it." (B4.1)

31. Does your child use pronouns (e.g., you, me, him, her, us, them, it) as the object in phrases and/or sentences? For example, your child says, "John hurt me." (B4.2)

32. Does your child use six different pronouns (e.g., my, your, her, its, our, their, mine, yours, hers, ours, theirs) to express possession in phrases and/or sentences? For example, your child says, "Those are her shoes." (B4.3)

33. Does your child use six different pronouns (e.g., some, any, none, every, anything, something, nothing, all, lots, many, more) to refer to an unspecified person or an object? For example, your child says, "He doesn't have any" or "I have some." (B4.4)

34. Does your child use two demonstrative pronouns (this, that, these, or those) to single out or demonstrate objectives? For example, your child says, "I want those." (B4.5)

_____**AEPS**_____   Social-Communication Domain

35. Does your child use adjectives to describe nouns and pronouns? For example, your child says, "Throw the *big* ball" or "I want the *red* pepper." (B5.1)

36. Does your child use adjectives to talk about how things are different from one another? For example, your child says, "I have the *biggest* ice cream," "My car is *best*," or "She is the *strongest*." (B5.2)

37. Does your child use adverbs to describe verbs? For example, your child says, "That tastes *bad*" or "Let's go *fast*." (B5.3)

38. Does your child use prepositions (in, on, out, up, down, under, by, of, for)? For example, your child says, "My books are *on* the bookshelf." (B5.4)

39. Does your child use connecting words (and, but, because, if, or)? For example, your child says, "We could play *or* take a nap." (B5.5)

40. Does your child correctly use articles (e.g., the, an, a)? For example, your child says, "I want *an* apple," or "Where's *the* ball?" (B5.6)

Priority Goals: _____

_____

_____

_____

Social Domain

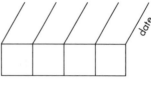

1. Does your child choose to play with other children? (A1)

2. Does your child initiate group activities with friends and encourage them to join in? For example, your child says to friends, "Come on, let's build a house" and then gives them jobs to do. (A2)

3. Does your child use all of the following strategies to resolve conflicts: (A3.0)

   (*Note:* If you scored Question 3 with an "S" or an "N," please indicate if your child is able to do a–c by placing a checkmark beside the item.)

   ____ a. Does your child try to find a solution to disagreements with playmates? For example, when your child is not getting along with a friend, your child says, "I'll play with the ball first, and then it's your turn." (A3.1)

   ____ b. Does your child tell an adult when he or she is having trouble with a friend? (A3.2)

   ____ c. Does your child claim a toy that belongs to him or her by taking the toy back or by saying, "That's mine!" (A3.3)

4. Does your child use all of the following strategies to meet physical needs: (B1)

   (*Note:* If you scored Question 4 with an "S" or an "N," please indicate if your child is able to do a–c by placing a checkmark beside the item.)

   ____ a. Does your child take care of him- or herself when uncomfortable, sick, hurt, or tired? For example, your child asks for help when hurt or takes a nap when tired. (B1.1)

   ____ b. Does your child take care of his or her own physical needs? For example, your child washes his or her dirty hands or takes off wet clothes. (B1.2)

   ____ c. Does your child ask for or get food or drink when hungry or thirsty? (B1.3)

Y = Yes; S = Sometimes; N = Not Yet.

_____**AEPS**_____ Social Domain

5. Does your child follow rules in places outside of his or her home or school? For example, your child follows rules to stay seated during a bus ride or follows directions to not touch food in the grocery store. (B2)

6. Does your child tell you what he or she likes and does not like? For example, your child says, "I love chocolate cake" or "I don't like to play football." (C1)

7. Does your child know all of the following pieces of information about self and others: (C2)

   (*Note:* If you scored Question 7 with an "S" or an "N," please indicate if your child is able to do a–f by placing a checkmark beside the item.)

   ____ a. His or her address, including number, street, and town? (C2.1)

   ____ b. His or her telephone number? (C2.2)

   ____ c. His or her birthday, including the month and day? (C2.3)

   ____ d. His or her brother's(s') and sister's(s') first names *and* own first and last name? (C2.4)

   ____ e. Whether he or she and others are boys or girls? (C2.5)

   ____ f. His or her first name and age? (C2.6)

8. Does your child tell you when he or she is happy and sad and when others are happy and sad? (C3)

Priority Goals: _____

_____

_____

_____

Family Report Summary Form

Child's Name: _____

| First Administration | | | | | Second Administration | | | | |

Date _____ Parent _____

Date _____ Parent _____

Domain	Domain Raw Score	Total Domain Score Possible	Domain Percent Score		Domain	Domain Raw Score	Total Domain Score Possible	Domain Percent Score
Fine Motor	____	10	____		Fine Motor	____	10	____
Gross Motor	____	12	____		Gross Motor	____	12	____
Adaptive	____	16	____		Adaptive	____	16	____
Cognitive	____	62	____		Cognitive	____	62	____
Social-Communication	____	80	____		Social-Communication	____	80	____
Social	____	16	____		Social	____	16	____
TOTAL	____	196	____		TOTAL	____	196	____

| Third Administration | | | | | Fourth Administration | | | | |

Date _____ Parent _____

Date _____ Parent _____

Domain	Domain Raw Score	Total Domain Score Possible	Domain Percent Score		Domain	Domain Raw Score	Total Domain Score Possible	Domain Percent Score
Fine Motor	____	10	____		Fine Motor	____	10	____
Gross Motor	____	12	____		Gross Motor	____	12	____
Adaptive	____	16	____		Adaptive	____	16	____
Cognitive	____	62	____		Cognitive	____	62	____
Social-Communication	____	80	____		Social-Communication	____	80	____
Social	____	16	____		Social	____	16	____
TOTAL	____	196	____		TOTAL	____	196	____

(See Chapter 10 for information on using this form.)

FAMILY INTEREST SURVEY

by

Juliann Cripe and Diane Bricker

for

Assessment, Evaluation, and Programming System (AEPS) for Infants and Children

edited by

Diane Bricker, Ph.D.

Child's name: _____

Child's date of birth: _____

Family name: _____

Name of person
   completing form: _____

Date: _____

Family's address: _____

_____

_____

The purpose of the Family Interest Survey is to assist family members and early interventionists in developing an individualized education program (IEP) or individualized family service plan (IFSP) and selecting family intervention outcomes. The survey is divided into three sections. The first section addresses child interests, the second section family interests, and the third section community interests.

DIRECTIONS

To complete the Family Interest Survey, read each item and then check whether it is a priority interest, an interest but not a current priority, or not an interest at this time. The survey is designed to be used twice, once to assist in planning for the initial IEP/IFSP meeting and then again at the IEP/IFSP review meeting. Space is available for indicating the dates of these two meetings.

For each date used, check one box in each row.

Date: _____ Date: _____

Child's Interests
I am interested in...

	Priority interest	Interest but not a current priority	Not an interest at this time	Priority interest	Interest but not a current priority	Not an interest at this time
Knowing more about my child's current strengths and needs						
Learning about services and programs for my child						
Knowing more about my child's condition/disability						
Making plans for future services and programs						
Knowing how my child grows and learns (such as social, motor, self-care)						
Learning ways to care for and help my child (such as positioning, diet, health)						
Learning about laws that affect my child, my rights, and how to advocate for my child						
Teaching my child						
Managing my child's behavior						
Learning to talk and play with my child						
Talking with teachers and professionals about my child's program						

Family's Interests
I am interested in...

	Priority interest	Interest but not a current priority	Not an interest at this time	Priority interest	Interest but not a current priority	Not an interest at this time
Explaining my child's special needs to siblings, grandparents, and friends						
Gaining support for my child's brothers and sisters						
Involving family and friends in my child's care or free time						
Counseling for my family						
Learning to solve family problems ourselves						

(continued)

AEPS   Family Interest Survey

Family's Interests
I am interested in...

	Priority interest	Interest but not a current priority	Not an interest at this time	Priority interest	Interest but not a current priority	Not an interest at this time
Gaining more support for myself (friends, partner, neighbors, minister)						
Gaining more support for my partner (friend, neighbors, minister)						
Having time for myself						
Having fun, recreation with my family						

Community Interests
I am interested in...

	Priority interest	Interest but not a current priority	Not an interest at this time	Priority interest	Interest but not a current priority	Not an interest at this time
Meeting other families						
Joining parent support groups or groups for children with special needs (e.g., United Cerebral Palsy)						
Learning about resources or agencies for help with:						
Medical care						
Dental care						
Financial assistance						
Food						
Housing						
Furniture, clothing, supplies						
Transportation						
Legal aid						
Health insurance						
Employment services						

(continued)

_____**AEPS**_____   Family Interest Survey

Community Interests
I am interested in...

	Priority interest	Interest but not a current priority	Not an interest at this time	Priority interest	Interest but not a current priority	Not an interest at this time
Vocational training						
Crisis intervention						
Toys, adaptive equipment						
Finding child care or preschools						
Finding babysitting or respite care						
Learning about Supplemental Security Income (SSI) and my child's eligibility						
Finding help to adapt the house for my child's needs						
Talking effectively about my child's and family's needs with professionals and agencies						
Including my child in activities (church, temple, recreation, camps)						
Volunteering with other families or projects						

Other interests or needs

_____

_____

_____

_____

CHILD PROGRESS RECORD

for

Assessment, Evaluation, and Programming System (AEPS) for Infants and Children

AEPS Measurement for Three to Six Years

edited by

Diane Bricker, Ph.D., and Kristie Pretti-Frontczak, Ph.D.

Child's name: _____

Child's date of birth: _____

Family name: _____

Name of person

   completing form: _____

Date: _____

Family's address: _____

_____

_____

The AEPS Child Progress Record was designed to assist caregivers and interventionists in monitoring child change through the use of a visual display of current abilities, intervention targets, and child progress. Paralleling the AEPS Test, the Child Progress Record is divided into six domains. Under each domain are listed the strands with their associated goals and objectives. Each goal and objective directly corresponds to an AEPS Test item.

Under each strand, the associated goals appear in the far right-hand box. To the left are one or more arrows that list the objectives leading to the specific goal located in the box to the right. The easiest objective is listed in the first arrow, followed by arrows listing increasingly more difficult objectives.

DIRECTIONS

The Child Progress Record can be used in conjunction with the AEPS Test. Shade and date goals and objectives for which the child has met criteria. Use an asterisk to indicate those goals and objectives selected by IEP/IFSP targets. As the child achieves each of the goals and objectives, shade and date each arrow and box following the direction of the arrows. This process provides a visual display of child progress over time.

Fine Motor Domain

Strand A: Manipulation of objects

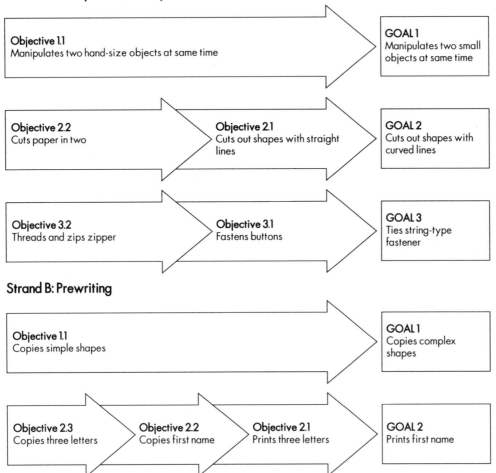

Objective 1.1
Manipulates two hand-size objects at same time

GOAL 1
Manipulates two small objects at same time

Objective 2.2
Cuts paper in two

Objective 2.1
Cuts out shapes with straight lines

GOAL 2
Cuts out shapes with curved lines

Objective 3.2
Threads and zips zipper

Objective 3.1
Fastens buttons

GOAL 3
Ties string-type fastener

Strand B: Prewriting

Objective 1.1
Copies simple shapes

GOAL 1
Copies complex shapes

Objective 2.3
Copies three letters

Objective 2.2
Copies first name

Objective 2.1
Prints three letters

GOAL 2
Prints first name

Gross Motor Domain

Strand A: Balance and mobility in standing and walking

Objective 1.1
Walks up and down stairs

GOAL 1
Alternates feet walking up and down stairs

Strand B: Play skills

Objective 1.4
Balances on one foot

Objective 1.3
Maintains balance in walking

Objective 1.2
Jumps from platform

Objective 1.1
Jumps in place

GOAL 1
Jumps forward

Objective 2.1
Runs

GOAL 2
Runs avoiding obstacles

Objective 3.4
Throws ball

Objective 3.3
Kicks ball

Objective 3.2
Catches ball

Objective 3.1
Bounces ball

GOAL 3
Bounces, catches, kicks, and throws ball

Objective 4.1
Hops

GOAL 4
Skips

Objective 5.1
Pedals and steers two-wheel bicycle with training wheels

GOAL 5
Rides and steers two-wheel bicycle

Adaptive Domain

Strand A: Dining

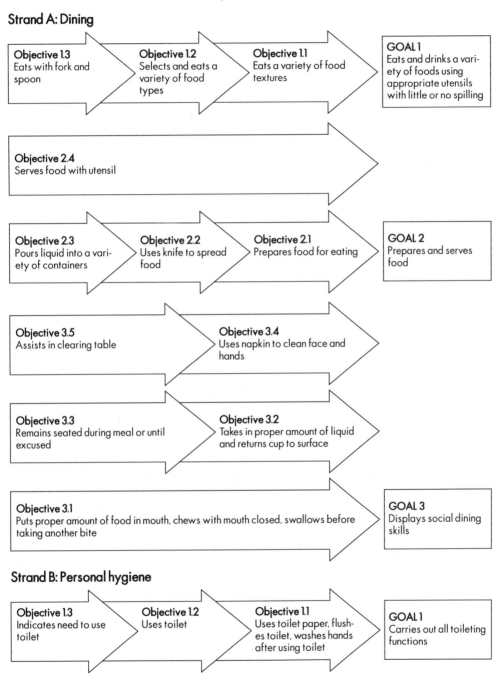

Objective 1.3
Eats with fork and spoon

Objective 1.2
Selects and eats a variety of food types

Objective 1.1
Eats a variety of food textures

GOAL 1
Eats and drinks a variety of foods using appropriate utensils with little or no spilling

Objective 2.4
Serves food with utensil

Objective 2.3
Pours liquid into a variety of containers

Objective 2.2
Uses knife to spread food

Objective 2.1
Prepares food for eating

GOAL 2
Prepares and serves food

Objective 3.5
Assists in clearing table

Objective 3.4
Uses napkin to clean face and hands

Objective 3.3
Remains seated during meal or until excused

Objective 3.2
Takes in proper amount of liquid and returns cup to surface

Objective 3.1
Puts proper amount of food in mouth, chews with mouth closed, swallows before taking another bite

GOAL 3
Displays social dining skills

Strand B: Personal hygiene

Objective 1.3
Indicates need to use toilet

Objective 1.2
Uses toilet

Objective 1.1
Uses toilet paper, flushes toilet, washes hands after using toilet

GOAL 1
Carries out all toileting functions

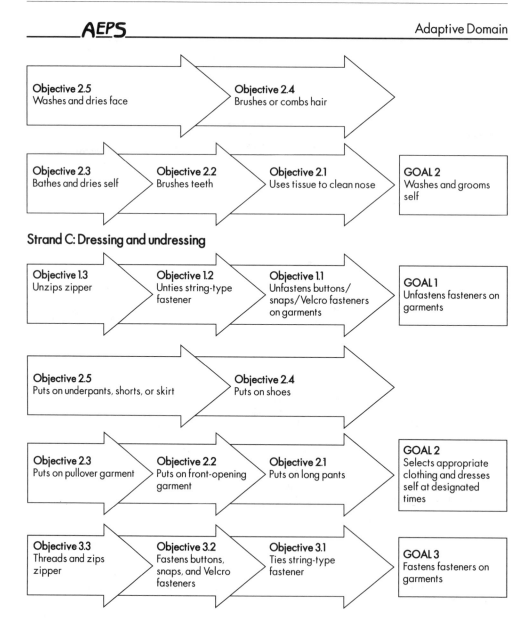

Objective 2.5
Washes and dries face

Objective 2.4
Brushes or combs hair

Objective 2.3
Bathes and dries self

Objective 2.2
Brushes teeth

Objective 2.1
Uses tissue to clean nose

GOAL 2
Washes and grooms self

Strand C: Dressing and undressing

Objective 1.3
Unzips zipper

Objective 1.2
Unties string-type fastener

Objective 1.1
Unfastens buttons/ snaps/Velcro fasteners on garments

GOAL 1
Unfastens fasteners on garments

Objective 2.5
Puts on underpants, shorts, or skirt

Objective 2.4
Puts on shoes

Objective 2.3
Puts on pullover garment

Objective 2.2
Puts on front-opening garment

Objective 2.1
Puts on long pants

GOAL 2
Selects appropriate clothing and dresses self at designated times

Objective 3.3
Threads and zips zipper

Objective 3.2
Fastens buttons, snaps, and Velcro fasteners

Objective 3.1
Ties string-type fastener

GOAL 3
Fastens fasteners on garments

Cognitive Domain

Strand A: Participation

Objective 1.2 Responds to request to begin activity	Objective 1.1 Responds to request to finish activity	GOAL 1 Initiates and completes age-appropriate activities

Objective 2.4 Remains with group during small group activities	Objective 2.3 Looks at appropriate object, person, or event during small group activities	

Objective 2.2 Responds appropriately to directions during small group activities	Objective 2.1 Interacts appropriately with materials during small group activities	GOAL 2 Watches, listens, and participates during small group activities

Objective 3.4 Remains with group during large group activities	Objective 3.3 Looks at appropriate object, person, or event during large group activities	

Objective 3.2 Responds appropriately to directions during large group activities	Objective 3.1 Interacts appropriately with materials during large group activities	GOAL 3 Watches, listens, and participates during large group activities

Strand B: Demonstrates understanding of concepts

Objective 1.2 Demonstrates understanding of three different colors	Objective 1.1 Demonstrates understanding of six different colors	GOAL 1 Demonstrates understanding of eight different colors

Objective 2.2 Demonstrates understanding of one shape	Objective 2.1 Demonstrates understanding of three different shapes	GOAL 2 Demonstrates understanding of five different shapes

Objective 3.2
Demonstrates understanding of two different size concepts

Objective 3.1
Demonstrates understanding of four different size concepts

GOAL 3
Demonstrates understanding of six different size concepts

Objective 4.3
Demonstrates understanding of two different qualitative concepts

Objective 4.2
Demonstrates understanding of four different qualitative concepts

Objective 4.1
Demonstrates understanding of six different qualitative concepts

GOAL 4
Demonstrates understanding of 10 different qualitative concepts

Objective 5.2
Demonstrates understanding of two different quantitative concepts

Objective 5.1
Demonstrates understanding of five different quantitative concepts

GOAL 5
Demonstrates understanding of eight different quantitative concepts

Objective 6.3
Demonstrates understanding of three different spatial relations concepts

Objective 6.2
Demonstrates understanding of six different spatial relations concepts

Objective 6.1
Demonstrates understanding of nine different spatial relations concepts

GOAL 6
Demonstrates understanding of 12 different spatial relations concepts

Objective 7.2
Demonstrates understanding of three different temporal relations concepts

Objective 7.1
Demonstrates understanding of five different temporal relations concepts

GOAL 7
Demonstrates understanding of seven different temporal relations concepts

Strand C: Categorizing

Objective 1.3
Groups objects on the basis of physical attribute

Objective 1.2
Groups objects on the basis of function

Objective 1.1
Groups objects, people, or events on the basis of category

GOAL 1
Groups objects, people, or events on the basis of specified criteria

AEPS   Cognitive Domain

Strand D: Sequencing

Objective 1.1
Follows directions of three or more related steps that are routinely given

GOAL 1
Follows directions of three or more related steps that are not routinely given

Objective 2.1
Fits one ordered set of objects to another

GOAL 2
Places objects in series according to length or size

Objective 3.1
Completes sequence of familiar story or event

GOAL 3
Retells event in sequence

Strand E: Recalling events

Objective 1.2
Recalls events immediately after they occur

Objective 1.1
Recalls events that occurred on same day, with contextual cues

GOAL 1
Recalls events that occurred on same day, without contextual cues

Objective 2.1
Recalls verbal information about self

GOAL 2
Recalls verbal sequences

Strand F: Problem solving

Objective 1.2
Identifies means to goal

Objective 1.1
Suggests acceptable solutions to problems

GOAL 1
Evaluates solutions to problems

Objective 2.3
Gives possible cause for some event

Objective 2.2
Makes prediction about future or hypothetical events

Objective 2.1
Gives reason for inference

GOAL 2
Makes statements and appropriately answers questions that require reasoning about objects, situations, or people

AEPS   Cognitive Domain

Strand G: Play

Objective 1.3
Uses imaginary props

Objective 1.2
Plans and acts out recognizable event, theme, or storyline

Objective 1.1
Enacts roles or identities

GOAL 1
Engages in imaginary play

Objective 2.2
Conforms to game rules

Objective 2.1
Maintains participation

GOAL 2
Engages in games with rules

Strand H: Premath

Objective 1.3
Recites numbers from 1 to 3

Objective 1.2
Recites numbers from 1 to 5

Objective 1.1
Recites numbers from 1 to 10

GOAL 1
Recites numbers from 1 to 20

Objective 2.3
Demonstrates understanding of one-to-one correspondence

Objective 2.2
Counts two objects

Objective 2.1
Counts five objects

GOAL 2
Counts 10 objects

Objective 3.3
Identifies printed numerals 1–3

Objective 3.2
Identifies printed numerals 1–5

Objective 3.1
Identifies printed numerals 1–8

GOAL 3
Identifies printed numerals 1–10

Objective 4.3
Matches printed numerals to sets of 1–3 object(s)

Objective 4.2
Matches printed numerals to sets of 1–5 object(s)

Objective 4.1
Matches printed numerals to sets of 1–8 object(s)

GOAL 4
Matches printed numerals to sets of 1–10 object(s)

Strand I: Prereading

Objective 1.3
Participates in story-
telling

Objective 1.2
Tells about pictures in
book

Objective 1.1
Demonstrates functional
use of books

GOAL 1
Demonstrates prereading skills

Objective 2.2
Rhymes words

Objective 2.1
Blends sounds

GOAL 2
Demonstrates prereading auditory skills

Objective 3.1
Produces phonetic sounds for letters

GOAL 3
Sounds out words

Objective 4.1
Identifies letters

GOAL 4
Reads words by sight

Social-Communication Domain

Strand A: Social-communicative interactions

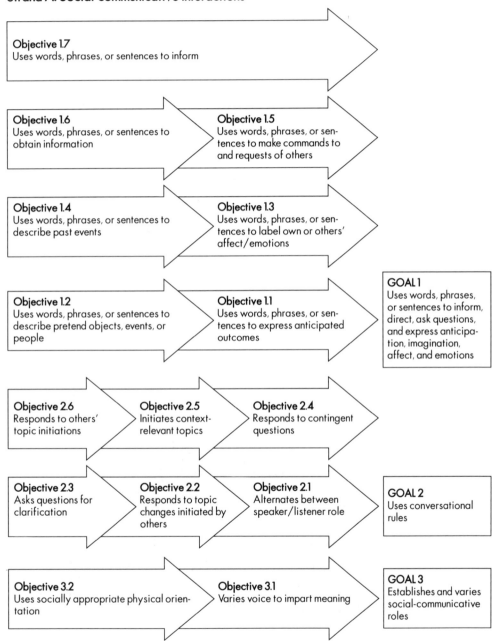

Objective 1.7
Uses words, phrases, or sentences to inform

Objective 1.6
Uses words, phrases, or sentences to obtain information

Objective 1.5
Uses words, phrases, or sentences to make commands to and requests of others

Objective 1.4
Uses words, phrases, or sentences to describe past events

Objective 1.3
Uses words, phrases, or sentences to label own or others' affect/emotions

Objective 1.2
Uses words, phrases, or sentences to describe pretend objects, events, or people

Objective 1.1
Uses words, phrases, or sentences to express anticipated outcomes

GOAL 1
Uses words, phrases, or sentences to inform, direct, ask questions, and express anticipation, imagination, affect, and emotions

Objective 2.6
Responds to others' topic initiations

Objective 2.5
Initiates context-relevant topics

Objective 2.4
Responds to contingent questions

Objective 2.3
Asks questions for clarification

Objective 2.2
Responds to topic changes initiated by others

Objective 2.1
Alternates between speaker/listener role

GOAL 2
Uses conversational rules

Objective 3.2
Uses socially appropriate physical orientation

Objective 3.1
Varies voice to impart meaning

GOAL 3
Establishes and varies social-communicative roles

AEPS   Social-Communication Domain

Strand B: Production of words, phrases, and sentences

Objective 1.6
Uses present progressive "ing"

Objective 1.5
Uses regular past tense verbs

Objective 1.4
Uses irregular past tense verbs

Objective 1.3
Uses third person singular verb forms

Objective 1.2
Uses copula verb "to be"

Objective 1.1
Uses auxiliary verbs

GOAL 1
Uses verbs

Objective 2.3
Uses regular plural nouns

Objective 2.2
Uses irregular plural nouns

Objective 2.1
Uses possessive "s"

GOAL 2
Uses noun inflections

Objective 3.6
Asks questions using rising inflection

Objective 3.5
Asks what and where questions

Objective 3.4
Asks why, who, and how questions

Objective 3.3
Asks when questions

Objective 3.2
Asks questions with inverted auxiliary

Objective 3.1
Asks yes/no questions

GOAL 3
Asks questions

Objective 4.5
Uses demonstrative pronouns

Objective 4.4
Uses indefinite pronouns

Objective 4.3
Uses possessive pronouns

Objective 4.2
Uses object pronouns

Objective 4.1
Uses subject pronouns

GOAL 4
Uses pronouns

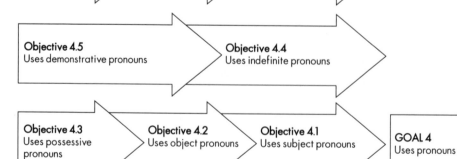

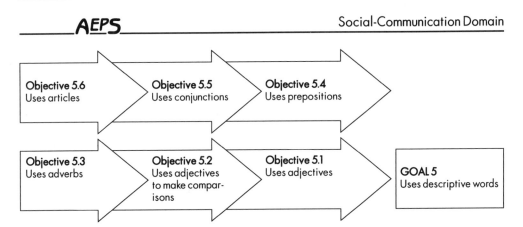

Social Domain

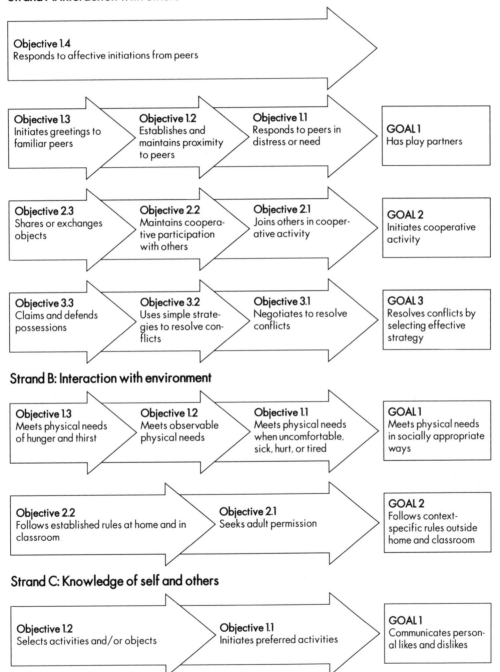

Strand A: Interaction with others

Objective 1.4
Responds to affective initiations from peers

Objective 1.3
Initiates greetings to familiar peers

Objective 1.2
Establishes and maintains proximity to peers

Objective 1.1
Responds to peers in distress or need

GOAL 1
Has play partners

Objective 2.3
Shares or exchanges objects

Objective 2.2
Maintains cooperative participation with others

Objective 2.1
Joins others in cooperative activity

GOAL 2
Initiates cooperative activity

Objective 3.3
Claims and defends possessions

Objective 3.2
Uses simple strategies to resolve conflicts

Objective 3.1
Negotiates to resolve conflicts

GOAL 3
Resolves conflicts by selecting effective strategy

Strand B: Interaction with environment

Objective 1.3
Meets physical needs of hunger and thirst

Objective 1.2
Meets observable physical needs

Objective 1.1
Meets physical needs when uncomfortable, sick, hurt, or tired

GOAL 1
Meets physical needs in socially appropriate ways

Objective 2.2
Follows established rules at home and in classroom

Objective 2.1
Seeks adult permission

GOAL 2
Follows context-specific rules outside home and classroom

Strand C: Knowledge of self and others

Objective 1.2
Selects activities and/or objects

Objective 1.1
Initiates preferred activities

GOAL 1
Communicates personal likes and dislikes

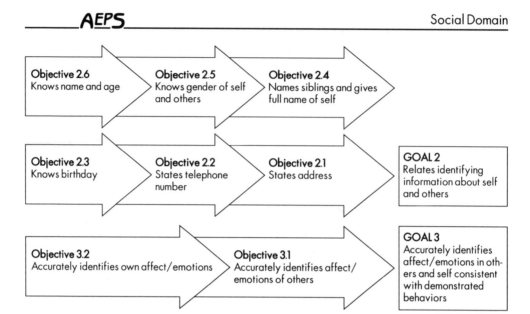

Objective 2.6
Knows name and age

Objective 2.5
Knows gender of self
and others

Objective 2.4
Names siblings and gives
full name of self

Objective 2.3
Knows birthday

Objective 2.2
States telephone
number

Objective 2.1
States address

GOAL 2
Relates identifying
information about self
and others

Objective 3.2
Accurately identifies own affect/emotions

Objective 3.1
Accurately identifies affect/
emotions of others

GOAL 3
Accurately identifies
affect/emotions in oth-
ers and self consistent
with demonstrated
behaviors

INDEX

Page numbers followed by *t* or *f* indicate tables or figures.